Deference in Human Rights Adjuc

Deference in Human Rights Adjudication

CORA CHAN
Professor, Faculty of Law, University of Hong Kong

OXFORD
UNIVERSITY PRESS

OXFORD
UNIVERSITY PRESS

Great Clarendon Street, Oxford, OX2 6DP,
United Kingdom

Oxford University Press is a department of the University of Oxford. It furthers the University's objective of excellence in research, scholarship, and education by publishing worldwide. Oxford is a registered trade mark of Oxford University Press in the UK and in certain other countries

Published in the United States of America by Oxford University Press
198 Madison Avenue, New York, NY 10016, United States of America

British Library Cataloguing in Publication Data

Data available

Library of Congress Control Number: 2024934054

ISBN 9780198921646

DOI: 10.1093/9780198921677.001.0001

Printed and bound by
CPI Group (UK) Ltd, Croydon, CR0 4YY

MIX
Paper | Supporting responsible forestry
FSC® C013604

Acknowledgements

This book started life as a doctoral thesis at the University of Oxford. My greatest debt of gratitude goes to my supervisors, Nick Barber and Paul Craig, for their intellectual guidance and mentorship. Their immeasurable generosity at every step of the journey, from the start of the thesis through to its publication as a book, exceeds anything that I could ever ask of a supervisor. It is an utmost privilege and honour to be their student.

I would also like to thank my examiners—Joanna Bell, Timothy Endicott, Alison Young, and Paul Yowell—for their instructive comments, from which I have benefitted enormously.

My heartfelt thanks are extended to the following colleagues for their helpful feedback on draft chapters of the book: Peter Chau, Albert Chen, Chen Jianlin, Daisy Cheung, Chong Bu, Lisa Burton Crawford, Tom Daly, Rosalind Dixon, Danny Gittings, Jeff Gordon, Aileen Kavanagh, Kelvin Kwok, Edward Lui, Will Partlett, Evan Rosevear, Amelia Simpson, Scott Stephenson, Alec Stone Sweet, Adrienne Stone, Lulu Weis, the late Julius Yam, Po Jen Yap, Simon Young, Angela Zhang, and participants at the UNSW Gilbert + Tobin Centre of Public Law Roundtable on Comparative Constitutional Law 2020, Melbourne Legal Theory Workshop 2021 and HKU Law Faculty works-in-progress research workshop 2021–2022.

I am grateful to Jeremias Adams-Prassl, Richard Albert, Terry Au, Johannes Chan, Joseph Chan, Ruth Chang, Sujit Choudhry, Thomas Cheng, Moshe Cohen-Eliya, Gráinne De Búrca, Fiona De Londras, David Dyzenhaus, Fu Hualing, Michaela Hailbronner, Ran Hirschl, Lusina Ho, Hayley Hooper, Michael Hor, Eric Ip, Swati Jhaveri, Madhav Khosla, David Law, Emily Lee, Hoong Phun Lee, Rebecca Lee, Ernest Lim, Becky Loo, Niels Petersen, Gila Stopler, Ioanna Tourkochoriti, Mark Tushnet, Scott Veitch, Sergio Verdugo, Marco Wan, Joseph Weiler, and Zhao Yun for their astute advice and guidance on the project.

Many ideas in the book were inspired by discussions with numerous colleagues over the years. In that context, I would particularly like to thank Trevor Allan, Anne Carter, Margit Cohn, Paul Daly, Mark Elliott, Jeff King, Lo Pui Yin, and Julian Rivers.

Thanks also to the many friends and colleagues who have supported me along the way: Shahla Ali, Shreya Atrey, Aslı Ü Bâli, Clement Chen, Anne Cheung, Richard Ekins, Chen Hui Wen, Mindy Chen-Wishart, Gabriel Cheung, Erin Delaney, Maartje de Visser, Anna Dziedic, Fang Yuxue, Gu Weixia, Elizabeth Huang, Agnes Ip, Michael Jackson, Julienne Jen, Puja Kapai, Humphrey Ko, Karen

Kong, Jedidiah Kroncke, Kuo Ming Sung, Victoria Kwok, Massimo Lando, Lee Sau Kong, Paul Lejot, Rachel Li, Sida Liu, Kelley Loper, John Lowry, Vanessa MacDonnell, Jaclyn Neo, Michael Ng, Catherine O'Regan, Stefano Osella, Victor Ramraj, Yaniv Roznai, Vivian Wong, and Cedric Yeung.

I thank Joanna Keung, Megan Louie, and Veronica Yu for their excellent research assistance.

It has been a delight to work with Brian Stone and Charlotte Kershaw at Oxford University Press. I am grateful for their help and support in enabling the publication of the book.

The ideas in this book were mainly developed at the Faculty of Law and Magdalen College of the University of Oxford and the Faculty of Law of the University of Hong Kong. I thank these institutions for their support. I also thank the Hong Kong Jockey Club Charities Trust for funding my DPhil studies at Oxford.

Above all, I am indebted to my parents and sisters for their unconditional love. This book is dedicated to them.

As the production of this book reached its final stage, a dear friend and colleague passed away. Julius Yam was a sterling academic, passionate teacher, and noble friend. His friendship was an indispensable source of strength and inspiration. I will sorely miss him. This book is also dedicated to his memory.

Summary Contents

Detailed Contents

Table of Cases

CANADA

HONG KONG

IRELAND

ISRAEL

NEW ZEALAND

UNITED KINGDOM

1
Introduction

I. Two Underexplored Questions

A perennial issue in public law is whether, and if so when, how, and how much, the courts should defer to the decisions of the executive or legislature in adjudication. The issue is particularly acute in the context of human rights adjudication, which in many jurisdictions has increased both the breadth and depth of the power of the courts vis-à-vis other branches of government. More subject matter is now within the jurisdiction of the courts, which are able to adjudicate human rights using proportionality, a legal test that is more demanding than orthodox tests of judicial review, such as *Wednesbury* unreasonableness.[1] Such an expansion of judicial power raises concerns over whether the courts will intrude into questions they lack the institutional or constitutional competence to adjudicate.[2] To allay such concerns, the courts sometimes defer to the judgments of the executive or legislature. In jurisdictions around the world, the rise of proportionality has—rather ironically—paralleled the rise of the doctrine of deference.[3] Deference is seen as a central tool for ensuring that human rights are protected without overstepping the executive or legislature's institutional competence and constitutional legitimacy.[4] It is a manifestation of the separation of powers and, in the rights context, the prime site for debating deeper normative questions concerning such separation.

The literature on deference is extensive.[5] There has been considerable discussion of whether, why, and when courts should defer,[6] as well as of whether there

[1] See eg Aharon Barak, *Proportionality: Constitutional Rights and their Limitations* (CUP 2012) part III; Robert Alexy, *A Theory of Constitutional Rights* (OUP 2010) chs 3, 6, postscript.

[2] See nn 3, 5–7, 10.

[3] Cora Chan, 'A Preliminary Framework for Measuring Deference in Rights Reasoning' (2016) 14(4) ICON 851, 851–52; cf Julian Rivers, 'Proportionality and Variable Intensity of Review' (2006) 65 CLJ 174, 176–77.

[4] Deference can be considered as one way of facilitating what theorists have called democratic or constitutional 'dialogue': see eg Alison L Young, *Democratic Dialogue and the Constitution* (OUP 2017) 226–29; Rosalind Dixon, 'Constitutional "Dialogue" and Deference' in Geoffrey Sigalet, Grégoire Webber and Rosalind Dixon (eds), *Constitutional Dialogue: Rights, Democracy, Institutions* (CUP 2019) 161, 177–85; Rosalind Dixon, 'The Supreme Court of Canada, Charter Dialogue, and Deference' (2009) 47 Osgoode Hall LJ 235.

[5] In addition to sources in nn 3, 6–7, 10; see also Richard A Edwards, 'Judicial Deference under the Human Rights Act' (2002) 65(6) MLR 859; Alan DP Brady, *Proportionality and Deference under the UK Human Rights Act: An Institutionally Sensitive Approach* (CUP 2012).

[6] Murray Hunt, 'Sovereignty's Blight: Why Public Law Needs "Due Deference"' in Nicholas Bamforth and Peter Leyland (eds), *Public Law in a Multi-Layered Constitution* (Hart 2003); Jeffrey Jowell, 'Judicial Deference: Servility, Civility or Institutional Capacity?' [2003] PL 592; Jeffrey Jowell,

Deference in Human Rights Adjudication. Cora Chan, Oxford University Press. © Cora Chan 2024.
DOI: 10.1093/9780198921677.003.0001

should be a doctrine of deference that is independent of ordinary principles of judicial review.[7] The general view seems to be that the courts should sometimes defer on epistemic grounds and that it is possible to formulate doctrine on the guiding factors for deference.[8] There has also been discussion of how the courts should determine whether a ground for deference exists, with many rejecting a crude approach that carves out certain subject matter as warranting more or less deference (the 'spatial' approach)[9] in preference for a more nuanced approach whereby the courts engage in multifactorial balancing on a case-by-case basis to determine the degree of deference due (the 'due deference', 'contextual', or 'multifactorial balancing' approach).[10] These discussions are helpful in furthering understanding of how powers in rights adjudication can be properly allocated, but two questions regarding how courts ought to defer remain underexplored.

The first question is how courts should give effect to the reasons they have for deferring. Courts have an array of devices to choose from; for example, they may defer by lowering the standard of review, lowering the standard of proof, reversing the burden of proof, or granting a deferential remedy. Which one of these devices or a combination thereof should courts choose if they wish to give effect to their reasons for deferring in a given case? If a court has, say, reasons of democratic legitimacy to defer to the legislature in a given case, should it defer by lowering the standard of review, reversing the burden of proof, lowering the standard of proof, or granting a deferential remedy? If the court seeks to give effect to the legislature's democratic legitimacy once in setting the standard of review, and then again in fashioning remedies, will that result in the double counting of deference?

The second underexplored question concerns how to render deference practicable without undue compromise of the reasons for deference in a particular case. Given human fallibility and resource constraints in the real world, how can deference be made more workable for judges, that is, enable them to understand how deference is to be applied and come to appropriate and consistent rulings on deference, as well as more predictable for litigants, that is, enable them to have some idea of how deference will be applied in the case at hand? For example, when and

'Judicial Deference and Human Rights: A Question of Competence' in Paul Craig and Richard Rawlings (eds), *Law and Administration in Europe: Essays in Honour of Carol Harlow* (OUP 2003).

[7] TRS Allan, 'Human Rights and Judicial Review: a Critique of "Due Deference"' (2006) 65 CLJ 671; Aileen Kavanagh, 'Defending Deference in Public Law and Constitutional Theory' (2010) 126 LQR 222; TRS Allan, 'Judicial Deference and Judicial Review: Legal Doctrine and Legal Theory' (2011) 127(Jan) LQR 96; TRS Allan, *The Sovereignty of Law: Freedom, Constitution, and Common Law* (OUP 2013) 241–85.

[8] A prominent exception is Allan. See Allan, 'Human Rights and Judicial Review' (n 7); Allan, 'Judicial Deference and Judicial Review' (n 7); Allan, *The Sovereignty of Law* (n 7).

[9] Hunt (n 6) 337.

[10] Alison Young, 'In Defence of Due Deference' (2009) 72(4) MLR 554; Aileen Kavanagh, *Constitutional Review under the UK Human Rights Act* (CUP 2009) part II; Kavanagh, 'Defending Deference' (n 7); Jeff King, *Judging Social Rights* (CUP 2012); Aileen Kavanagh, *The Collaborative Constitution* (CUP 2023) 281–95.

how should more guidance on deference in the form of bright-line rules be given to judges and litigants? Is the spatial approach always unjustified? Can the multi-factorial balancing exercise be rendered more workable and predictable, and if so how?

I call these two questions, both of which relate to how courts ought to defer (the first concerns how courts should express deference,[11] and the second how they should determine when, how much, and how to defer), questions that concern the 'method of deference'. This book is one of the first studies to systematically explore these two—important—questions. If the devices chosen by a court cannot reflect its reasons for deference (or reflect them to the appropriate degree), then those reasons cannot be properly accounted for, thereby defying principled adjudication and leading to too much or too little deference (and, correspondingly, to too little rights protection or too great a sacrifice of the countervailing public interest). If the method for determining when, how, and how much to defer is too complex or vague, then legal certainty for litigants may be compromised, and there may also be insufficient guidance for judges, leading to the wrong choice of device(s), mistaken identification of situations calling for deference, or inconsistent rulings, again flouting principled adjudication and leading to too much or too little deference.[12] The answers to the two questions of interest are therefore key to maintenance of the separation of powers and the courts functioning as forums of principle and adhering to the rule of law.

The significance of the issues explored in this book can be illustrated by *R (on the application of DA and others) v Secretary of State for Work and Pensions*,[13] one of a series of challenges to the UK government's cap on welfare benefits. In this case, the applicants argued that regulations exempting those entitled to a working tax credit were discriminatory against lone parents of young children, whose ability to work was constrained. The UK Supreme Court upheld the arrangement. In determining whether it was proportionate, the majority judges held that because the case involved socio-economic policy, an area in which the elected branches of government have relative institutional and constitutional competence, the courts should give the government considerable leeway.[14] Deference was then expressed by adjusting the standard of review attached to the four-limb proportionality test

[11] This book speaks at various points of judges using devices to 'express' deference. In ordinary parlance, the term 'express' can be understood in both a communicative sense (ie conveying a message to a target audience) and a non-communicative sense (eg giving effect to certain considerations). When referring to judges using certain devices to 'express' deference, the book is using the term in the latter sense. What I mean is that judges can use these devices to give effect to the normative considerations that underlie deference. Whether those considerations need to be given effect through communication is a question on which I am agnostic. I thank the reviewer for prompting me to clarify this.

[12] On the importance of workability and legal certainty, see eg Lon L Fuller, *The Morality of Law* (Yale University Press 1964).

[13] [2019] UKSC 21, [2020] 1 All ER 573.

[14] ibid [56]–[66] (Lord Wilson), [110]–[118] (Lord Carnwath), [125] (Lord Hodge).

from correctness to 'manifestly without reasonable foundation'.[15] Arguably, deference was also expressed by reversing the burden of proof, putting the onus on the applicant to show that the challenged measure was manifestly without reasonable foundation.[16] Lord Wilson also floated the idea that if discrimination were found, then deference could be expressed at the remedial stage: the 'same ... concept of institutional propriety' that led to relaxation of the standard of review may militate against issuing a declaration of incompatibility.[17]

DA raises several questions about the propriety of the court's method of deference. First, the court was faced with a choice of devices for expressing deference, namely, the standard of review, burden of proof, or remedies.[18] How should that choice have been made? Was it right for the majority judges to defer by lowering the standard of review, and arguably also the burden of proof, and in the way that they did, that is, by adding the filter of 'manifestly without reasonable foundation' to and reversing the onus on all four limbs of the proportionality test, an approach that Lord Kerr, in dissent, disputed?[19] Do the different deference devices reflect different reasons for deference such that some reasons can be expressed only by using certain devices? If the same reasons for deference are expressed through more than one device—for example, once by lowering the standard of review, and then again at the remedial stage—does that constitute double counting? When, if ever, would it be justified for the courts to defer for the same reason using more than one device? Second, the court in the case in question treated the subject matter of the decision—that is, socio-economic policy—as an indicator of institutional and constitutional competence. Was it justified in doing so? Whilst such a spatial approach has been heavily criticized for being insufficiently sensitive to context, it has the advantage of workability for judges and certainty for litigants. The alternative case-by-case multifactorial balancing exercise has the advantage of sufficient flexibility to cater for context but provides less guidance to judges and litigants. Even if the use of doctrinal categories such as those used by the court in

[15] ibid. For subsequent development of the 'manifestly without reasonable foundation' principle, see *R (on the application of SC, CB and 8 children) v Secretary of State for Work and Pensions and others* [2021] UKSC 26, [2022] AC 223, discussed in Chapter 6.

[16] This would appear to be the effect of the ruling, although some may dispute that. See, for comparison, n 13 [62], [66] (Lord Wilson) and [177] (Lord Kerr).

[17] ibid [90].

[18] This book describes the standard of review, burden of proof, and so on as 'devices' for deference. This usage may seem unfamiliar given that the term 'device' is normally used to refer to something that is instrumental in bringing about an effect, and, in this context, the standard of review and burden of proof per se are unable to bring about any deferential effect. It is the *adjustment of* the standard of review and *reversal of* the burden of proof rather than *the standard and burden themselves* that can bring about a deferential effect. In describing the latter as devices, the book is using the term in a broader sense to include opportunities in the course of adjudication for the courts to exercise deference, opportunities that allow for a judicial choice on whether and how to defer. I thank the reviewer for prompting me to reflect on the 'device' terminology.

[19] n 13 [162]–[177].

DA sacrifices some sensitivity to context, is it nonetheless justified, or sometimes justified, all things considered?

The aforementioned case allows us to see how significant the consequences of an inappropriate method can be: if, by deferring through more than one device, the court in that case afforded the decision-maker an excessive dose of deference, then it failed to protect the right to equality to a sufficient degree. If, in truth, the way in which the court relaxed the standard of review and burden of proof did not reflect the institutional and constitutional considerations for deference in the case, or the level thereof, then the court afforded those considerations too little weight. The court adopted a spatial approach at the expense of close contextual analysis, potentially sacrificing rights protection. If it had instead adopted multi-factorial balancing, however, then its analysis would have been more tailored to the case, albeit at the cost of limiting certainty for future litigants and guidance for future courts. It remains unclear how the balance between flexibility and certainty should and can be struck. At stake, therefore, concerning questions about the method of deference are important constitutional principles: the separation of powers, human rights protection, and the rule of law. This book provides conceptual resources for understanding how courts ought to defer.

The remainder of this introductory chapter is organized as follows. In section II, I first provide a brief definition of deference and outline the scope and methodology of the book. Section III then explains that the answers to the two focal questions of this book will enable us to formulate methods of deference that meet two corresponding criteria, one internal and one external. Section IV situates the book within the relevant literature, and section V considers potential objections to my project. Section VI concludes by sketching a roadmap of the book.

II. Definition, Scope, and Methodology

This book defines deference as occurring when a court grants leeway to the legislature or executive—leeway that it would not have granted had it merely considered its own balance of reasons bearing on the rights issue before the court[20]—for reasons that arise from its comparative institutional position[21] (eg that the legislature is more likely than the court to arrive at a correct answer on, or has more constitutional legitimacy to determine, the issue). This definition is further elaborated in Chapter 2. For now, it suffices to note the following core elements of deference: its consequence, that is, the court grants leeway to the political branches that it would not have granted had it considered only its own balance of reasons on

[20] Philip Soper, *The Ethics of Deference: Learning from Law's Morals* (CUP 2002) 22–24.
[21] Andrew Legg, *The Margin of Appreciation in International Human Rights Law: Deference and Proportionality* (OUP 2012) 1–2.

the rights issue before the court; and the reasoning process leading to that consequence, that is, the granted leeway is the result of a special kind of reasons, namely, reasons that arise from the comparative institutional positions of the courts and the political branches of government.

The book focuses on deference in cases in which an executive or legislative act is challenged in a national court on the ground that the act violates a constitutional right that is subject to a limitation clause (qualified right[22]). I focus on rights rather than on another area or all areas of public law adjudication because rights are an arena in which deference is most prevalent and most commonly discussed and one in which theoretical resources are most urgently required. I exclude supranational courts because the imperatives for and against deference may differ in the national and supranational contexts. I focus on qualified rights (as opposed to, say, all rights, including absolute rights) because the globally embraced three-stage framework for adjudicating qualified rights gives judicial reasoning a predictable core. That core in turn presents numerous deference devices upon which systematic analysis can be anchored.[23] Under the three-stage framework, courts first assess whether there has been a prima facie limitation of a right (the rights definition stage)[24] and, if so, then examine whether the limitation is justified under a proportionality test (the rights limitation stage). If the limitation fails the proportionality test, the court then decides what remedies, if any, to grant (the remedial stage). The arguments in this book are applicable to jurisdictions that embrace this three-stage framework for adjudicating qualified rights. Chapter 3 explains how the framework enables systematic analysis of how courts ought to defer. Although the book focuses on qualified rights and national courts, its arguments may well be applicable outside those contexts as well.

The three-stage framework has been adopted by courts around the world, but its adoption is not uncontroversial. Criticisms have been levied against, for example, distinguishing the definition and limitation stages.[25] In developing arguments using the three-stage framework, the book assumes rather than defends the framework's adoption in rights adjudication. It seeks to examine how deference should be exercised if the framework is adopted—as it indeed is in cases across the globe—leaving a response to criticisms of such adoption to another occasion.

[22] Barak (n 1) 32–37, 133–45.

[23] See Chan, 'A Preliminary Framework' (n 3) 857.

[24] cf Aharon Barak, 'A Research Agenda for the Future' in Vicki C Jackson and Mark Tushnet (eds), *Proportionality: New Frontiers, New Challenges* (CUP 2017) 325–29.

[25] See eg Bradley W Miller, 'Justification and Rights Limitations' in Grant Huscroft (ed), *Expounding the Constitution: Essays in Constitutional Theory* (CUP 2008) 93; Grégoire CN Webber, *The Negotiable Constitution: On the Limitation of Rights* (CUP 2009); Allan, *The Sovereignty of Law* (n 7) 283–84; Grégoire Webber, 'On the Loss of Rights' in Grant Huscroft, Bradley W Miller, and Grégoire Webber (eds), *Proportionality and the Rule of Law: Rights, Justification, Reasoning* (CUP 2014) 123; Francisco J Urbina, *A Critique of Proportionality and Balancing* (CUP 2017) 247–51.

My project is theoretical and normative. I seek to provide the conceptual resources needed to analyse how courts ought to defer in particular contexts. The methodology is primarily theoretical, although doctrinal methodology is also used insofar as it is relevant to answering the normative enquiry. For example, I draw on case law to illustrate some existing methods of deference. The case law I draw upon is from common law jurisdictions that embrace both the aforementioned three-stage framework for adjudicating qualified rights and a structured, multi-limb proportionality test that probes in a sequential manner whether a given rights limitation (i) pursues a sufficiently important or legitimate aim; (ii) is rationally connected to that aim; (iii) is no more than necessary to achieve the aim; and (iv) strikes a fair balance between the individual right and the public interest.[26] Those jurisdictions are Canada, Hong Kong, Ireland, Israel, New Zealand, and the United Kingdom. This choice of jurisdictions is made for a practical reason: these jurisdictions provide the elaborate reasoning on methods of deference required for this study. In principle, however, nothing prevents my arguments from being applicable to common law jurisdictions that adopt the three-stage framework for adjudicating rights but apply a non-structured proportionality test (eg India and South Africa) or to civil law jurisdictions that adopt the framework (eg Germany).

My case illustrations are drawn primarily from supreme courts, with particular attention to cases that laid down doctrine on deference, although lower court judgments are also referenced when useful for illustration purposes. The criterion for selecting cases for illustration is their relevance in exemplifying the key conceptual and normative issues with which this book is concerned. The book draws primarily on constitutional rights cases and the constitutional rights literature, although administrative law materials are also consulted where they shed light on relevant issues in the rights context. The literature on criminal and evidence law is drawn upon as well in the discussion of devices for deference. Constitutional rights adjudication traverses a wide range of contexts with diverse emphases (eg some cases turn primarily on factual and evidential issues, whereas others turn more on disputes over legal principles). Although the book does not draw illustrations from all terrains of constitutional rights adjudication, nor does it draw conclusive observations on the method of deference that should be adopted in specific rights contexts, it does develop general arguments that can be applied across qualified rights adjudication that uses the aforementioned three-stage framework.

[26] Or a test comprising the first three limbs alone, see eg *de Freitas v Permanent Secretary of Ministry of Agriculture, Fisheries, Lands and Housing* [1998] UKPC 30, [1999] 1 AC 69 [25]. The second to fourth limbs are referred to as suitability, necessity, and balance in some jurisdictions, eg Germany. The four-limb formulation used herein was developed in *R v Oakes* [1986] 1 SCR 103, [69]–[70]. For the spread of proportionality globally, see eg Alec Stone Sweet and Jud Mathews, *Proportionality Balancing and Constitutional Governance* (OUP 2019); Moshe Cohen-Eliya and Iddo Porat, *Proportionality and Constitutional Culture* (CUP 2013).

The book has both theoretical and practical aims, seeking both to enhance theoretical understanding of and provide practical guidelines on how courts ought to defer, and it is developed with these dual aims in mind. Whilst the bulk of the book contains in-depth conceptual analysis, Chapters 4–6 constitute the core chapters, and each of these chapters ends with key takeaway points for judges who wish to apply the theoretical arguments therein. Those who are interested only in the practical implications of these chapters can skip to those points, which contain cross-references to sections with the theoretical underpinnings of those implications. The translation of theory into practice necessarily passes over certain nuances in theoretical analysis, and hence the guidelines herein should be understood not as summaries of that analysis, but rather as practical steps that are consistent with and flow from it. Although the guidelines are tailored for judges, who in the jurisdictions under study form the key group determining how deference is practised, they are also of use to policymakers who wish to formulate laws and policies on deference.

III. Internal Logic and External Constraints

The answers to the two focal questions of this book will guide the formulation of methods of deference that satisfy two corresponding criteria. The first criterion (which corresponds to the first question) is whether a method of deference appropriately reflects the reasons for deference in a particular case, that is, why the court should defer in the first place. It is an internal criterion—or a criterion of what I call the 'internal logic' of deference—because it pertains to normative considerations that justify the practice of deference itself. The second criterion (which corresponds to the second question) is external; it concerns whether a method of deference is workable for judges and predictable for litigants. Unlike such factors as relative institutional and constitutional competence, which, as will be explained in Chapter 2, are reasons why courts should defer in the first place, the question of whether a method of deference is workable and predictable is not such a reason, and, in that sense, is external to the practice of deference. The latter considerations, which I call 'external constraints' or 'practicability considerations', should nevertheless constrain that practice.

These two criteria do not exhaust the criteria for deciding how courts ought to defer. For example, in deciding which deference device to use, a court may have to take into account considerations other than reasons for deference, workability, and predictability, such as the financial burden that the use of various devices would likely impose on the respective parties to the litigation. Nevertheless, the internal criterion and external criterion outlined above undoubtedly constitute two of the most important criteria, as their fulfilment is necessary to justify a given approach to deference. Accordingly, this book focuses on these two criteria.

IV. Existing Discussions

Although this book's two questions on how courts ought to defer have been understudied, a number of important works have paved the way for the in-depth exploration of these questions undertaken herein. These works are discussed in detail later in the book. Here, I merely outline some of them in brief, and discuss how my book builds upon them and where its originality lies.

On the question of what devices courts should use to express their reasons for deference, theorists have identified various devices through which deference can be expressed. For example, Mark Elliott,[27] Alison Young,[28] Paul Craig,[29] Richard Edwards,[30] Rosalind Dixon,[31] and myself,[32] amongst others,[33] have recognized that deference can be expressed by lowering the standard of review and giving extra weight to the government's case; Sujit Choudhry[34] and Kent Roach[35] have analysed the standard of proof device; Guy Davidov,[36] Brian Foley,[37] and Alison Young[38] have suggested that the choice of a deferential definition of a right could be a means of deference; Julian Rivers,[39] Aharon Barak,[40] Janneke Gerards,[41] and David Kenny,[42] amongst others,[43] have analysed the burden of proof as a means of

[27] Mark Elliott, 'Proportionality and Deference: the Importance of a Structured Approach' in Christopher Forsyth, Mark Elliott, Swati Jhaveri, Anne Scully-Hill, and Michael Ramsden (eds), *Effective Judicial Review: A Cornerstone of Good Governance* (OUP 2010) 269.

[28] Young, 'In Defence of Due Deference' (n 10) 555; Alison L Young, 'Will You, Won't You, Will You Join the Deference Dance?' (2014) 34(2) OJLS 375, 389–90; Young, *Democratic Dialogue and the Constitution* (n 4) 227.

[29] Paul Craig, *Administrative Law* (8th edn, Sweet & Maxwell 2016) 617–27, 652–68.

[30] Edwards (n 5) 872–82.

[31] Rosalind Dixon, *Responsive Judicial Review: Democracy and Dysfunction in the Modern Age* (OUP 2023) 130–31.

[32] Cora Chan, 'Proportionality and Invariable Baseline Intensity of Review' (2013) 33(1) LS 1, 5–6; Chan, 'A Preliminary Framework' (n 3) 858–60.

[33] See eg Janneke Gerards, 'Pluralism, Deference and the Margin of Appreciation Doctrine' (2011) 17(1) ELJ 80, 88; Kirsty McLean, *Constitutional Deference, Courts and Socio-Economic Rights in South Africa* (Pretoria University Law Press 2009) 144–45.

[34] Sujit Choudhry, 'So What is the Real Legacy of Oakes? Two Decades of Proportionality Analysis under the Canadian Charter's Section 1' (2006) 34 Supreme Court L Rev 501.

[35] Kent Roach, *The Supreme Court on Trial: Judicial Activism or Democratic Dialogue* (rev edn, Irwin Law Inc 2016) 181–83, 195–96.

[36] Guy Davidov, 'Judicial Deference and the Constitutional Protection of Human Rights' (1998) Thesis submitted in conformity with the requirements for the degree of Master of Laws at Faculty of Law of University of Toronto 56.

[37] Brian Foley, *Deference and the Presumption of Constitutionality* (Institute of Public Administration 2008) ch 3.

[38] Young, *Democratic Dialogue and the Constitution* (n 4) 228.

[39] Julian Rivers, 'The Presumption of Proportionality' (2014) 77(3) MLR 409. For my reply to him, see Cora Chan, 'The Burden of Proof Under the Human Rights Act' [2014] JR 46.

[40] Barak (n 1) ch 16.

[41] Gerards (n 33) 88.

[42] David Kenny, 'Proportionality, the Burden of Proof, and Some Signs of Reconsideration' (2014) 52 IJ 141.

[43] See eg Guy Davidov, 'The Paradox of Judicial Deference' (2000–01) 12 NJCL 133, 154, 162–63. See also David Bilchitz, 'Necessity and Proportionality: Towards A Balanced Approach' in Liora Lazarus, Christopher McCrudden, and Nigel Bowles (eds), *Reasoning Rights: Comparative Judicial Engagement*

deference; and Kent Roach,[44] Robert Leckey,[45] and Aruna Sathanapally,[46] amongst others,[47] have considered how the choice of remedies can affect the degree of deference.[48] My book builds upon these works by systematically collating the various devices into a scheme, articulating the methodology for such collation, and explaining how the devices can function as devices for deference with illustrations from various jurisdictions.

There is a dearth of discussion on how the reasons for deference should guide the choice of devices for deference. However, recent years have seen calls for elaboration on how the use of various devices is determined, as well as an important attempt to expressly map the normative drivers of deference onto various devices. For example, Rebecca Williams advocates for the articulation of why particular intensities of review are adopted across the four devices she propounds.[49] In a ground-breaking piece, Mark Elliott maps the prevalent normative considerations determining deference, namely, the importance of the right at stake and the primary decision-maker's relative institutional and constitutional competence, onto, inter alia, the standard of review and the degree of weight that should be afforded the decision-maker in determining whether that standard has been satisfied, respectively.[50] This piece constitutes one of the first attempts to identify an internal logic to the use of various devices for deference. Regrettably, as we will see in Chapter 4, Elliott's reasoning for his conclusions is brief, and his coverage of

(Hart Publishing 2014) 46–47, which suggests devices akin to the standard of proof, burden of proof, and standard of review.

[44] See eg Kent Roach, *Constitutional Remedies in Canada* (2nd edn, Thomson Reuters 2019).

[45] Robert Leckey, *Bills of Rights in the Common Law* (CUP 2015).

[46] Aruna Sathanapally, *Beyond Disagreement: Open Remedies in Human Rights Adjudication* (OUP 2012).

[47] See eg Dixon, *Responsive Judicial Review* (n 31), 176–80, 204–41; Rosalind Dixon, 'The Forms, Functions, and Varieties of Weak(ened) Judicial Review' (2019) 17(3) ICON 904, 912–14; Erin F Delaney, 'Analyzing Avoidance: Judicial Strategy in Comparative Perspective' (2016) 66 Duke LJ 1, 43–57.

[48] For ways to measure judicial activism, see Bradley C. Canon, 'A Framework for the Analysis of Judicial Activism' in Stephen C Halpern and Charles M Lamb (eds), *Supreme Court Activism and Restraint* (Lexington Books 1982) 385; Margit Cohn and Mordechai Kremnitzer, 'Judicial Activism: A Multidimensional Model' (July 2005) 18(2) CJLJ 333; Stefanie A Lindquist and Frank B Cross, *Measuring Judicial Activism* (OUP 2009); Benjamin Goold, Liora Lazarus, and Gabriel Swiney, 'Public Protection, Proportionality, and the Search for Balance' [2007] 10/07 Ministry of Justice Research 1–3, 20; Guy Davidov and Amnon Reichman, 'Prolonged Armed Conflict and Diminished Deference to the Military: Lessons from Israel' [2010] 35(4) L & Soc Inquiry 919; William P Marshall, 'Conservatives and the Seven Sins of Judicial Activism' [2002] 73 U Colom L Rev 1217; Ernest A Young, 'Judicial Activism and Conservative Politics' [2002] 73 U Colom L Rev 1139; Sujit Choudhry and Claire E Hunter, 'Measuring Judicial Activism on the Supreme Court of Canada: A Comment on *Newfoundland (Treasury Board) v NAPE*' [2003] 48(3) McGill L J 525; Margit Cohn, 'Judicial Activism in the House of Lords: A Composite Constitutionalist Approach' (2007) PL 95; Chan, 'A Preliminary Framework' (n 3).

[49] Rebecca Williams, 'Structuring Substantive Review' [2017] PL 99, 100–01, 122–23.

[50] Mark Elliott, 'From Bifurcation to Calibration: Twin-Track Deference and the Culture of Justification' in Hanna Wilberg and Mark Elliott (eds), *The Scope and Intensity of Substantive Review: Traversing Taggart's Rainbow* (Hart 2015) 70–73, 80–82.

the considerations underlying devices for deference is insufficiently comprehensive. My book constitutes a continuation and expansion of Elliott's endeavour to 'expos[e] and harness[s] the relationship between underlying normative factors' and public law's 'doctrinal superstructure',[51] that is, to construct doctrinal tools that reflect the normative considerations that ought to shape deference.

The question of the double counting of deference has received some attention, with theorists warning of the risk thereof. Alison Young, for example, highlights several possible forms of double counting, including the court deferring for the same reason in both determining the standard of review and giving weight to the public authority's views in deciding whether the standard has been satisfied.[52] Similarly, Trevor Allan argues that because deference considerations are 'already embodied in traditional doctrine' on, inter alia, distinguishing appeal from review, which rules out a standard of review that calls for the substitution of full merits, deferring over and above that doctrine constitutes double counting.[53] However, no one has hitherto probed into the questions of when the double counting of deference actually occurs (eg does it occur every time the court defers in more than one way for the same reason?) and how different deference devices can legitimately be combined, questions that this book explores.

On the issue of how methods of deference can be made workable for judges and predictable for litigants, there has been much discussion of the relative advantages of contextual, multifactorial balancing over the spatial approach in meeting the normative imperatives for deference in a particular case,[54] but little analysis of how the potential problem of non-practicability in the former approach can be addressed. There is awareness of the problem. For example, Michael Taggart argues that 'signposts on the review rainbow or map'[55] need to be developed, as otherwise public law 'will continue to be rather chaotic, unprincipled, and result-oriented', 'partially negat[ing] the rule of law that judicial review is meant to instantiate'.[56] He further argues that 'a deliberate and concerted effort' to articulate the contextual approach is needed: 'We must get beyond simply talking about context and actually contextualize in a way that can generate generalizable conclusions.'[57] Elliott posits that the mapping of normative considerations onto the devices for deference could 'avoid reducing the field to a state of unhelpful shapelessness'.[58]

There have also been attempts to articulate and refine the principles that should guide judicial deference.[59] Jeff King's work represents by far the most

[51] ibid 76.
[52] Young, 'In Defence of Due Deference' (n 10) 570.
[53] Allan 'Human Rights and Judicial Review' (n 7) 679–80.
[54] Kavanagh, 'Defending Deference' (n 7) 223–26; Young, 'In Defence of Due Deference' (n 10) 566–79; Hunt (n 6) 349–70.
[55] Michael Taggart, 'Proportionality, Deference, Wednesbury' (2008) 2008 NZ L Rev 423, 453, 460.
[56] ibid 454.
[57] ibid 453–54.
[58] Elliott (n 50) 75.
[59] Kavanagh, *Constitutional Review* (n 10) chs 7–9; Young, 'In Defence of Due Deference' (n 10).

comprehensive and sophisticated attempt at making the contextual approach more practicable. In his seminal book, King distils four factors that should guide judicial restraint in social rights adjudication in polities that satisfy certain background political conditions that are salient in the United Kingdom and in some other Commonwealth jurisdictions, expounds how courts can assess each factor, and combines his multifactorial analysis with a default position of judicial minimalism.[60] The full richness of King's analysis cannot be captured by this short outline. Suffice it to say at this point that it constitutes a significant step towards rendering the multifactorial approach more tailored to the normative considerations underpinning deference (fulfilment of the internal criterion) and more practicable (fulfilment of the external criterion), and that this book seeks to develop the enterprise of deference along the same course. Herein, I build upon the ideas of King and other theorists who have sought to refine the principles of judicial restraint, as well as upon the literature on rule-based decision-making,[61] to explain how judges can determine the extent to which bright-line rules on deference should be relied upon and to formulate a list of techniques for balancing the two criteria.

A recent work that examines the modality of deference in depth is worth mentioning here at greater length, namely, Dean Knight's *Vigilance and Restraint in the Common Law of Judicial Review*.[62] In the book, Knight identifies four prevalent approaches—in England, Australia, New Zealand, and Canada—to calibrating deference in judicial review (including but not limited to human rights cases): scope of review, grounds of review, intensity of review, and contextual review. His ambitions are both descriptive and normative: the book both traces trends in the use of these approaches across the Commonwealth and evaluates the strengths and weaknesses of each with a view to guiding the choice amongst them. His criteria for normative evaluation focus on legality (or what I call the external criterion). Knight concludes, inter alia, that the grounds of review and intensity of review fare better in general than the other two approaches in terms of his normative criteria.

Knight's work draws attention to the overlooked question of how courts ought to defer. He also convincingly establishes that the external criterion is an important criterion for guiding the practice of deference. Moreover, he suggests when rule-based decision-making would be least problematic, as well as the judicial techniques for enhancing such decision-making. All of this informs my analysis of the external criterion in important ways. However, Knight's normative project ultimately suffers from two limitations, which justifies the complementarity offered herein.

[60] King, *Judging Social Rights* (n 10).

[61] Eg Frederick Schauer, *Playing by the Rules: A Philosophical Examination of Rule-Based Decision-Making in Law and in Life* (OUP 1991); Cass R Sunstein and Adrian Vermeule, 'Interpretation and Institutions' (2003) 101 Mich L Rev 885.

[62] Dean R Knight, *Vigilance and Restraint in the Common Law of Judicial Review* (CUP 2018).

First, Knight's benchmark for evaluating which method of deference should be used is ostensibly limited to the external criterion. Yet, as explained above, the internal criterion of whether a method of deference can express the underlying normative considerations is core to justification of the practice of deference, and cannot be ignored. A normative project that omits consideration of an approach to deference's ability to fulfil that criterion is incomplete.

Second, because Knight's analysis is derived from an examination and categorization of decided cases alone, it at best reflects the four prevalent approaches to deference that courts have adopted. However, the most appropriate approach to deference may be one that no court has yet adopted. It is true that there is value in assessments that focus on existing approaches, especially because common law judges tend to develop their approaches incrementally, building on existing approaches. However, it is often necessary to think beyond what has been done in considering what ought to be done. As will become clear in Chapters 3–6, my book identifies possible approaches to deference conceptually, going beyond the methods that courts have adopted in practice.

V. Potential Objections

My ambition to formulate guidance on deference might meet with objections from 'non-doctrinalists',[63] who would argue against any attempt to erect a further doctrinal edifice on the subject. The softer camp of non-doctrinalists represented by Tom Hickman would argue that factorial balancing on a case-by-case basis is the best the courts can do in deciding how to defer. Given the myriad contexts in which human rights cases take place, further doctrinal scaffolding governing the court's giving of weight to the executive or legislature's judgments would, if based on high-level abstractions (eg merely highlighting that expertise and democratic legitimacy are relevant factors for determining deference), be unable to enhance guidance/practicability to judges and litigants in any meaningful way, and, if based on more specific categories (eg certain subject matters attract more or less deference), be able to enhance guidance but be insufficiently sensitive to the facts.[64] My reply is that whilst enhancement of guidance/practicability indeed comes at the cost of sensitivity to context, that trade-off is sometimes necessary; that is, it is sometimes necessary, all things considered, to sacrifice sensitivity to context for greater guidance/practicability. These arguments are elaborated in Chapter 6. As a whole, the book not only analyses (in my discussions of the internal criterion) how deference can be made more context-sensitive but also fleshes out (in my discussions of the

[63] Jeff King, 'Institutional Approaches to Judicial Restraint' (2008) 28(3) OJLS 409, 411–14; Tom Hickman, *Public Law after the Human Rights Act* (Hart 2010) 130–43.

[64] Hickman (n 63) 137–39.

external criterion) the considerations that should determine where the balance between enhancing context sensitivity and increasing practicability lies, and proposes tools for striking that balance.

The harder camp of non-doctrinalists represented by Allan would argue against any form of independent doctrine on deference; even the fleshing out of the factors of a multifactorial balancing test would be unacceptable. Allan argues that any doctrine of deference is 'either empty or pernicious'.[65] It is empty if it merely repeats separation of power considerations that are already reflected in traditional judicial review principles.[66] It is pernicious if it counsels the courts to give leeway to the executive or legislature over and above what such principles mandate.[67] The argument on perniciousness is addressed in Chapter 2, where I argue that courts sometimes have to resort to reasoning that is external to the merits of the case, and in Chapter 5, where I explore when double counting occurs. Here, I focus on addressing Allan's argument on emptiness. As Paul Craig argues, even if considerations of judicial deference are part of the traditional principles of judicial review, it does not follow that such considerations would not benefit from open articulation and refinement.[68] The works of due deference theorists, as well as the present book, are precisely efforts to provide such articulation and refinement, thereby offering more guidance to judges and litigants on the crucial principle of deference. Such guidance is needed because of human fallibility and resource constraints in the real world. In the absence of doctrinal guidance, judges may arrive at wrong or inconsistent rulings, and litigants may be unable to plan their cases.[69] Thus, even granting that considerations of deference are part of the traditional principles of judicial review, that does not mean that attempts to elaborate and clarify those considerations, such as the present attempt, are insignificant.

VI. Roadmap of the Book

This book contains seven chapters (including the present chapter). Chapters 2 and 3 are the building blocks for Chapters 4–6, which constitute the crux of the book. Chapters 4 and 5 address the first of the two questions the book seeks to tackle, that is, how courts ought to defer to give effect to the reasons for deference in a

[65] Allan, 'Human Rights and Judicial Review' (n 7) 675.
[66] ibid 675, 679.
[67] ibid 675–82.
[68] Paul Craig, *UK, EU and Global Administrative Law: Foundations and Challenges* (CUP 2015) 246–48.
[69] See eg King, 'Institutional Approaches' (n 63) 411–13. Allan concedes the role of public law doctrine in 'promoting consistency and discipline in the exercise and development of judicial review': Allan, *The Sovereignty of Law* (n 7) 243.

particular case. Chapter 6 addresses the second question, that is, how methods of deference can be made more practicable without undue compromise of the normative underpinnings for deference. Chapter 7 concludes.

To answer the two questions, the book first explains, in Chapter 2, what reasons courts have for deference. The chapter draws a distinction between grounds for deference (which are tied to the fulfilment of objective values[70]) and factors for considering whether such grounds exist. It argues that in polities that satisfy certain background conditions (which include the jurisdictions whose case law the book draws upon), the courts have three sets of grounds for exercising deference: grounds that relate to arriving at the correct outcome on the rights issue in question, grounds that relate to respect for constitutional legitimacy, and a residual category of grounds that relate to other considerations that courts should take into account in adjudication. Chapter 2 maps out the relationship between such grounds and the main factors involved in considering their existence.

Chapter 3 then explains that the courts have at their disposal six devices for exercising deference: the burden of proof, standard of proof, standard of review, giving of weight to views, choice of interpretation (ie adopting an interpretation of a constitutional provision that affords the executive or legislature more decision-making room), and choice of remedy. Using case law, it illustrates how these devices operate at the three stages of rights adjudication.

With the reasons and devices for deference now explained, the foundation for exploration of the two key questions is laid. Chapters 4 and 5 explore the first question. They analyse how courts should deploy the six devices to fulfil the reasons for deference. Chapter 4 focuses on what we may call the 'qualitative' aspect of the analysis: it explores how courts should choose which device to use (and which issue to apply the device to) to fulfil a certain reason for deference. The chapter analyses the nature of each device, compares the normative considerations justifying the use of each device and deference on different substantive issues, and highlights situations in which the use of one device (or its application to a specific substantive issue) is needed to express a particular reason for deference. For example, the standard of review, a device that caters exclusively to the court–defendant relationship, cannot express the imperative to minimize the social costs of an erroneous ruling, which should be expressed using the burden and standard of proof, devices that cater to a three-way relationship (ie court–defendant–applicant). Moreover, sometimes the facts that give rise to reasons for deference discriminate between deference on various issues, in which case the court should determine which issue to defer on according to which set of facts exists. For example, if the public authority has superior expertise on the third but not the second limb of the proportionality test,

[70] Joseph Raz, *Practical Reasons and Norms* (OUP 1999) 34.

the court should defer on the former but not the latter so as to give effect to the expertise reason for deference.

Chapter 5 focuses on what we may call the 'quantitative' aspect of the first key question: it explores how courts should choose which device or combination of devices to use, and which stage of adjudication to defer at, to give effect to the strength of the reason for deference, that is, to express the right *degree* of deference. I first compare the range of deference (determined by the minimum and maximum degrees of deference) and granularity of deference (ie how fine-grained the degree of deference is) expressible by the six devices and argue, inter alia, that both the range and granularity of deference that the burden of proof can express are smaller/less than those of the other devices. I then explain how the degree of deference expressible by particular devices can be compared, and compare the degree of deference expressible at the three stages of adjudication. I argue that in the jurisdictions covered by this study, when deference at the definition and limitation stages is exercised in ways that lead to favourable outcomes for the primary decision-maker at those stages, the degree of deference manifested at the three stages—definition, limitation, remedy—is in decreasing order. The chapter then examines the combinability of devices. It offers a definition of the double counting of deference: that is, it occurs when a court gives undue additional weight to a ground (as defined in Chapter 2) served by deference. Understood as such, deference using more than one device, deferring for the same kind of reason more than once, or taking into account more than once a factor suggesting deference does not necessarily lead to double counting. Chapter 5 closes by highlighting three non-exhaustive categories of cases that raise suspicions of double counting.

The analysis in Chapters 4 and 5 concerns the internal logic of deference. It does not take into account the considerations of formulating deference methods that are workable for judges and predictable for litigants. Such external constraints are addressed in Chapter 6, which explores the second of this book's two questions, that is, how the methods of determining when, how, and how much to defer can be made more workable and predictable without undue compromise of those methods' ability to reflect the normative reasons for deference in a particular case. Noting that there is an inevitable trade-off between making methods of deference more practicable and making them more flexible to account for variations in the degree and means of deference across contexts, Chapter 6 expounds the factors that determine where the balance between these two considerations should lie and introduces four sets of techniques for striking that balance: the use of rules, presumptions, and factorial analysis; mapping certain normative considerations onto specific deference devices; developing clear and reliable indicators of deference; and developing finite scales for various devices and levels of scrutiny that combine various devices.

Chapter 7 concludes the book. It offers four examples of how the various techniques proposed in Chapter 6 can be combined and illustrates how they can be put into practice using the case of Hong Kong. It then draws together the previous chapters by highlighting examples of the sacrifices to internal logic that are entailed by greater accommodation of external constraints. It also presents examples of the empirical data needed to draw conclusive observations using the ideas in this book and suggests several directions for future research.

2
Reasons for Deference

I. Introduction

In Chapter 1, I explained that this book interrogates two questions, namely, how a court should defer to give effect to the reasons it has for deferring and how methods of deference can be made more practicable. To answer these questions, we need two building blocks: the reasons (if any) courts have for deferring and the devices available to courts for expressing deference. This chapter constructs the first of these two blocks. It begins, in section II, by analysing how judicial reasoning in the deference context works. Section III then draws a distinction between two kinds of reasons for deference: grounds and factors for considering whether said grounds exist. Section IV argues that in polities that satisfy certain background conditions, the courts have three sets of grounds for deference: grounds that relate to arriving at the correct outcome on the rights issue at hand; grounds that relate to respect for constitutional legitimacy; and grounds that relate to other considerations that the court should take into account in adjudication. Following on from this argument, section V maps out the relationship between such grounds and the main factors for considering their existence. Section VI then explains the relative merits of a taxonomy of reasons that uses grounds as a skeleton structure to organize factors. In sections VII–IX, I elaborate on when said grounds and factors can be taken to exist and anticipate and respond to potential objections. Section X recaps the normative foundations of the three sets of grounds. As will be seen, the analysis in this chapter lays the foundation for analysing what devices the courts should use to express the various reasons for deference (the subject of Chapter 4), when such devices may be combined (the subject of Chapter 5), and the potential and limits of using rule-bound methods of deference formulated on the basis of factors (the subject of Chapter 6). Section XI concludes with a summary.

Two preliminary points are in order. First, this chapter explores what reasons the courts have for deferring at a theoretical level; it does not aim to *directly* provide a deliberative guide to judges in particular jurisdictions or contexts. Whilst the book as a whole, and Chapter 6 on practicability in particular, is meant to offer practical guidance, the present chapter is not intended to offer guidance to the courts directly. Second, except for in section III and unless the context indicates otherwise, terms such as 'reasons to defer' are used throughout the chapter to cover both reasons for deference offered by grounds and those offered by factors,

Deference in Human Rights Adjudication. Cora Chan, Oxford University Press. © Cora Chan 2024.
DOI: 10.1093/9780198921677.003.0002

a distinction I elaborate on in section III. With these points in mind, let us now begin by examining what deference is.

II. Deference and Judicial Reasoning

In Chapter 1, I define judicial deference as occurring when a court grants leeway to the legislature or executive[1]—leeway that it would not have granted if it had merely considered its own balance of reasons on the rights issue at hand[2]—for reasons that arise from the comparative institutional positions of the court and the two political branches of government[3] (eg that the legislature is more likely than the court to arrive at a correct answer to, or has greater constitutional legitimacy to determine, a given issue). Let us now examine more closely how judicial reasoning in the deference context works.

The reasons that arise from the comparative institutional positions of the court and the primary decision-maker may function as first- or second-order reasons. Adopting Joseph Raz's distinction between first- and second-order reasons, a first-order reason is a reason that bears directly on an issue, whereas a second-order reason is *a reason about a first-order reason*: a 'reason to act for ... or to refrain from acting for' a first-order reason.[4]

Following Raz's account of the distinction between first- and second-order reasons, and departing from the understanding of some public lawyers that reasons for deference are exclusively second-order reasons,[5] this book allows for the possibility of reasons for deference operating in both the first- and second-order reasoning of the court. To see why that is possible, we need to understand that first-order reasons can bear on two types of questions. The first type concerns the merits of the case, that is, which party—the primary decision-maker or the applicant—has the stronger case on the rights issue before the court. The second concerns whether the court should grant leeway to the primary decision-maker *regardless of* the strength of its case on the merits. Hence, the fact that a reason does not pertain directly to the merits of the case does not automatically mean that it is

[1] I explain in Chapter 3 how the various devices for deference discussed in this book can be conceptualized using the idea of 'giving leeway'. cf Aileen Kavanagh, *The Collaborative Constitution* (CUP 2023) 272.

[2] Philip Soper, *The Ethics of Deference: Learning from Law's Morals* (CUP 2002) 22–24.

[3] Andrew Legg, *The Margin of Appreciation in International Human Rights Law: Deference and Proportionality* (OUP 2012) 1–2. For the concept of deference in law generally, see Gary Lawson and Guy I Seidman, *Deference: the Legal Concept and the Legal Practice* (OUP 2020).

[4] Joseph Raz, *Practical Reasons and Norms* (OUP 1999) 39.

[5] Eg Kavanagh, *The Collaborative Constitution* (n 1) 268–69; Dimitrios Kyritsis, 'What is Good about Legal Conventionalism' (2008) 14 LEG 135, 156; TRS Allan, 'Judicial Deference and Judicial Review: Legal Doctrine and Legal Theory' (2011) 127(Jan) LQR 96, 108–12; TRS Allan, *The Sovereignty of Law: Freedom, Constitution, and Common Law* (OUP 2013) 277.

a second-order reason; it may be a first-order reason pertaining to the second type of questions outlined herein.

Institutional-based reasons function as second-order reasons for deference when they reweigh[6] or pre-empt[7] the court's own balance of first-order reasons. Typically, this happens when the court adds weight to the public authority's case on the merits in view of the latter's superior expertise; that is, such expertise leads the court to reweigh its first-order reasons on the first type of questions outlined above.

Institutional-based reasons function as first-order reasons for deference when they do not affect the court's balance of reasons on the merits, but constitute reasons for granting leeway to the primary decision-maker *regardless of the strength of its case on the merits*, that is, reasons that relate to the second type of questions outlined above. They are reasons that reduce the relative importance (to the court) of arriving at a correct outcome on the merits.[8] An example is when a court believes that the legislature is wrong on a rights issue but nonetheless grants it significant leeway because the democratic reasons for doing so are so weighty that they *override* the importance of getting the issue correct in the case concerned, in which case the democratic reasons function as reasons for deference at the first-order level.

If a court is persuaded by first-order reasons to change its view on the merits of an individual rights claim, then it is not deferring; it is simply agreeing with the decision-maker or has been persuaded on the merits. The court is not acting 'contrary to the way [it] would normally act if [it] simply considered the balance of reasons'[9] on the rights issue before it. Hence, when institutional-based reasons function at the first-order level, only those that do not change the court's view on the merits of the rights issue are reasons for deference. This last point is further elaborated in section VII.1 on epistemic deference.

In relying on the distinction between first- and second-order reasons, and that between reasons that arise from the comparative institutional positions of the court and the primary decision-maker and those that do not, I am not saying that it is always easy to distinguish these reasons in concrete cases.[10] The reasons the courts consider may be 'submerged beneath legal doctrines' that reflect conclusions on

[6] Stephen Perry, 'Second-order Reasons, Uncertainty and Legal Theory' (1988–89) 62 S Cal L Rev 913, 932; Aileen Kavanagh, 'Defending Deference in Public Law and Constitutional Theory' (2010) 126 LQR 222, 233; Cora Chan, 'Deference, Expertise and Intelligence-gathering Powers' (2013) 33(4) LS 598, 600.

[7] For the treatment of second-order reasons as exclusionary reasons, see Joseph Raz, *The Morality of Freedom* (OUP 1986) ch 3; Soper (n 2) 38–47. The distinction between reweighting and pre-emption corresponds roughly to Yoav Dotan's distinction between 'disagreement deference' and 'avoidance deference': Yoav Dotan, 'Deference and Disagreement in Administrative Law' (2020) 71(4) Adm L Rev 761, 772–74.

[8] For the distinction between overriding and pre-emption, see Raz, *Practical Reasons* (n 4) 25–47.

[9] Soper (n 2) 22.

[10] cf Allan, 'Judicial Deference' (n 5) 96, 99–101.

the balance between those reasons.[11] The theorization of deference seeks to shed light on its 'deep structure' rather than its 'surface characteristics'.[12]

III. Grounds Versus Factors

Before I assess what reasons (if any) the courts have for deferring, I would first like to distinguish between grounds and factors. Grounds are reasons for the conclusion that deference is more likely than non-deference to fulfil the objective values[13] that deference can serve (eg arriving at the correct outcome on the rights issue in question, respect for constitutional legitimacy, coherence in related areas of law). Achievement of a value is an integral part of the formulation of a ground. Where a ground exists, the court has a conclusive reason to defer in relation to the value(s) concerned. This does not, however, mean that said reason cannot be outweighed by considerations of other values in a particular instance. For example, that there is a ground for deference in relation to the value of respecting constitutional legitimacy does not mean that the court should defer in the case in question. The value of respecting constitutional legitimacy may be outweighed in a particular instance by, say, the value of obtaining the correct outcome on the rights issue at hand, which demands non-deference. Hence, even if there is a reason to defer based on constitutional legitimacy, it may be that taking into account all relevant values the court should still not defer.

Grounds are to be distinguished from factors, which are *indicators*, presenting defeasible reasons to believe that a ground for deference is present. For example, in the jurisdictions covered by this book, a high degree of polycentricity over an issue is a factor that indicates that a ground, such as that deference is more likely than non-deference to lead to a correct outcome on the rights issue before the court, exists. Where a factor exists, there is a presumption that deference is more likely to fulfil a value, although that presumption can be rebutted. A court may be able to benefit from a non-conventional institutional setup in a particular case, for example, the use of amicus briefs, such that it is as competent as the original decision-maker to assess the polycentric issue at stake,[14] in which case the presumption offered by the polycentricity factor is rebutted. Where a presumption is not rebutted, a factor offers a good reason to defer. It is convenient to note at this point that although factors offer presumptive reasons for deference conceptually, Chapter 6 explains how there may be good reasons for the *court* to treat factors

[11] Dimitrios Kyritsis, *Where Our Protection Lies: Separation of Powers and Constitutional Review* (OUP 2017) 178.

[12] ibid, emphasis omitted.

[13] Raz, *Practical Reasons* (n 4) 34.

[14] cf eg Jeff King, *Judging Social Rights* (CUP 2012) 203–08.

as giving rise not merely to presumptions about deference but to bright-line rules as well.

Some factors are reliable indicators, but that does not turn them into grounds themselves. For example, in many contexts the fact that the original decision-maker has more expertise to assess a particular technical issue generally suggests that deference will likely lead to a correct outcome on the rights issue concerned. However, it may be that in a particular instance the decision-making process does not allow for that expertise to be applied to the given issue, in which case the presumption that the decision-maker is more likely than the court to arrive at the correct answer is rebutted. Therefore, indicators, even if reliable, still do not have the necessary connection with the achievement of values that grounds have.

The distinction between grounds and factors is conceptual rather than descriptive. My point is not that judges in fact reason about deference by making the distinction, but rather that a distinction exists at the conceptual level. The distinction between grounds and factors is normative in one sense but not in another. It is normative in that I argue that the distinction ought to be drawn in reasoning about when and how judges should defer. It provides the conceptual clarity needed for such analysis. Only by recognizing the distinction is one able to see that factors are relevant only insofar as they suggest the existence of a ground. If the distinction is elided, there is a risk of arriving at wrong conclusions on deference, for example, concluding that deference is warranted when a factor exists even though that factor fails to suggest that deference is more likely than non-deference to fulfil a value in a particular instance, or concluding that deference is not warranted merely because a factor is absent. Also, only by recognizing the distinction are we drawn to investigate the relationship between grounds and factors, investigation that is needed to probe such questions as whether double counting occurs when a court defers for the same factor more than once (which is the subject of Chapter 5) and what is lost in terms of the achievement of values when we rely on bright-line rules suggested by factors (which is the subject of Chapter 6).

However, I am not arguing that judges must take the distinction into account and rely on grounds directly in day-to-day adjudication. Whether they should do so depends, inter alia, on the ability of the judges in the given polity or context to assess whether certain values could be fulfilled by deference. Given the possibility of judicial fallibility, it might well be that courts could make better judgments on deference if they focused solely on factors without thinking about the underlying values (in the grounds formula). I explore guidelines that could be given to judges in light of judicial fallibilities in Chapter 6. For now, it suffices to note that this chapter is agnostic on whether judges should directly take the distinction between factors and grounds into account in adjudicating rights.

Despite the distinction's importance for theoretical analysis, it is often elided in scholarship. Some jurists place values (or grounds) and factors alongside each other, giving the impression that they operate at the same level of reasoning. For example, Jeff King identifies democratic legitimacy, polycentricity, expertise, and flexibility as the four main considerations informing the principles of judicial restraint.[15] As I explain below, whilst democratic legitimacy and flexibility are grounds, polycentricity and expertise are factors. Moreover, although some scholars and judges seem to be aware of the distinction,[16] there has been little analysis of the relationship between grounds and factors, for example, of which factors are presumptively suggestive of which grounds and how, bearing in mind that one factor may be suggestive of more than one ground. In sections IV–VI, I provide broad justification for three sets of grounds for deference, analyse the relationship between such grounds and certain key factors, and assess the relative merits of my taxonomy. Sections VII–IX then elaborate on when such grounds and factors can be taken to exist and deal with possible objections. Section X recaps the normative foundations of the three sets of grounds.

IV. Three Sets of Grounds for Deference

The question of when deference is due (if at all) in constitutional rights adjudication is part of a broader enquiry into how powers should be allocated between various branches of government, an enquiry that in turn depends on the political conditions that prevail in a given jurisdiction. The following discussion assumes the following background conditions,[17] which are prevalent in the jurisdictions that this book covers (which are common law jurisdictions that adopt the three-stage framework and a structured proportionality test in rights adjudication). The arguments in this chapter hold if these background conditions hold, although they may also hold in jurisdictions that do not meet all of the conditions.

1) The constitution was arrived at through a legitimate process, and its goals and allocation of powers are generally just and worthy of support.
2) Protection of constitutional rights is a key constitutional goal, and the courts have been granted powers to review legislative and executive acts for compatibility with constitutional rights.[18]

[15] ibid part II. See also eg Kirsty McLean, *Constitutional Deference, Courts and Socio-Economic Rights in South Africa* (Pretoria University Law Press 2009) ch 2.

[16] See eg Kavanagh, 'Defending Deference' (n 6) 246. See also Kavanagh, *The Collaborative Constitution* (n 1) 278–79.

[17] cf King, *Judging Social Rights* (n 14) 10–11.

[18] Such powers are covered under both (what are known as) 'strong-form' review and 'weak-form' review (or the 'New Commonwealth model'). See Mark Tushnet, 'Alternative Forms of Judicial Review' (2003) 101 Mich L Rev 2781; Stephen Gardbaum, *The New Commonwealth Model of Constitutionalism: Theory and Practice* (CUP 2013); Scott Stephenson, *From Dialogue to Disagreement in Comparative Rights Constitutionalism* (The Federation Press 2016).

3) The three main branches of government—legislative, executive, and judicial—bear the characteristics we commonly identify with the respective institutions of liberal democracies: that is, the legislature is relatively large, amateur, representative, and democratically accountable; the executive possesses force and technical capacities; and the courts are a triadic and reasoned forum, with a judiciary that has legal expertise and is relatively small and unelected.[19] Given their respective features, we can expect the three branches to have certain weaknesses, as well as strengths, even in the best of circumstances.
4) The three main branches of government engage in the joint enterprise of governing, with each having a distinct role to play. Governance is a matter of inter-institutional collaboration, with institutions complementing one another to 'achiev[e] good government under the constitution'.[20]
5) 'Circumstances of politics' and 'burdens of judgment' exist; that is, there are reasonable disagreements about, inter alia, what constitutes the content of rights and what that content requires, and action has to be taken in spite of such disagreements.[21]

In polities that satisfy these conditions, the courts have three main tasks and corresponding sets of grounds for deference in constitutional rights adjudication. First, they should strive to do justice to the applicant by arriving at correct answers to the rights issue before them, that is, to appropriately balance the considerations that determine what right the individual applicant has against the state. By 'right', I mean both the primary right to certain acts (or non-acts) by the state, as well as the secondary right of remedy to which the individual is entitled if his or her primary right is breached. In referring to 'correct' answers or outcomes, I do not mean to imply that there is necessarily a single right answer to any given rights issue.[22] There may be multiple correct answers. Nevertheless, the question of which institution—the court or the executive or legislature—is more likely to arrive at those answers would still arise.[23] To arrive at correct answers to rights issues, the courts may sometimes need to defer to the executive or legislature's view.

[19] See NW Barber, *The Principles of Constitutionalism* (OUP 2018) 57–70.

[20] Kavanagh, *The Collaborative Constitution* (n 1) 98, 115, 269, see also 4–5, 86–120; Kyritsis (n 11) ch 2; Aileen Kavanagh, 'The Constitutional Separation of Powers' in David Dyzenhaus and Malcolm Thorburn (eds), *Philosophical Foundations of Constitutional Law* (OUP 2016) 230–35; Jeff King, 'Institutional Approaches to Judicial Restraint' (2008) 28(3) OJLS 409, 427–28; King, *Judging Social Rights* (n 14) 11; Eoin Carolan, *The New Separation of Powers: A Theory for the Modern State* (OUP 2009) ch 5.

[21] Jeremy Waldron, *Law and Disagreement* (OUP 1999) chs 5, 7, 10; Jeremy Waldron, 'The Core of the Case Against Judicial Review' (2006) 115(6) Yale LJ 1346, 1368. For the concept of 'burdens of judgment', see John Rawls, *Political Liberalism* (Expanded edition, Columbia University Press 2005), 54–58.

[22] cf eg Ronald Dworkin, *Taking Rights Seriously* (Duckworth 1977) ch 13, 327–38.

[23] In the main this book does not take a position on the correct answers in particular cases; it merely assumes the possibility of correct answers.

Rights adjudication traverses all policy areas, and there are bound to be questions that the political organs have superior epistemic abilities to decide, particularly those involving a determination of the substance and priority of various collective interests.[24] Where it has been established that the primary decision-maker is more likely than the courts to arrive at the correct answer to a given question, it is rational for the courts to defer on that question.[25] The first set of grounds for deference is thus stated as follows: deference is more likely than non-deference to lead to the correct outcome for the rights issue concerned.

Second, the courts should respect constitutional legitimacy in deciding cases. There are at least two sources of constitutional legitimacy, which are sometimes conflated in discussions of the constitutional grounds for deference.[26] One is constitutional intent—expressed in, for example, constitutional provisions that allocate powers—which reflects where society thinks powers should lie. The allocation may be direct, for example, the constitution specifies that a certain matter is to be decided by a particular body. The allocation may also be indirect, for example, the constitution mandates compliance by the courts with certain standards (say, international treaties) or certain bodies (say, an international court), which in turn sets the threshold for judicial intervention on the matter in question. The other source of legitimacy is process values, including democracy, participation, and public accountability. Given the circumstances of politics, there has to be a fair way of resolving disagreements.[27] If the constitution specifies such a resolution mechanism, then constitutional intent provides a reason for following it. Even if the constitution does not specify a resolution mechanism, however, the fairness of the mechanism used provides an independent moral reason for adherence to it. The process values of democracy, participation, and public accountability thus give rise to legitimacy grounds for deference. Whilst constitutional rights adjudication can instantiate the process value of public accountability[28]—compelling and offering public justification for state encroachment on rights[29]—and in polities where the

[24] See eg Kavanagh, *The Collaborative Constitution* (n 1) 208–09.

[25] See eg Chan, 'Deference' (n 6) 603; Murray Hunt, 'Sovereignty's Blight: Why Public Law Needs "Due Deference"' in Nicholas Bamforth and Peter Leyland (eds), *Public Law in a Multi-Layered Constitution* (Hart 2003) 337; Kavanagh, 'Defending Deference' (n 6); Alison Young, 'In Defence of Due Deference' (2009) 72(4) MLR 554; Julian Rivers, 'Proportionality and Variable Intensity of Review' [2006] CLJ 174; Jeffrey Jowell, 'Judicial Deference: Servility, Civility or Institutional Capacity?' [2003] PL 592; Tom Hickman, *Public Law after the Human Rights Act* (Hart 2010) 142.

[26] cf Hickman, who distinguishes the 'allocation of functions' argument from the 'ballot box' argument: Hickman, *Public Law* (n 25) 156–59.

[27] See eg Waldron, *Law and Disagreement* (n 21) chs 5, 7, 10; Waldron, 'The Core of the Case' (n 21) 1371–75.

[28] Deference may be compatible with the value of public accountability when the original decision-maker has court-like qualities of independence and impartiality. See text to n 56.

[29] See eg Carolan (n 20) 103; Mattias Kumm, 'Institutionalising Socratic Contestation: The Rationalist Human Rights Paradigm, Legitimate Authority and the Point of Judicial Review' (2007) 1(2) EJLS 153; Mattias Kumm, 'The Idea of Socratic Contestation and the Right to Justification: The Point of Rights-Based Proportionality Review' (2010) 4(2) LEHR 141; for the idea of public reason see Rawls (n 21) 212–54.

constitution grants the courts rights review powers, constitutional intent is an added legitimacy reason for instituting such a review mechanism, there are also process grounds for judicial deference to decisions arrived at through democratic or participatory processes. In the case of democratic processes, deference is justified by the concept of political equality, that is, that decision-making by a democratic, representative institution 'publicly embodies the equal advancement of the interests of the citizens of a society when there is disagreement about how best to organize their shared life',[30] as well as the concept of liberty or self-determination.[31] Democratic processes enable citizens to have a say—and an equal one at that—in collective decision-making.[32] Self-determination also justifies judicial respect for decisions that are arrived at through processes involving stakeholder participation. The second set of grounds for deference is thus stated as follows: deference is more likely than non-deference to fulfil the demands of respect for constitutional legitimacy.

The third set of grounds for deference is a residual category comprising considerations that the court should take into account in adjudication but that do not relate to or go beyond the individual rights claim and do not concern constitutional legitimacy. Some of these grounds instead relate to the broader social and systemic effects of the court's decision, and become salient only at the remedial stage when the court needs to face head-on the potential impact of the coercive and immediate enforcement of an applicant's rights on the governmental system with respect to serving the public.[33] Examples of considerations that the courts have taken into account in determining deference, or that have been discussed in the literature and can be categorized under this set of grounds, include:

preserving the courts' long-term ability to protect rights (a consideration that usually arises in the context of a court decision with the potential to provoke a government backlash, say, in the form of curbing the court's competence);[34]

[30] Tom Christiano, 'Democracy', *The Stanford Encyclopedia of Philosophy* (Fall 2018 Edition), Edward N Zalta (ed), <https://plato.stanford.edu/archives/fall2018/entries/democracy/> section 2.2.3, last accessed 14 April 2024.

[31] ibid section 2.2.1.

[32] See eg Waldron, 'The Core of the Case' (n 21) 1386–395; Waldron, *Law and Disagreement* (n 21) ch 5. I should not be taken to endorse all of Waldron's arguments on voting equality.

[33] For the potential systemic impact of individual remedies, see eg Ernest J Weinrib, *Corrective Justice* (OUP 2012) 107–15; Kent Roach, 'Remedies for Laws that Violate Human Rights' in John Bell, Mark Elliott, Jason NE Varuhas, and Philip Murray (eds), *Public Law Adjudication in Common Law Systems: Process and Substance* (Hart 2016) 269; Robert Leckey, *Bills of Rights in the Common Law* (CUP 2015) 128–69; Aruna Sathanapally, *Beyond Disagreement: Open Remedies in Human Rights Adjudication* (OUP 2012) 26–29, 87–100.

[34] See eg Aileen Kavanagh, *Constitutional Review under the UK Human Rights Act* (CUP 2009) 199–200; Aileen Kavanagh, 'Judicial Restraint in the Pursuit of Justice' (2010) 60 U of Toronto LJ 23, 35–36; Rosalind Dixon, *Responsive Judicial Review: Democracy and Dysfunction in the Modern Age* (OUP 2023) 194–99. See also Mark Tushnet, 'New Forms of Judicial Review and the Persistence of

enhancing the efficacy of a rights decision for the applicant (a consideration that usually arises in the context of a rights decision potentially being better received by a hostile public if introduced by elected branches of government rather than imposed by judges);[35]

avoiding decisions that undermine the rights culture of the political branches,[36] diminish their sense of obligation and ability to protect rights,[37] or otherwise weaken the 'democratic responsiveness' of the political branches;[38]

ensuring coherence in government policy on related issues (eg when it is possible to allow the government to decide all related issues in one go);[39]

ensuring that a court decision will not have knock-on effects that the court is unable to assess or foresee;[40]

affording state institutions the flexibility to respond to new information or circumstances[41] (ie enabling them to arrive at appropriate policies and reach the right legal answers in future); and

respecting inter-institutional comity when another branch of government is considering the issue in question.[42]

Rights—and Democracy-Based Worries' (2003) 38 Wake Forest L Rev 813, 830; James B Thayer, 'The Origin and Scope of the American Doctrine of Constitutional Law' (1893) 7(3) Harv L Rev 129, 142–46; Julius Yam, 'Judging Under Authoritarianism' MLR, forthcoming. Early access: https://onlinelibrary.wiley.com/doi/10.1111/1468-2230.12861.

[35] Kavanagh, *Constitutional Review* (n 34) 200–01; Kavanagh, 'Judicial Restraint in the Pursuit of Justice' (n 34) 32–33. See also Richard H Fallon, Jr, 'Foreword: Implementing the Constitution' (1997) 111 Harv L Rev 54, 148–49.

[36] Thomas Poole, 'The Reformation of English Administrative Law' (2009) 68(1) CLJ 142, 162–64.

[37] Mark Tushnet, *Taking the Constitution Away from the Courts* (Princeton University Press 1999) 57–70; Alexander M Bickel, *The Least Dangerous Branch: The Supreme Court at the Bar of Politics* (2nd edn, Yale University Press 1986) 147–48; Thayer (n 34) 155–56; Dixon (n 34) 200–01.

[38] Dixon (n 34) 2–8. See also John Hart Ely, *Democracy and Distrust: A Theory of Judicial Review* (HUP, 1980); Sathanapally (n 33) 28–29; Leckey (n 33) 154–69; Cass R Sunstein, 'Foreword: Leaving Things Undecided' (1996) 110(4) Harv Law Review 6, 7.

[39] Kavanagh, *Constitutional Review* (n 34) 182–83. A classic example is *Bellinger v Bellinger* [2003] UKHL 21, [2003] 2 AC 467 [39]–[49]. Coherence here refers to coherence in the normative justifications given by the policymaker in related areas of law. It is to be distinguished from the consideration of ensuring that the courts can hand down consistent judgments on deference, a consideration that is discussed in Chapter 6 on workability and legal certainty.

[40] See eg *In Re S (Minors) (Care Order: Implementation of Care Plan)* [2002] UKHL 10, [2002] 2 AC 291 [35]–[44]. See also Michael Taggart, 'Proportionality, Deference, Wednesbury' (2008) NZ L Rev 423, 458.

[41] King, *Judging Social Rights* (n 14) ch 9; Sunstein (n 38) 8. This concern partly motivated Lords Neuberger, Mance and Wilson in *R (on the application of Nicklinson and another) v Ministry of Justice* [2014] UKSC 38, [2015] 1 AC 657 not to grant a remedy after finding a rights violation [120], [127]–[128].

[42] Kavanagh, *The Collaborative Constitution* (n 1) 98, 272, 294; *Nicklinson* (n 41) [116]–[128]; *The Queen on the application of The National Council of Civil Liberties (Liberty) v Secretary of State for the Home Department and another* [2018] EWHC 975 (Admin), [2019] QB 481 ('*NCCL*') [93]; also *Bellinger* (n 39) [37]; cf *R (Steinfeld and another) v Secretary of State for International Development* [2018] UKSC 32, [2020] AC 1 [58].

As part of the joint enterprise of governance, it is improper for the courts to decide a case without regard for the potential impact of its decision on the collective good.[43] Borrowing Alexander Bickel's words, 'however much judicial review may always' lead to drastic policy consequences 'uncertainly, inconclusively, and unavoidably', 'it should surely not do so knowingly, demonstrably and avoidably'.[44] A conception of the courts' role would be 'unduly narrow' if it focused solely on the first two grounds to the exclusion of other considerations.[45] Dimitrios Kyritsis puts the argument in these terms:

> the courts must be aware that they are partners in a project that they share with the other branches of government. This project is structured in a way that implements important constitutional principles like democracy and furthers aims like efficiency, and expediency ... [T]hat courts are partners in a joint project with the political branches has normative force that is independent of the content of the decisions that they are called upon to review.[46]

To fulfil their partnership role, courts may sometimes be required to 'assign normative weight to inputs that are morally sub-optimal'[47] from the perspective of the grounds of correct legal outcomes on rights issues or constitutional legitimacy.[48] The third set of grounds for deference is thus stated as follows: deference is more likely than non-deference to achieve other values that the court should take into account in adjudication.

The three sets of grounds for deference, and the grounds within each set, may pull in different directions. Resolution of the tension amongst them depends on the relative weight the court should grant the relevant grounds in a given case. Such weight is a function of the importance of the values at stake (eg how important it is to arrive at the correct outcomes for the rights issues in question), as well as the likelihood of deference being able to fulfil those values, with the court's assessment of such likelihood hinging on its ability to assess the original decision-maker's relative competence and legitimacy. All of these elements vary by context, and this chapter in the main discusses the issue of weight at only a general level. However, section IX on the third set of grounds discusses the issue at greater length to pre-empt objections. Chapter 6 then addresses the implications of the issue of judicial competence to assess questions of deference.

[43] Kavanagh, *The Collaborative Constitution* (n 1) 86–117.

[44] Bickel (n 37) 156.

[45] Kavanagh, *Constitutional Review* (n 34) 199. See also Fallon (n 35) 141–52. cf Allan, *The Sovereignty of Law* (n 5) 266–68, 319–23, which appear to reject all pragmatic or strategic considerations in judicial reasoning.

[46] Kyritsis (n 11) 162.

[47] ibid 193.

[48] See Kavanagh, 'Judicial Restraint in the Pursuit of Justice' (n 34) 32–34.

V. Factors Indicating Grounds

With the distinction between grounds and factors drawn, and the three sets of grounds for deference identified, we are now in a position to flesh out the key factors relevant to each set.[49] Let us begin by examining the first set: deference is more likely than non-deference to lead to correct answers to the rights issue in question. In polities that satisfy the aforementioned background conditions, a non-exhaustive list of factors for considering whether this ground exists includes the following:

1) The relative epistemic abilities or expertise of the original decision-maker, which is a culmination of that institution's qualifications, experience, track record, information, and institutional features, including the method by which it was formed and its decision-making processes. For questions whose correct answers depend on gauging the views of the public or particular stakeholders, the fact that a decision-making body is democratically elected or makes decisions through participatory processes (the factors relevant to assessing whether this is the case are presented in the discussion on constitutional legitimacy later in this section) is also a relevant factor.[50]
2) The nature of the right, which is an indicator of factor 1. The general assumption is that the courts have greater competence to assess questions of absolute rights than qualified rights because the latter involve assessments of collective interests, assessments that the political branches may be better positioned to make.
3) The complexity of the issue and degree of polycentricity, which are also indicators of factor 1. The general assumption is that the more polycentric[51] and complex the issue is, the less competence the court has to assess it.
4) The degree of judicial uncertainty over the legal answer, an indicator of factor 1, suggesting that the court may be less able to arrive at the correct answer than the original decision-maker.
5) The nature and importance of the right and extent of the rights limitation, which are indicators of factor 4. Assuming that the harm to the countervailing interest remains constant, the more unqualified and important the right, and the more serious its limitation, the more certain the court will be

[49] See Kavanagh, *The Collaborative Constitution* (n 1) 278–79 for a helpful list of factors.

[50] For an account of how the democratic features of the legislature may be relevant for both epistemic and legitimacy reasons, see Young, 'In Defence of Due Deference' (n 25) 565–66; Jeffrey Jowell, 'Judicial Deference and Human Rights: A Question of Competence' in Paul Craig and Richard Rawlings (eds), *Law and Administration in Europe: Essays in Honour of Carol Harlow* (OUP 2003) 80.

[51] See Lon L Fuller, 'The Forms and Limits of Adjudication' (Dec 1978) 92(2) Harv L Rev 353; King, *Judging Social Rights* (n 14) ch 7.

of an unjustified rights violation, and hence the less need it will have to defer for epistemic reasons.

Factor 1 is generally more proximate to the first ground for deference than the other factors, but it is nonetheless merely a factor suggesting that the ground exists rather than the ground itself. The presumptions stated in all the factors are rebuttable. For example, uncertainty over the legal answer tells us only that the court may lack the competence to decide the question. It tells us nothing about the other side of the equation—the executive or legislature may be similarly or even less competent,[52] in which case the presumptive reason to defer offered by legal uncertainty would be rebutted.

The factors listed above (both for this ground and the other grounds) do not all arise at the same time in adjudication.[53] Some can be ascertained at an earlier point in the adjudication process than others. For example, whilst a court may be able to ascertain polycentricity (factor 3) without assessing the merits of the case, it can ascertain the extent of a rights limitation (factor 5) only after assessing those merits to some degree. Nonetheless, all of the factors can be ascertained either without engaging with the merits of the case or before the court has fully reasoned through those merits, and can therefore act as a presumption about when, how, and how much to defer.[54] How factors can operate as presumptions is further explained in Chapter 6.

The second set of grounds for deference concerns respect for constitutional legitimacy. A non-exhaustive list of factors for determining whether the grounds in this set exist is as follows:

1) The importance of and potential harm to the countervailing societal interest, which are indicators of whether deference is more likely to meet the demands of respect for democratic values: the assumption is that the more that

[52] Komesar stresses the importance of assessing institutional competence in a comparative light: Neil K Komesar, *Imperfect Alternatives: Choosing Institutions in Law, Economics and Public Policy* (University of Chicago Press 1994).

[53] I thank the reviewer for highlighting this point.

[54] For example, whilst the degree of a rights limitation cannot be ascertained without looking at the facts of the case *at all*, it can be ascertained without full deliberation on whether the limitation of the right is justified overall. The court may therefore rely on this factor, ie the degree of the rights limitation, as a presumption about what standard of proportionality review to apply. For example, the court may take the view that when the degree of rights limitation is high, the strict necessity proportionality test presumably applies. If the court does take this view, then once it has ascertained that there is a serious limitation of a right in the case before it, it can presume that the strict necessity test applies. The factors can operate as presumptions even if they are contingent on the ascertaining of certain facts. The earlier those facts can be ascertained, the earlier they can function as presumptions for the court. Nevertheless, the ascertaining of factors may frontload certain issues in the merits of the case. For example, but for the need to ascertain how important a right is and the degree of the rights limitation in order to determine, say, whether a presumed standard of review applies, these questions would be assessed only when the court examines the third and fourth limbs of the proportionality test. For further elaboration on how factors can operate as presumptions, see Chapter 6.

is at stake for society as a whole, the greater the need for the decision to be made by those who are democratically accountable.

2) The nature of the impugned decision, which is an indicator of whether deference to a particular institution is more likely to meet the demands of respect for democratic values: the assumption is that a decision with a stronger democratic pedigree warrants more deference on legitimacy grounds.[55]
3) The degree of polycentricity, which is an indicator of whether deference is more likely to meet the demands of respect for democratic and participatory values: the assumption is that the more polycentric an issue, the less likely it is that the interests of all of those affected will be reflected in the judicial process, and hence the more relative legitimacy that participatory or democratic decision-making processes have.
4) The institutional features of the primary decision-maker and the court, which are indicators of whether deference is more likely to meet the demands of respect for constitutional legitimacy: the assumptions are that the more democratic or participatory the original decision-maker's processes are, the more that deference would enhance democratic or participatory values, and that the more independent and impartial the original decision-maker is, the more that deference would be compatible with the demands of public accountability.[56]
5) Whether the political branches of government would be willing and able to step in if the court did not intervene,[57] which is an indicator of whether deference is more likely to meet the demands of respect for constitutional legitimacy.
6) Whether there is reasonable disagreement over the rights issue, whether there is more than one way of remedying the rights violation or whether an alternative scheme needs to be established, and whether remedying a violation would entail radical and controversial legal reform, which would affect whether there is a heightened need to instantiate the value of democracy: if the answer is positive, more leeway should be afforded democratic decision-making processes.
7) Judicial uncertainty over the legal answer to an issue, which is an indicator of whether there is reasonable disagreement over the rights issue.

[55] Note, however, that deference on grounds of constitutional legitimacy is not necessarily limited to directly elected decision-makers. For a discussion of how reasoned administration can contribute to democratic values, see eg Jerry L Mashaw, *Reasoned Administration and Democratic Legitimacy: Reasoned Administration and Democratic Legitimacy* (CUP 2018). See also Matthew Lewans, *Administrative Law and Judicial Deference* (Hart 2018) 184–223.

[56] See eg *R (Cart) v Upper Tribunal* [2011] UKSC 28, [2012] 1 AC 663, a landmark decision on the UK courts' role in supervising the restructured tribunal system. On the implications of this decision, see Joanna Bell, 'Rethinking the Story of *Cart v Upper Tribunal* and Its Implications for Administrative Law' (2019) 39(1) OJLS 74. The effect of *Cart* was reversed by s 2 of the Judicial Review and Courts Act 2022.

[57] Kavanagh, *The Collaborative Constitution* (n 1) 322–27.

8) The nature and importance of the right and extent of the rights limitation, which affect whether there is a heightened need for the value of public accountability to be instantiated: the assumption is that the more unqualified and important the right, and the more serious its limitation, the stronger the need for public accountability, and thus the less deference the courts should grant.[58]
9) Whether the rights in question pertain to those 'particularly vulnerable to majoritarian bias and neglect',[59] which affects whether there is a heightened need for the value of public accountability to be instantiated: the assumption is that when such rights are involved, there is a stronger need to compel public accountability from government institutions, and hence the courts should grant less deference.[60]

The third set of grounds for deference concerns the fulfilment of other values that the court should take into account in adjudication. A non-exhaustive list of factors relevant to assessing whether deference can serve the values listed in section IV is as follows:

1) The importance of and potential harm to the countervailing societal interest, which is an indicator of whether deference is more likely to protect the long-term ability of the court to do justice: the higher the stakes for society, the greater the risk of a government or societal backlash.
2) The nature of the impugned decision, which is an indicator of whether deference is needed to avoid undesirable or unforeseeable systemic effects, with legislation and policies generally having a more far-reaching impact than individualized administrative decisions.
3) The institutional features of the decision-maker in question and the court, which constitute an indicator of whether deference is more likely to lead to coherence in related areas of law and prevent the decision from having undesirable or unforeseeable systemic effects.
4) Whether other branches of government would be willing and able to step in if the court did not intervene, which is an indicator of whether deference is more likely to enhance the efficacy of the rights decision and enhance coherence in related areas of law.

[58] Julian Rivers went so far as to suggest that the intensity of review (ie degree of deference) should be determined solely by the seriousness of the rights limitation. Rivers (n 25) 205. King argues that democratic legitimacy is not a valid reason for deference when absolute constitutional rights are at stake. King, *Judging Social Rights* (n 14) 173–74.

[59] King, *Judging Social Rights* (n 14) 177–85.

[60] See the arguments in ibid 176–85 and Ely, *Democracy and Distrust* (n 38). cf Richard Ekins, *The Nature of Legislative Intent* (OUP 2012) chs 4–5; Waldron, 'The Core of the Case' (n 21) 1395–401; Paul Yowell, *Constitutional Rights and Constitutional Design: Moral and Empirical Reasoning in Judicial Review* (Hart 2018) 115–30.

5) How well democratic processes are functioning in practice and the level of societal respect for the court and elected branches of government, which are indicators of whether deference is more likely to enhance the efficacy of a rights decision.
6) Whether the circumstances are likely to change and new information come to light, thereby calling for a revisitation of the judicial decision, which is an indicator of whether deference is more likely to enable state institutions to arrive at correct decisions in future.[61]

Two observations, both harking back to our earlier discussion of the importance of recognizing the grounds versus factors distinction, can be made based on the analysis thus far. First, a factor may be relevant to more than one ground. For example, the institutional features of the original decision-maker and court are relevant to assessing the existence of all three sets of grounds. This mapping of grounds and factors sheds light, inter alia, on whether, and if so when, it is justified for the court to defer to a decision-maker's institutional features more than once, and sets the scene for Chapter 5. Second, the systematic exposition of what values the factors are indicative of reveals the potential and limits of achieving those values by following bright-line rules formulated on the basis of factors, thus setting the stage for the discussion in Chapter 6.

VI. Relative Merits of the Taxonomy

The taxonomy of reasons proposed herein is distinct in that it uses grounds exclusively as an umbrella structure for fitting factors. It therefore differs from many of the taxonomies in the literature, which place factors—especially those that are reliable indicators of more than one ground (which can be called 'super indicators')—at the forefront, either exclusively or alongside grounds.[62] Whether the proposed taxonomy is preferable to these other taxonomies depends, inter alia, on the purpose for which the taxonomy is formulated. A taxonomy that places such factors as the institutional features of the political branches and courts at the forefront may be preferable if that purpose is descriptive: such a taxonomy may more accurately reflect how judges in a particular jurisdiction or context reason about deference because reliable indicators may play an important role in judicial reasoning. A taxonomy that features reliable indicators may also be preferable if the purpose is to devise a guide to help judges to arrive at correct judgments on deference in specific jurisdictions or contexts. If the identified factors are indeed reliable indicators of

[61] See King, *Judging Social Rights* (n 14) ch 9; *Nicklinson* (n 41) [112], [116]–[120], [127]–[128].
[62] See eg Paul Craig, *UK, EU and Global Administrative Law: Foundations and Challenges* (CUP 2015) 249–55; Kavanagh, *Constitutional Review* (n 34) ch 7; King, *Judging Social Rights* (n 14) part II.

grounds in a given jurisdiction or context—that is, if their existence generally suggests that deference will more likely than non-deference fulfil underlying values—then the risk of an erroneous judgment on deference arising from a focus on those factors is likely to be small. Given the possibility of judicial fallibility in assessing whether a factor will fulfil a value in a given situation, it may well be that in certain polities and contexts, correct judgments on deference can be maximized by guiding judges to focus on reliable factors.

However, the purpose of my taxonomy is not descriptive, and nor is it to *directly* provide a guide for judges in a particular jurisdiction or context. Rather, it is to offer the conceptual resources needed for theoretical analysis of deference. For *this* purpose, a taxonomy that uses grounds to structure factors is preferable to one that places reliable factors at the forefront for two reasons. First, the proposed structure helps to reorient reasoning on deference around the ultimate values being served by the factors, thereby reducing the risk of the erroneous analysis of deference that might result from overemphasis on factors, a point I allude to in section III.

Second, because the conceptual resources developed herein are intended to be applicable to jurisdictions that fit the aforementioned background conditions and across various human rights contexts, the taxonomy needs to be structured around elements that are common to said jurisdictions and contexts. Whilst it is relatively easy to identify the grounds and factors shared by jurisdictions and contexts, it is harder to identify shared reliable factors because whether a factor is reliable is highly context dependent. The pool of common denominators would be smaller if the focus were on reliable factors, and the utility of the resulting taxonomy weaker. For present purposes, therefore, a taxonomy that features grounds rather than reliable factors is preferable.

The advantages and limitations of taxonomies that place reliable factors at the forefront can be demonstrated by assessing the desirability of taxonomies that feature 'institutional grounds for deference' that are independent of epistemic considerations. Writing in the context of the UK Human Rights Act 1998 (HRA), Paul Craig and Aileen Kavanagh intend 'institutional grounds for deference' to cover situations in which the primary decision-maker, by virtue of possessing law-making competence that the court lacks (such possession is classified as a factor under my schema), is in a better position to resolve an issue over and above any epistemic considerations.[63] The values served by deference in such situations include respect for the constitutional allocation of powers and democratic processes (which I categorize under the second set of grounds) and flexibility, coherence in related areas of law, and the avoidance of knock-on effects (which I categorize under the third set of grounds). The typical cases with 'institutional grounds for deference' are those in which the courts defer or consider deferring when assessing

[63] Craig (n 62) 249 and Kavanagh, *Constitutional Review* (n 34) 182–83.

what remedies would be appropriate[64] because they are concerned that granting a relatively intrusive remedy would lead to systemic effects that are undesirable, unforeseeable, or beyond the court's ability to assess; tie the government's hands on a matter that requires flexibility; pre-empt a decision being considered by parliament, thereby breaching inter-institutional comity; or lead to an overhaul of the law or judicial selection of one of numerous options to remedy the situation, a move that the court lacks the constitutional legitimacy to make.[65]

I have no substantive disagreement with these authors. We agree that the identified considerations are reasons for deference. However, they place the relative institutional competence of the political branches and courts in the driver's seat of their taxonomy, whereas I place such competence in a comparatively backseat position. The appeal of their approach in terms of reflecting how judges actually reason in the United Kingdom is evident: the aforementioned typical cases are common in the HRA context, and the courts in such cases often refer to the government's lawmaking competence as a reason for deference, using such wording as 'institutional propriety' and 'institutional competence' to encapsulate relevant considerations,[66] which demonstrates that the government's lawmaking competence figures prominently in the courts' reasoning on whether to defer. The appeal of these authors' approach in terms of offering a deliberative guide for judges in most human rights contexts in the United Kingdom is also evident: in the United Kingdom, that the government possesses lawmaking competence that the court lacks generally means that if the court defers and passes the ball back to the government, the latter will duly exercise its lawmaking competence, thereby allowing the underlying values of coherence in how the government treats related issues, the avoidance of undesirable systemic effects and respect for constitutional legitimacy to be achieved. The government's lawmaking competence can, in the context of the HRA, be taken as a 'super indicator' for deference achieving numerous underlying values.

However, even the UK government may fail to heed the court in rare circumstances.[67] A taxonomy oriented around grounds rather than reliable factors better enables theorists to recognize situations in which institutional features should not attract deference because they do not suggest a ground. In addition, the government's possession of lawmaking competence cannot be taken as a reliable

[64] The question of what remedies are more deferential than others will be explored in Chapter 3.

[65] See eg *Nicklinson* (n 41) [110]–[128]; *Re S* (n 40) [35]–[44]; *International Transport Roth GmbH and others v Secretary of State for the Home Department* [2002] EWCA Civ 158, [2003] QB 728 [156]–[184]; *Bellinger* (n 39) [37]–[49].

[66] See eg *R (on the application of DA and others) v Secretary of State for Work and Pensions* [2019] UKSC 21, [2020] 1 All ER 573 [90]–[91]; *Alconbury Developments Limited v Secretary of State for the Environment, Transport and the Regions* [2001] HRLR 2 [95]–[106].

[67] Consider eg the UK government's defiance (for many years) on prisoners' voting rights. Notwithstanding that the court involved was the ECtHR rather than a UK court, the point being made remains valid, ie that one cannot rule out that in rare circumstances the UK government may fail to act on a cue given by the court to introduce rights reform. See also Hayley Hooper, 'Trust As A Core Principle of the Constitution' (2022) 81(2) CLJ 228.

factor across all contexts in all jurisdictions that meet the aforesaid conditions. In Hong Kong, for example, it cannot be assumed that the government will generally exercise its lawmaking competence if the court passes the ball back to it in relation to, say, sexual minority rights. The difference from the United Kingdom in this scenario is the result, inter alia, of differing levels of public concern for sexual minority rights and the ability and determination of the governments in the respective jurisdictions to introduce controversial rights reform.

A pair of cases from the United Kingdom and Hong Kong serves to demonstrate that whether a factor is reliable is context dependent. In *Bellinger v Bellinger*[68] and *W v Registrar of Marriages*,[69] the UK House of Lords (UKHL) and Hong Kong Court of Final Appeal (HKCFA), respectively, held that the then prevailing marriage laws violated the right to marry insofar as they made no provision for the right of those who had undergone gender reassignment surgery to marry in their post-operative gender. Both courts chose a relatively deferential option from amongst the remedies open to them: the UKHL granted a declaration of incompatibility rather than remedially interpret 'female' as including the applicant, whereas the HKCFA ordered a remedial interpretation but suspended the order for twelve months, thereby giving the government time to introduce comprehensive legislation.[70] The two courts' choice of a relatively deferential remedy was driven by similar concerns, including enabling coherence in policy across related areas of law.[71] Both courts concluded that it was best to leave it to the government, which had lawmaking competence, to introduce comprehensive reform.

The UK Parliament did eventually pass said comprehensive legislation,[72] but the Hong Kong government institutions did not. In fact, the latter did not even pass the minimum legislative revisions needed to allow the applicant to marry because the Hong Kong legislature is dominated by members hostile to sexual minority rights[73] and the executive does not have the political muscle to introduce controversial rights reform. These divergent outcomes suggest that the fact that a government possesses lawmaking competence cannot be considered a reliable indicator of deference enhancing coherence in the law *across the board in all jurisdictions* that meet the background conditions. It is certainly not a reliable factor in the context of sexual minority rights in Hong Kong. A taxonomy that places institutional features at the forefront not only risks erroneous assessments of deference; it is also non-transferable as a guide to contexts and jurisdictions in which those features cannot be taken as a reliable indicator.

68 *Bellinger* (n 39).
69 [2013] HKCFA 39, [2013] 3 HKC 375.
70 *Bellinger* (n 39) [34]–[55]; *W* (n 69) [120]–[150].
71 *Bellinger* (n 39) [39]–[49]; *W* (n 69) [120]–[148].
72 In fact, preparation for legislation was already underway when the case was being decided.
73 Note that even the minority of legislators who were pro-LGBT rights vetoed the proposed legislative revisions because they thought that they did not go far enough.

The proposed taxonomy may or may not be a good guide for helping judges to arrive at correct judgments on deference. Whether it is depends, inter alia, on the ability of judges in the given jurisdiction and context to arrive at appropriate judgments on deference through reasoning using both grounds and factors rather than the latter alone. What can be said with certainty, however, is that it offers conceptual building blocks for constructing other taxonomies that can serve as useful deliberative guides for judges in particular polities or contexts. For example, jurists may take from my taxonomy certain factors, assess for particular jurisdictions or contexts the proximity of said factors to the underlying values therein, sift out the most proximate ones, and feature them in a taxonomy meant to guide judges in those jurisdictions or contexts.

Having laid down a taxonomy of grounds and factors, I now examine in greater detail when such grounds and factors can be taken to have been established.

VII. Arriving at Correct Answers to Rights Issues Before the Court

1. First- versus second-order epistemic competence

As explained above, an indicator of whether deference can lead to correct outcomes is the relative epistemic abilities of the court and primary decision-maker. To understand how epistemic deference works, it should be noted that the executive or legislature's superior epistemic ability can be relevant to the court's reasoning at both the first- and second-order levels, a point alluded to in section II.[74] At both levels, such ability generates reasons for the court to believe that the primary decision-maker is correct on the rights issue before the court, but it does so in different ways. Superior epistemic ability figures in the court's first-order reasoning when such ability is demonstrated by sound arguments on the merits that persuade the court that the primary decision-maker is correct. In this case, its superior epistemic ability strengthens the primary decision-maker's case, albeit only indirectly via the persuasive arguments on the merits. The court agrees with the decision-maker (or agrees with it to a greater extent than it would in the absence of such arguments); it does not defer.

In contrast, the primary decision-maker's superior epistemic ability figures in the court's second-order reasoning when such ability is not demonstrated by persuasive arguments on the merits, but nonetheless suggests there are reasons to believe that the primary decision-maker is more likely than the court to be correct; for example, the original decision-maker has a good track record or credentials in the subject matter concerned. In this case, its superior epistemic ability strengthens

[74] I first drew this distinction in Chan, 'Deference' (n 6) 600–01.

the decision-maker's case directly without being mediated through persuasive arguments on the merits. The court views the decision-maker's case more favourably than it ordinarily would if it simply considered its own balance of first-order reasons on the rights issue; it has deferred to the decision-maker's case.

For example, if the executive is able to demonstrate its superior information-gathering powers by revealing information to the court, and the court is convinced by that information, then those powers will figure into the court's first-order reasoning. However, if the executive is unable to disclose to the court the information underpinning its conclusions, say, for national security reasons, but the court nevertheless trusts those conclusions, then the executive's information-gathering abilities will figure into the court's second-order reasoning.[75] Similarly, if the primary decision-maker is able to demonstrate its expertise by proffering convincing reasons on the merits of the rights issue in question, then such expertise will be factored into the court's first-order reasoning. If the decision-maker's expertise cannot be demonstrated by such persuasive reasons, but is nevertheless given weight by the court, then it is relevant as second-order reasoning. Second-order arguments of expertise often take the form of the primary decision-maker possessing certain institutional features that make it more likely to be correct in the *type* of question at hand.[76]

Understanding the two different ways in which the primary decision-maker's expertise can figure into the court's reasoning helps us to understand a key issue that divides Trevor Allan and due deference theorists, an issue upon which I elaborate in section VII.5. For now, it suffices to highlight that for the purposes of this book, the first set of grounds for deference refers to reasons concerning arriving at correct outcomes on the rights issue in question that arise directly from the superior epistemic ability of the original decision-maker, that is, when that ability figures in the court's *second*-order reasoning.

2. The role of judicial uncertainty

Some scholars have argued that deference is appropriate when the courts are uncertain about the correct answer.[77] As indicated in section V, however, uncertainty itself is not a ground for deference. That a court is uncertain does not mean that it is in a worse position than the executive or legislature to arrive at the correct answer. Uncertainty is, however, an indicator of the court's epistemic limitations in resolving the issue in question. Despite not being a ground for deference itself,

[75] See eg *The Queen on the Application of Louis Farrakhan v Secretary of State for the Home Department* [2002] EWCA Civ 606, [2002] QB 1391 [73].

[76] See Chan, 'Deference' (n 6) 601–02 for illustrations of the distinction.

[77] See eg Kavanagh, *Constitutional Review* (n 34) 171–72.

uncertainty nonetheless offers a prima facie reason to believe that deference is likelier to lead to correct outcomes than non-deference, and hence it is right for scholars to treat it as a trigger or, in Aileen Kavanagh's words, 'constitutional cue'[78] for considerations of deference.

Uncertainty here refers to a court being uncertain of the proper weight of one or both sides of the case at hand or taking the view that the weight is finely balanced between the two.[79] The courts face both empirical and normative epistemic uncertainty in rights adjudication.[80] The former occurs when a court is unsure of the factual state of affairs, whilst the latter occurs when it is unsure of certain moral or value judgments. That both types of uncertainty occur in rights adjudication becomes clear when we consider the rights limitation stage. Consider, for example, an instance of the government raising the minimum age for being granted a marriage visa from 18 to 21, purportedly to tackle the problem of forced marriages, the facts of *R (on the application of Quila and another) (FC) v Secretary of State for the Home Department*.[81] In assessing whether this measure is a proportionate limitation on the right to marry of those between the ages of eighteen and twenty-one, the court may face both empirical and normative uncertainty.[82] Empirical uncertainty may arise at all four limbs of the proportionality test.[83] At the first limb, the court may be uncertain about the extent of the problem of forced marriage, and hence of whether preventing it is a sufficiently important reason to justify the limitation of the right to marry. Empirical uncertainty may also arise at the second limb, with the court unsure of whether the measure in question is capable of deterring forced marriages. At the third limb, the court may be uncertain about the existence of less restrictive measures that could deter such marriages to the same extent. Finally, at the fourth limb, the court may be unsure of both the number of unforced marriages that would be affected by the measure and the degree of deterrence of forced marriages likely to be effected by it, and hence of whether the two are fairly balanced.

Normative epistemic uncertainty can arise at the first and fourth limbs of the proportionality test.[84] To continue with the foregoing illustrative case, even if the

[78] Kavanagh, *The Collaborative Constitution* (n 1) 279.

[79] Chan, 'Deference' (n 6) 603.

[80] Alan DP Brady, *Proportionality and Deference under the UK Human Rights Act* (CUP 2012) 68–73. See also Niels Petersen, 'The Construction of Judicial Deference and the Use of Scientific Evidence in Constitutional Jurisprudence' (on file with author).

[81] [2011] UKSC 45, [2012] 1 AC 621. See also the analysis of this case in Alison L Young, 'Will You, Won't You, Will You Join the Deference Dance?' (2014) 34(2) OJLS 375, 378–80.

[82] I am not saying that the court in *Quila* did face these two forms of uncertainty, but rather that they may arise in a case like it.

[83] Brady (n 80) 69.

[84] ibid 72. Normative epistemic reasons for deference are distinct from democratic legitimacy reasons for deference. A court may be sure of its own normative judgment and have no normative epistemic reason to defer but may still have legitimacy reasons to give weight to the legislature's judgment, and vice versa.

court knows the extent of the problem of forced marriages at the first limb, it may still be uncertain about whether tackling that problem is sufficiently important to warrant the rights limitation, which is a value judgment. At the fourth limb, even if the court knows the extent of the harm to the right and benefit to society brought about by the measure, it may still be unsure of whether a fair balance has been struck between the two, an assessment that involves a value judgment.

3. Weighing first- and second-order reasons

Deference on the ground that it is more likely than non-deference to lead to correct outcomes would be justified were a court to conclude, after taking into account both first- and second- order reasons relevant to that ground, that deference would indeed be likelier to lead to such outcomes. Such a balancing act depends, inter alia, on how certain the court is of its own answer on the merits or of its ability to arrive at the right answer on the merits and how compelling the second-order epistemic reasons are. For example, if the court's first-order reasoning yields considerable uncertainty over whether there has been a rights violation, and the government proffers solid second-order evidence to show that it is likelier to be correct than the court, then there is a strong case for deference. Conversely, if the court is very sure that there has been a rights violation, and there is no strong second-order evidence that the government is likelier to be correct, then the case for deference is weaker.

4. Establishing second-order epistemic competence

Much has been written on the types of expertise that particular government institutions may possess and the limitations thereof.[85] It is beyond the scope of this chapter to conduct the type of comprehensive analysis that is already on offer, and I thus highlight just a few general points here.

First, epistemic abilities vary greatly across institutions and individuals, and accurate assessment of whether a decision-maker is in a superior epistemic position requires identification of the precise issue with which the court is faced and sensitivity to the relative competence of the courts and decision-maker in question.

Second, expertise may be more or less specific to the question at issue. The more specific it is to the question, the more reliable expertise is as an indicator that deference will lead to correct outcomes. Assume that the executive has prohibited X from entering the country, claiming that there is secret intelligence information

[85] See eg Elizabeth Fisher and Sidney A Shapiro, *Administrative Competence: Reimagining Administrative Law* (CUP 2020) chs 2–3; King, *Judging Social Rights* (n 14) ch 8; Yowell (n 60) chs 4–5; Waldron, 'The Core of the Case' (n 21) 1376–86.

showing him to be a terrorist who poses a threat to national security. In the absence of the intelligence information upon which the executive has relied, the court has to decide whether to believe that X poses a national security threat. The executive may try to demonstrate its superior expertise in assessing the matter by pointing to its general institutional features (eg information-gathering powers), seeking to show that it possesses more information than the court in general for making national security assessments. Alternatively, it may point to its track record and to specific institutional features to demonstrate that it is a reliable judge of whether someone is a terrorist. The latter demonstration is more specific to the question at issue. It shows not only that the executive has greater capacity to garner useful information than the court, but also that it has, in the context of judging whether an individual is a terrorist, applied that capacity and made reliable risk assessments based on the information collected. The latter claim of epistemic superiority should attract more deference than the former.

Third, although expertise is often associated with administrators,[86] it is possible for a legislature to also possess superior expertise. I elaborate upon this point together with my fourth and final point, namely, that superior expertise can be established in relation to both empirical and normative matters. Yowell argues that certain institutional features of courts and legislatures render the latter more competent in general than the former to make the empirical and normative assessments needed to resolve constitutional rights cases.[87] My argument here is less ambitious. I do not claim that legislatures are generally more competent to make such assessments. Instead, based on the features highlighted by Yowell, I argue that they could be so. The fact that legislatures are elected and relatively large enables them to acquire certain facts about the society (eg constituent preferences) that the courts—being unelected and bivalent—are less able to acquire. Insofar as the correct answer to an issue depends on such facts, a legislature can be considered an expert. For example, consider that a court has to decide whether allowing a satirical publication on Christianity would seriously injure religious sentiments. The legislature's proximity to its constituents may equip it with knowledge of the Christian community's feelings that the court lacks. To give another example, if the urgency of a social problem depends partly on how frustrated the public is with that problem, then the legislature may again be in a better position than the courts to assess whether the problem's resolution is a sufficiently important aim to limit rights. The legislature may also have superior knowledge of its own internal workings. For example, in situations such as that in the Hong Kong case of *Kwok Cheuk Kin v Secretary for Constitutional and Mainland Affairs*,[88] where the court needed

[86] See eg King, *Judging Social Rights* (n 14) 221. For a comprehensive and sophisticated account of administrative capacity and accountability and how administrative law can promote it, see Fisher and Shapiro, *Administrative Competence* (n 85).

[87] Yowell (n 60) chs 4–5.

[88] [2017] HKCFA 44, [2017] 5 HKC 242.

to decide whether it was necessary to adopt a law preventing legislators from resigning to set in motion a de facto referendum in order to protect the integrity of the legislature, it is possible that the legislature itself may be better able to predict the law's necessity, given its superior knowledge of how legislators generally behave.

It seems that the courts do not commonly defer for normative epistemic reasons in practice. Such a stance may be justified—although I remain agnostic about whether it is—given that the courts do not seem to have less access to moral truth than the executive or legislature. Be that as it may, it cannot be ruled out that particular instances may arise in which the courts fare worse in moral reasoning. Waldron and Yowell argue that sound decisions concerning morality are more likely to be reached when deliberation is open-ended and upfront[89] (uncluttered by legal procedures, doctrine and other technicalities) and involves people with diverse backgrounds, features that are generally present in legislatures and absent in the courts.[90] Normative assessments by the political branches thus deserve a degree of judicial deference, at least in situations where their deliberations have been thorough, based on public reasons, and involve voices not represented in the judicial process.

5. Objections

Although deference for epistemic reasons is relatively uncontroversial, objections have been raised by critics who reject any doctrine of deference, the most prominent of whom is Trevor Allan. In Chapter 1, I respond to his argument that any doctrine of deference is empty, by explaining how such doctrine adds value to our understanding of how the courts should reason. Here, I address his criticism that deference is pernicious. His remarks that due considerations of deference can and should be accommodated in the court's reasoning on the merits[91] may give the impression that he in fact agrees in large part with the deference approach advanced by due deference theorists, objecting only to the distillation of the considerations on deference into a theory. However, closer examination of his position reveals a key difference with such theorists. Whilst both camps accept that epistemic abilities can be relevant to the court's first-order reasoning on the merits, they disagree on their relevance to its second-order reasoning.[92] Allan insists that expertise matters only if it is able to generate convincing reasons on the merits of the case,[93]

[89] Yowell (n 60) 109.

[90] ibid 110; Waldron, 'The Core of the Case' (n 21), 1376–86.

[91] Allan, 'Judicial Deference' (n 5).

[92] Chan, 'Deference' (n 6) 602.

[93] See eg TRS Allan 'Human Rights and Judicial Review: A Critique of "Due Deference"' (2006) 65 CLJ 671, 672, 674–76, 683, 688–89; Allan, 'Judicial Deference' (n 5) 107; TRS Allan 'Deference,

whilst the due deference camp contends that the courts are sometimes justified in giving weight to expertise that fails to generate such reasons.[94] Allan argues that the courts abdicate their responsibility to enforce their 'own best judgment of a party's legal rights'[95] and compromise judicial impartiality if they consider factors extrinsic to the merits of the case.[96]

To the objection that the courts abdicate their judicial responsibility if they defer for second-order reasons, my reply is that there is no reason to believe that the judicial duty to arrive at the correct answer on rights issues can be fulfilled only by relying on first-order reasons.[97] If, after taking both first- and second-order reasons into account, the court believes that deference is more likely than non-deference to lead to the correct outcome, then it is obliged by its judicial role to defer. Deference for validly established epistemic reasons helps the courts to arrive at the best judgment concerning the parties' legal rights rather than compels them to discard such judgment.[98] It helps them to discharge their judicial duty rather than asks them to abdicate it. Such aid is needed, not least because the answers to rights issues are not always straightforward, a position that Allan himself accepts in acknowledging that there can be reasonable epistemic disagreements over the correct legal answer to a given issue.[99]

To the objection based on compromised judicial impartiality, I would argue that the courts do not give the primary decision-maker undue advantage merely by deferring for validly established second-order reasons. There is no reason to believe that adjudication can be fair only if it proceeds solely on the basis of first-order reasons. The courts rely on second-order epistemic reasons all the time. When they have to decide between equally strong conflicting opinions, for instance, they may legitimately consider the qualifications of the experts involved to determine which one to rely on.[100] In such a situation, it cannot seriously be argued that the court gave an undue advantage to the expert who eventually secured its trust by virtue of his or her superior qualifications. The applicants in a rights case may themselves need to rely on second-order reasons if they are seeking to proffer expert evidence. The court is giving neither party undue advantage by relying on validly established

Defiance and Doctrine: Defining the Limits of Judicial Review' (2010) 60 U of Toronto LJ 41, 51; Allan, *The Sovereignty of Law* (n 5) 246–49, 275.

[94] See eg Kavanagh, 'Defending Deference' (n 6) 233–35; King, 'Institutional Approaches' (n 20) 438–39; Young, 'In Defence of Due Deference' (n 25) 566, 570, 573.

[95] Allan, 'Judicial Deference' (n 5) 100, 101, 109; Allan, 'Human Rights' (n 93) 688.

[96] Allan, 'Human Rights' (n 93) 676, 692–94.

[97] Chan, 'Deference' (n 6) 606.

[98] See Tom Hickman 'The Substance and Structure of Proportionality' (2008) PL 694, 697; Cora Chan, 'Proportionality and Invariable Baseline Intensity of Review' (2013) 33(1) LS 1, 21; Chan, 'Deference' (n 6) 605. Déirdre Dwyer, *Judicial Assessment of Expert Evidence* (CUP 2008) ch 2 explains why courts possesses some epistemic competence to evaluate the soundness of expert evidence generally.

[99] Allan, 'Judicial Deference' (n 5) 102. Allan, *The Sovereignty of Law* (n 5) 271.

[100] Chan, 'Deference' (n 6) 604.

second-order epistemic reasons. What matters, insofar as rational and fair adjudication is concerned, is that the reasons the court relies upon are cogent ones, not whether they are of the first or second order.[101]

VIII. Respect for Constitutional Legitimacy

1. Preliminary points

As indicated in section V, a decision-maker's democratic features can be relevant to assessing the existence of all three sets of grounds. The focus here is on the second set of grounds, that is, the courts deferring for the intrinsic value of constitutional legitimacy. This issue is the crux of the debate between those who argue for and against deference on legitimacy grounds. Even the latter camp, represented by Tom Hickman[102] and Jeffrey Jowell,[103] can agree with the former, which includes Murray Hunt,[104] Aileen Kavanagh,[105] and Alison Young,[106] that the courts can defer to a democratic institution if doing so is likely to lead to the correct outcome on the rights issue concerned. It is nevertheless worth reiterating before proceeding that constitutional legitimacy can have both instrumental and intrinsic value because the two types of value are sometimes fused, leading to conceptual confusion in the debate over whether the courts should defer on legitimacy grounds. For example, Kavanagh argues that the courts have reason to defer on the grounds of 'democratic legitimacy' when a decision has a better chance of being accepted by the public if it is introduced by an elected body.[107] This argument is in fact a defence of prudential grounds for deference (which fall under the third set of grounds for deference outlined in this chapter) rather than of the legitimacy ground itself. To defend the latter, one needs to defend the intrinsic rather than instrumental value of constitutional legitimacy.

The debate over whether the courts should defer on grounds of constitutional legitimacy focuses predominantly on whether *democratic* legitimacy is a ground for deferring through *one* deference device alone, namely, the giving of weight to the legislature or executive's views in assessing whether a measure fulfils the proportionality test. The present analysis offers a broader view in two ways. First, it covers not only the process value of democracy but other sources of constitutional legitimacy as well, including the constitutional allocation of powers and the

[101] Chan, 'Proportionality' (n 98) 18–21.
[102] Hickman, 'Public Law' (n 25) 165.
[103] Jowell 'Judicial Deference and Human Rights' (n 50) 80.
[104] Hunt (n 25) 350–54.
[105] Kavanagh, *Constitutional Review* (n 34) 190–96.
[106] Young, 'In Defence of Due Deference' (n 25) 566–67.
[107] Kavanagh, *Constitutional Review* (n 34) 193.

process values of participation and public accountability. Second, it assesses the relevance of constitutional legitimacy to the deployment of a wider array of devices for deference, including the setting of appropriate standards of review and the formulation of remedies.

2. Relevance of constitutional legitimacy in rights adjudication

I now explain how each of the two sources of constitutional legitimacy identified above—the constitutional allocation of powers and process values—can figure into judicial reasoning in rights adjudication. With respect to the former, constitutional documents and conventions reflect constitutional expectations of what standards of good governance the state should abide by and what role the courts should play in enforcing those standards. For example, the UK courts are mandated by the European Convention on Human Rights (ECHR) and the HRA to not fall below the minimum legal standards set by the European Court of Human Rights (ECtHR). Also, they are mandated by section 3 of the HRA to give legislative provisions a reading that is compatible with the HRA but only 'so far as it is possible' to do so; they have no power to fundamentally rewrite legislation. Another example is where a constitution allocates the powers of making laws and policies to the elected branches of government while allocating the powers of judicial or constitutional review to the courts. Such allocation accounts for the distinction between review and appeal. No matter how rigorous the courts are in their review, they are secondary decision-makers. They must not become the primary lawmakers and policymakers, and the standard of review must not be formulated to collapse the distinction altogether. Here, I adopt Kavanagh's distinction between 'minimal' and 'substantive' deference. Minimal deference, that is, deference embodied in the review versus appeal distinction, 'applies across the board to all legislative and executive decisions', whereas substantive deference, that is, deference over and beyond recognizing that the courts are secondary decision-makers, is warranted only in limited situations,[108] situations in which, I argue, process values require it, a point to which I now turn.

Some decisions call for stronger instantiation of the value of public accountability, and hence less or no substantive deference, for example, decisions involving important individual rights or the rights of individuals or groups who are 'particularly vulnerable to majoritarian bias and neglect'.[109] On the other hand, some cases require stronger instantiation of the value of community or stakeholder participation, and hence justify more substantive deference to genuinely democratic or participatory processes—at the rights definition and limitation stages, where

[108] ibid 227–28.

[109] See King, *Judging Social Rights* (n 14) 177–85.

reasonable disagreements over rights are involved,[110] and at the remedial stage, where there is more than one way of remedying a rights violation, where the setting up of an alternative scheme is needed,[111] or where remedying the violation would entail radical and controversial legal reform.[112]

3. Ascertaining whether legitimacy grounds exist

Ascertaining what the constitutional allocation of powers is in relation to rights adjudication involves, inter alia, constitutional interpretation. The constitutional text (where there is one) may indicate judicial review standards and where the burden of proof lies. For example, the Canadian Charter of Rights and Freedoms states that rights may be subject only to 'reasonable limits prescribed by law as can be demonstrably justified in a free and democratic society',[113] suggesting that the burden is on the state to justify rights limitations and that such limitations must be reasonable in a free and democratic society. Israel's Basic Law on Human Dignity and Liberty also stipulates that there shall be no violations of rights 'except by a law befitting the values of the State of Israel, enacted for a proper purpose, and to an extent no greater than is required',[114] suggesting that proportionality is the test for vetting rights limitations. Constitutional intent is also relevant. For example, the intent of the UK Parliament to use the HRA to 'bring rights home'—providing a domestic remedy for violations of ECHR rights—suggests that the UK courts should use 'correctness' as the standard of review in reviewing the compatibility of government acts with the HRA.[115] Where a polity has signed up to international rights instruments, the text of those instruments and the jurisprudence of the international body concerned (where relevant) are also indicative. For example, the United Kingdom is expected to not fall below the legal standards set by the ECtHR.

It has been argued that the fact that a constitution has allocated a particular policymaking function to a political branch of government in itself suggests that the courts should grant more deference on constitutional legitimacy grounds in reviewing that branch's exercise of its policymaking function.[116] This is true, but only insofar as it suggests that the courts should not collapse the distinction between review and appeal. Beyond that, the fact that a law or policy function is allocated to a

[110] See eg Waldron, *Law and Disagreement* (n 21) chs 5, 7, 10; Waldron, 'The Core of the Case' (n 21) 1367–68, 1371–72, 1387–95. cf Joseph Raz 'Disagreement in politics' (1998) 43 Am J Juris 25, 45–47.

[111] See eg *NCCL* (n 42) [85].

[112] See eg *Nicklinson* (n 41) [116]; and general discussions in Sathanapally, Leckey, and Roach (n 33).

[113] Section 1.

[114] Section 8.

[115] Hickman, *Public Law* (n 25) 111. For the distinction between the standard of review and what Hickman calls 'standard of legality', see Hickman, *Public Law* (n 25) 99–111.

[116] See the discussion in Brian Foley, *Deference and the Presumption of Constitutionality* (Institute of Public Administration 2008) 165; Thayer (n 34) 144.

particular branch of government does not in itself provide a constitutional ground for deference. Just as the constitution of a given jurisdiction may have allocated the primary lawmaking and policymaking functions to the legislature and executive, in polities that meet the background conditions stated above the constitution also gives the courts the power to ensure that the exercise of such functions complies with constitutional rights.[117] That the primary function is vested elsewhere does not provide a constitutional ground for the relaxed exercise of the secondary function by the courts.[118] Both functions are backed by a constitutional mandate, and as far as constitutional authority is concerned the existence of one cannot justify the relaxation of the other.

With respect to process values, in deciding whether respecting such values requires deference, the courts should assess whether the issue at stake is one in which heightened attention to such values is warranted. As noted above, the triggers for such attention include the involvement of important rights or the rights of those vulnerable to majoritarian bias and neglect, in which case there should be more instantiation of public accountability, and hence less or no substantive deference; questions of reasonable rights disagreements, in which case more substantive deference to democratic and participatory processes is warranted; and situations in which there is more than one way to remedy the rights violation, an alternative scheme has to be established, or remedying the right would entail a radical and controversial legal change, in which case more deference should be granted at the remedial stage. If these triggers are present, then the courts should assess the relative degree to which the pertinent process value has been (or can be) manifested by the decision-making process involved. Such assessment requires an evaluation of the composition and decision-making processes of the courts and government decision-makers involved to compare how well they have expressed (or can express) the values of public accountability, democracy, and participation.[119] As with deference on the ground of arriving at correct outcomes, deference on constitutional legitimacy grounds also admits of degrees.

4. Objections

Jowell, Hickman, and Allan object to the courts giving weight to the executive or legislature's assessments of proportionality on the grounds of constitutional legitimacy. Several arguments have been proffered to justify that objection, but none ultimately justifies the wholesale rejection of affording such weight. The first argument concerns the risk of double counting. Allan argues that constitutional

[117] Hickman, *Public Law* (n 25) 160.
[118] See Foley (n 116) 167.
[119] See Kavanagh, *The Collaborative Constitution* (n 1) 302–08. See also n 55.

legitimacy has already been taken into account when the standard of review is set as proportionality rather than correctness and that to defer again on that ground when applying that standard would be to count it twice.[120] It is worth noting here that in accepting that constitutional legitimacy can be relevant to the setting of criteria of legality, Allan is in fact accepting that it can be relevant as a consideration that does not relate directly to the specific claim of right. Double counting is indeed possible, but as I will show in Chapter 5, it does not follow that taking a reason for deference into account more than once in the adjudication process automatically leads to it.

The second objection to constitutional deference is that it leads to the risk of crude 'spatial approaches' to deference.[121] For example, Jowell argues that it leads to the risk of the courts withholding intervention whenever the elected branches purport to limit a qualified right in the public interest, thereby abdicating their constitutional role to protect rights.[122] There are also concerns that constitutional deference may lead to wholesale deference to, say, legislative decisions.[123] My reply is that according to the model of deference conceived here (and also put forward by Kavanagh, Young, Hunt, and other due deference theorists), deference can admit of degrees, and the fact that the elected branches are charged with determining the public interest, or that the decision in question was made via a democratic process, is not *in itself* a reason for total submission.[124] That the constitution allocates primary policymaking functions to other branches of government is a reason for recognizing the appeal versus review distinction only, not for further deference.[125] Democratic decision-making processes would attract substantive deference at the rights limitation stage only if reasonable rights disagreements were involved. Even then, such deference could admit of varying degrees depending on, inter alia, the democratic quality of the decision. How the process of calibrating deference can be simplified for practical reasons is discussed in Chapter 6.

The third argument, put forward by Hickman, is that if the constitutional rights instrument in question (the HRA in the UK context in Hickman's argument, although it could equally be applied to the other jurisdictions covered by this book) applies equally to all acts of the executive and legislature, and does not indicate that constitutional rights should be less safe from intrusions by decision-makers who are democratically accountable, there is no reason for the courts to defer on democratic grounds.[126] My response is that under the model of deference conceived here, substantive deference on legitimacy grounds is not automatically accorded

[120] Allan, 'Human Rights' (n 93) 679–80; Allan, 'Judicial Deference' (n 5) 97. This and other potential forms of double counting are highlighted in Young, 'In Defence of Due Deference' (n 25) 570, 577–78.

[121] See Young, 'In Defence of Due Deference' (n 25) 570.

[122] Jowell, 'Judicial Deference and Human Rights' (n 50) 73–74.

[123] Young, 'In Defence of Due Deference' (n 25) 571.

[124] See eg Kavanagh, *Constitutional Review* (n 34) 191.

[125] See the discussion on Kavanagh's distinction between minimal and substantive deference in text to n 108.

[126] Hickman, *Public Law* (n 25) 160.

to democratically accountable decision-makers (and so rights are not necessarily less secure against encroachments by such decision-makers). Whether it should be depends on whether the aforementioned triggers for heightened attention to the process values of democracy and participation are present. If there is indeed a heightened need to attend to such values, then there are good reasons (eg political equality, self-determination) for the courts to accord more respect to decisions made through democratic or participatory processes.[127]

The fourth and by far the strongest argument against the giving of weight on constitutional grounds relates to the court's legitimacy to conduct constitutional rights review. There are several strands to this argument. The first does not dispute the importance of majority rule to democratic legitimacy. It posits that because the constitutional mandate for the courts to exercise constitutional rights review powers itself has a majority basis (eg the HRA was passed by Parliament itself), the courts have no less a democratic mandate for determining constitutional rights issues than the elected branches, and hence should not defer on the basis that the latter has more democratic legitimacy.[128] This argument elides the majoritarian legitimacy that the courts enjoy for constitutional rights review *as a whole* with that which they enjoy for deciding particular questions. Although the courts' jurisdiction of constitutional rights review has a majority basis, this does not mean that in adjudicating particular questions therein the courts do not lack majoritarian legitimacy vis-à-vis the elected branches of government.

A second, and related, strand also does not dispute the importance of majority rule to democratic legitimacy. It is the flipside of the first strand: because the courts have a majority mandate to exercise constitutional rights review powers, it would be undemocratic for them to abstain from such exercise.[129] My response is that it would indeed be democratically illegitimate for a court to refuse its job altogether,[130] as would occur if it declined jurisdiction over rights adjudication on democratic grounds. Yet there is nothing illegitimate in the courts according a degree of weight to choices made by the majority in reasonable disagreements over rights. As Craig argues, '[t]o afford such respect is not inconsistent with the HRA, its wording or the principles underlying it. The argument is not for the courts to abstain or capitulate, but to take cognizance of the legislative choice when making its own final determination.'[131]

The third and final strand disputes the importance of majoritarian rule to democratic legitimacy. The argument goes that the inception of constitutional rights

[127] See text to nn 109–112.

[128] Jowell, 'Judicial Deference: Servility, Civility or Institutional Capacity?' (n 25) 597; Jowell 'Judicial Deference and Human Rights' (n 50) 74; Hickman, *Public Law* (n 25) 160.

[129] King, *Judging Social Rights* (n 14) 153.

[130] ibid.

[131] Craig (n 62) 252.

review redefined democracy: it is no longer equated with majoritarian rule but includes fundamental rights as well. This new constitutional order assigns the role of guardian of rights to the courts, giving them a constitutional mandate to intervene in rights cases. That they are unelected thus poses no constitutional impediment to such intervention.[132]

My response is that even though majority rule no longer equates to democracy, it is nonetheless still an important part of it.[133] In addition to the constitutional allocation of powers, majority rule remains an important source of constitutional legitimacy. Although in a constitutional rights democracy, the courts enjoy the former source of legitimacy for adjudicating constitutional rights as a general matter, they may still fare worse on the latter source than the elected branches of government when it comes to adjudicating particular rights questions. Granted that there are reasonable disagreements over rights, democratic legitimacy cannot be discarded altogether as a source of legitimacy in rights adjudication. When the courts adjudicate questions over which such disagreements exist, democratic legitimacy becomes relevant. Against the backdrop of reasonable disputes over rights, we need, as Hunt puts it, a 'vision of constitutionalism' that combines a 'meaningful role' for both the courts and democratic institutions in the furtherance of rights.[134]

In addition, in polities where the constitution specifies democracy as the system of government, the constitutional allocation of powers provides an extra reason (in addition to the process values of democracy and participation) for the courts to sometimes give weight to the decisions of democratic institutions. In these polities, it is safe to assume that the constitution envisions a role for democratic processes to resolve reasonable disagreements over rights.

My response to the third strand also addresses the final argument against giving weight on democratic grounds. Allan argues that if the courts forsake their judgment of parties' legal rights on the ground that the original decision-maker has more democratic credentials, then they (just as in the case of deferring on second-order epistemic reasons) also abdicate their responsibility to do justice in the individual case and undermine judicial impartiality.[135] My response is that if it is part of the courts' role to take democratic legitimacy into account in situations of contestable rights, then it is not an abdication of duty or violation of impartiality for the courts to give weight to such legitimacy.

[132] Hickman, *Public Law* (n 25) 160–61; Jowell, 'Judicial Deference and Human Rights' (n 50) 70, 74–75, 80; Jowell, 'Judicial Deference: Servility, Civility or Institutional Capacity?' (n 25) 597–98; Guy Davidov, 'The Paradox of Judicial Deference' (2000–01) 12 NJCL 133, 144–46.

[133] See eg Hunt (n 25) 350–51; Kavanagh, *Constitutional Review* (n 34) 192.

[134] Hunt (n 25) 340. See also Kavanagh, *The Collaborative Constitution* (n 1) 1–2.

[135] Allan, 'Human Rights' (n 93) 675–676.

IX. Residual Category

1. Validity and weight of specific grounds

Deference on the grounds in this residual category is relatively little discussed outside the US discourse, although indications of support for deference on such grounds can be found even in non-US discourse. Some of the oft-cited reasons for deference are in fact just such grounds, although they are generally not expressly couched as such. For example, the common argument that the courts should defer to preserve the state's ability to respond flexibly to changing circumstances[136] falls into this residual category: the aim is to preserve the state's ability to make correct decisions in future. The arguments for and against introducing a procedure-based proportionality review in rights cases also fall into this category; that is, such introduction would encourage a rights culture in—or, conversely, ossify—the administration.[137]

Admittedly, this category is a mixed bag of many and varied reasons. Not all of the grounds listed under the residual category in section IV are valid over time and across jurisdictions, but it is possible to envisage situations in which they could be established in jurisdictions that meet the stated background conditions. For example, particular legal and constitutional contexts may render it illegitimate for the courts to take into account strategic considerations in choosing amongst remedies,[138] considerations that would be legitimate in a different context. And whilst it might seem implausible that a controversial rights reform would be better received if introduced by the elected branches of government than by the courts in polities in which these institutions are equally respected, such a state of affairs can certainly be envisaged in polities in which the courts enjoy less respect than the political branches.

This leads us to a crucial point, namely, that the weight of the various grounds in the residual category can vary greatly. Recall that the weight that each ground should attract depends on the importance of the value realized by deference on that ground and on how certain the court is that deference will realize that value, variables that are highly context dependent. Nonetheless, two general remarks can be made with respect to polities that satisfy the background conditions. The first is that, as I have argued elsewhere,[139] given the configuration and constitutional role of the courts in those polities, the courts should in general give little weight to

[136] See eg King, *Judging Social Rights* (n 14) ch 9.

[137] See eg Poole (n 36) 155, 164.

[138] See eg Gavin Phillipson, 'Deference, Discretion, and Democracy in the Human Rights Act Era' (2007) 60 CLP 40, 61–68 for an argument on why the UK courts should maximize the use of remedial interpretation under the HRA 1998.

[139] Cora Chan, 'Can Hong Kong Remain a Liberal Enclave within China? Analysis of the Hong Kong National Security Law' [2021] PL 271, 292.

considerations related to a potential government or public backlash. Their political independence and disconnection from the public are likely to hinder their ability to assess how the government and public might respond, and hence whether such a backlash is likely to occur.[140] Moreover, giving in to a potential backlash would inevitably exert *some* harm on the value that deference in such a situation is intended to achieve, namely, preserving the courts' long-term credibility and ability to do justice:

> [i]f the courts act out of political expediency concerns, they compromise their impartiality, and if they do not articulate those concerns openly, as is often the case, they also compromise the transparency of their reasoning, and it is impartiality and transparency that give the courts credibility in the eyes of the public.[141]

Furthermore, yielding to threats of a government backlash may encourage the government to bully the courts into compliance in future, thereby harming the courts' long-term ability to do justice. One implication of this analysis is that if the outcome and legitimacy grounds for deference point decidedly against deference, then it is unlikely that backlash considerations can outweigh them.

Notwithstanding this analysis, we cannot rule out situations in which the harm to a court's credibility and ability caused by a backlash would be so serious as to exceed that brought about by the court yielding to the backlash (ie there is a *net* harm) *and* the court is fairly certain that the former harm will materialize because, say, it is experienced in assessing the credibility of threats to reduce its powers, in which case backlash considerations might well tip the balance.[142] My observation of the polities under study is that this high threshold for affording significant weight to backlash considerations is seldom met, although in principle it could be.

The second general remark is that considerations that relate to the rule of law such as those pertaining to a court decision's impact on coherence of the law in related areas—concerns that led the court in *Bellinger* to grant a remedy that gave the government more lawmaking leeway—should attract special weight. These considerations have a special standing because, as I explain in Chapter 1, enforcement of the rule of law is a core part of the judicial role. Also, being trained in law, judges have the expertise to assess rule of law considerations, for example, to discern the knock-on effects of their decisions on various areas of law and whether they can effect changes therein.

[140] See eg Dixon (n 34) 183.

[141] Chan, 'Can Hong Kong Remain a Liberal Enclave within China?' (n 139) 292. See Kyritsis (n 11) 195–97. See also Allan, 'Judicial Deference' (n 5) 101; Lawrence G. Sager, *Justice in Plainclothes: A Theory of American Constitutional Practice* (Yale University Press 2004) 207–13; Kavanagh, *Constitutional Review* (n 34) 198–99.

[142] Kavanagh, 'Judicial Restraint in the Pursuit of Justice' (n 34) 36.

2. Objections

Most objections to deference on the third set of grounds target deference for fear of a backlash.[143] The objections to such deference outlined above—for example, that by so deferring the courts compromise their credibility and that the courts lack the competence to second-guess reactions to their decisions—lead to objections in stronger and weaker forms. The stronger-form objection, made by Allan, is that the courts should never take prudential considerations into account.[144] My response is that to entirely exclude prudential considerations from judicial consideration is to adopt an 'unduly narrow conception of the judicial role'[145] and to disregard the fact that the courts are part of the joint enterprise of governance. The weaker-form objection, made by Kyritsis, is that such considerations should be taken into account only when 'the stakes are inordinately high—but these are bound to be exceptional'.[146] I believe that Kyritsis would agree with my account of deference, according to which, as explained in section IX.1, courts should afford significant weight to backlash considerations only when they are fairly certain that the net harm brought about by a backlash will materialize, a situation that appears to be rare in the polities under study.

My tripartite scheme of grounds may raise the query of how reasons for deference should be categorized under the scheme given that courts often take considerations of public interest into account in rights adjudication. For example, the proportionality test requires balancing the harm to an individual right against the benefit to broader societal interests. How do we distinguish considerations of public interest that pertain to the merits of the case—that is, to what right the individual applicant has against the state, and are hence also incidentally relevant to determining the first set of grounds for deference—from those that pertain to the third set of grounds? This is an important question, but one which this book does not attempt to answer. My tripartite scheme assumes that a distinction can be drawn between the considerations under each category, an assumption that is uncontroversial. My arguments do not hinge on controversial views concerning where the lines between the three categories should be drawn. Whether a consideration of public interest pertains to what right the litigant has or to other considerations that the court should take into account depends on one's theory about what 'right' an applicant has against the state.[147] It is beyond the scope of this book

[143] An exception is Allan, which appears to reject all considerations that this book categorizes as falling under the third set of grounds: Allan, *The Sovereignty of Law* (n 5) 266–68.

[144] Allan, 'Judicial Deference' (n 5) 101.

[145] Kavanagh, *Constitutional Review* (n 34) 199.

[146] Kyritsis (n 11) 196–97.

[147] For example, in *Her Majesty's Treasury v Mohammed Jabar Ahmed and others (FC)* [2010] UKSC 5, [2010] 2 AC 534, the UK Supreme Court had to decide whether to grant the government's request for a more deferential remedy, namely, *suspension* of the court's order that certain anti-terrorism restrictions be declared ultra vires and quashed. The government argued that suspension was needed

to offer such a theory. Moreover, the examples given in section IV of the considerations in each category are largely uncontroversial. For instance, I doubt that anyone would seriously disagree with the proposition that preserving the long-term ability of the courts to do justice, enhancing the efficacy of a rights decision, avoiding undermining the rights culture of the political branches, ensuring coherence in government policy, avoiding the knock-on effects of a court decision, and affording flexibility are considerations that relate to neither an applicant's rights nor to constitutional legitimacy. In any case, the examples are given for illustrative purposes alone. Even if someone were to disagree with the way in which I categorize a particular consideration, that would not affect my argument that a distinction between the categories of considerations can be drawn.

X. The Normativity of the Three Grounds

In section IX.2, I have sought to establish that in polities that satisfy the aforementioned background conditions, the courts have three sets of grounds for deference. The value of the first set has been largely assumed, as there is no dispute that arriving at the correct outcome on rights issues matters. I have sought to defend the value of the second set against critics. In short, a fair way of resolving reasonable rights disagreements is needed, and respecting social expectations in constitutional documents and stakeholder or community participation imbue the decision-making process with legitimacy. Although in polities that satisfy the background conditions the courts have a constitutional mandate to conduct constitutional rights reviews, they may still lack the legitimacy to decide particular

to enable it to address the order's effects by introducing legislation. The majority judges, who rejected the request, appeared to diverge from the dissenting judge on two grounds. First, the two camps had different assessments of whether suspension would harm the rule of law. The majority judges emphasized the harm that a suspended remedy would do to the effectiveness of the court judgment, whereas the dissenting judge emphasized the harm that non-suspension would do to the state's ability to comply with its obligations under international law. Second, the dissenting judge took the view that non-suspension would harm national security interests, harm that did not appear to be a concern for the majority judges. Whether the two considerations—threat to the rule of law and threat to national security—pertain to the merits of the case or to the third ground for deference depends on one's conception of what 'right' an applicant has. Compare two possible views that agree that the court ought to take both considerations into account in deciding what remedy to grant but diverge on what right an applicant has. One view sees an applicant as having a right only to the remedies that the court should grant, all things considered. In this view, the two considerations speak to the question of merits, ie what remedy the applicant has a right to. The other view sees the applicant as having a right to immediate vindication upon a breach of his primary rights. In this view, the national security consideration speaks to the third ground for deference rather than to the question of merits. Correspondingly, the former view may see the dispute between the majority and minority judges as merely a dispute over the merits, whereas the latter may see it as pertaining at least in part to whether the court should defer on national security grounds. I thank Joanna Bell and Alison Young for helpful discussions on this case and for prompting me to reflect on which considerations speak to the merits of the case and which to deference. For the distinction between questions of merits and questions of deference, see section II.

questions in rights adjudication relative to the elected branches of government. Although with the inception of constitutional rights review, majority rule no longer equates to democracy, it is still an important part of it and remains an important source of constitutional legitimacy.

The third set of grounds seems the most controversial. However, it is important to note the modest scope of my argument, which is this: in addition to reasons that relate to determining an applicant's rights (the first set of grounds) and pertain to constitutional legitimacy (the second set), there are other considerations that the court should take into account in determining questions of deference (the third set). I have given examples of grounds raised by courts or commentators that can be categorized under the third and residual category of grounds. It would be impossible to justify the value of each and every ground that falls into this category because the grounds are not exhaustive, but I have sought to do two things. First, I have provided a broad justification for why the courts should not limit themselves to considering reasons in the first and second sets of grounds. As part of the joint enterprise of governance, it would be irresponsible for the courts to ignore the impact of their decisions on the wider society and system of governance. Second, I have provided justification for what is perhaps one of the most controversial grounds within the third set: political backlash. In sum, given the configuration and constitutional role of the courts, they should in general give little weight to backlash considerations. However, we cannot rule out situations in which the harm caused by a potential political backlash that the court is fairly certain will materialize is so serious that it would exceed that brought about by the court yielding to it. In that case, the court would be justified in affording significant weight to backlash considerations. One need not agree that all (or any) of the examples of grounds raised by theorists and courts listed under the residual category in section IV are valid to accept the argument that there is a residual category of grounds for deference, and, indeed, I need not justify each and every one of those grounds to make that argument.

XI. Conclusion

In this chapter, I draw a distinction between two types of reasons—grounds and factors—and propose a taxonomy of reasons for deference oriented around three sets of grounds for deference: grounds that relate to arriving at the correct outcomes on the rights issue before the court; grounds that relate to respect for constitutional legitimacy; and grounds that relate to other considerations that the court should take into account in adjudication. I have elaborated on when these grounds and corresponding factors can be said to exist and dealt with objections to deference on said grounds. This analysis enables us to see the ultimate values served by deference and the relationship between grounds and factors, thereby providing the theoretical resources necessary to assess what devices the courts should use to express the values underlying deference (the subject of Chapters 4–5) and what is lost in terms of value achievement by the use of rule-bound methods to communicate deference to future judges and litigants (the subject of Chapter 6). With this foundation laid, Chapter 3 constructs the other building block of this book's central arguments, namely, what devices are available to the courts for expressing deference.

3
Devices for Deference

I. Introduction

In Chapter 2, I explain that the courts have three categories of grounds for deference: those relating to arriving at correct outcomes on the rights issue in question, those relating to respect for constitutional legitimacy, and those relating to other considerations that the court should take into account in adjudication. In this chapter, I turn to the issue of the devices that courts have at their disposal to express deference and identify six such devices: the burden of proof, standard of proof, standard of review, giving of weight to views, choice of interpretation, and choice of remedy. This chapter, together with Chapter 2, lays the foundation for my exploration in subsequent chapters of the methods of deference that the courts should adopt.

In what follows, I first provide an overview of my proposed schema of devices and then, in section III, compare the six devices. Section IV explains the methodology used to distil the devices and the schema's originality. The three subsequent sections are devoted to explaining how the devices operate at the rights definition, limitation, and remedial stages, respectively, using illustrative case law from the selected jurisdictions.

Before proceeding, it would be helpful to note a preliminary point about the illustrative cases. It is sometimes difficult to ascertain which device a court used solely by reading its written judgment. For example, it may be unclear whether references to allowing a policy to stand as long as it falls within 'a range of reasonable options' involves use of the standard of proof device or standard of review device. Such a lack of clarity would pose a problem if the cases were being used to make an empirical assessment of how frequently each device is used. However, for present purposes, namely, illustration of what devices are conceptually available, it raises no issues. My interpretations of particular devices being used in particular cases do not preclude alternative readings suggesting the use of other devices.

II. Overview of Schema

As noted, the proposed schema includes six devices for deference. The first is the burden of proof, which is determined by a court rule stipulating the default

Deference in Human Rights Adjudication. Cora Chan, Oxford University Press. © Cora Chan 2024.
DOI: 10.1093/9780198921677.003.0003

position,[1] and hence which party should bear the risk of the non-availability of evidence.[2] If the court adopts a rule stating that unless X is shown to be true, not-X will be deemed to be true, then not-X is the default position, and the side that advocates for X bears the burden of proof. That burden serves to allocate argumentative responsibility in an adversarial adjudicative setting.[3]

The burden of proof works hand in hand with the standard of proof, the second device in my schema. The standard of proof sets the degree of certainty (eg balance of probabilities) at which the party bearing the burden must demonstrate a proposition before it is deemed to be true.[4] When the standard is set at a balance of probabilities or above, the burden and standard of proof function together as a tie- or uncertainty-breaker.[5]

The burden and standard of proof are important concepts in human rights adjudication, which requires 'final authoritative'[6] judgments on assessments made by public bodies, often in circumstances of factual uncertainty—based on 'approximations and extrapolations from the available evidence, inferences from comparative data, and, on occasion, even educated guesses'[7]—or on the basis of normative judgments that can be legitimately disputed.[8] Although in adjudication generally, the concepts of the burden and standard of proof are more commonly applied to questions of fact than of law, they are applicable to the latter as well. When applied to questions of law, they convey the level of confidence that the court must have in a normative or evaluative proposition before ruling in favour of it.[9] As the examples in sections V and VI will show, the courts have used these concepts in assessing

[1] See David Kenny, 'Proportionality, the Burden of Proof, and Some Signs of Reconsideration' (2014) 52 IJ 141, 147. See also Julian Rivers, 'The Presumption of Proportionality' (2014) 77(3) MLR 409.

[2] This evidence includes both the evidence that is proffered in court as well as 'background information' and the 'prior odds' of certain propositions being true. See Dale A Nance, *The Burdens of Proof: Discriminatory Power, Weight of Evidence, and Tenacity of Belief* (CUP 2016) 95, 210.

[3] cf Charles-Maxime Panaccio, 'In Defence of Two-Step Balancing and Proportionality in Rights Adjudication' (2011) 24 CJLJ 109, 120–21.

[4] For competing theories of forensic proof (eg subjective or objective, Pascalian or Baconian), see eg Alex Stein, *Foundations of Evidence Law* (OUP 2005) chs 2–4; Ho Hock Lai, *A Philosophy of Evidence Law* (OUP 2008) chs 1–4; Georgi Gardiner, 'The Reasonable and the Relevant: Legal Standards of Proof' (2019) 47(3) Philosophy & Public Affairs 288; Nance (n 2) chs 2–5; Mike Redmayne, 'Objective Probability and the Assessment of Evidence' (2003) 2 Law, Probability and Risk 275; Gustavo Ribeiro, 'Can There be a Burden of the Best Explanation?' (2018) 22(2) Intl J of Evidence & Proof 91; Mike Redmayne, 'Standards of Proof in Civil Litigation' (1999) 62(2) MLR 167, 194 fn 133; sources in fn 421 of Roderick Munday, *Cross and Tapper on Evidence* (13th edn, OUP 2018) 173.

[5] See David Wiseman, 'Managing the Burden of Doubt: Social Science Evidence, the Institutional Competence of Courts and the Prospects for Anti-Poverty Charter Claims' (2014) 33 NJCL 1, 3.

[6] Panaccio (n 3) 124–25. See Nance (n 2) 16–17; Déirdre Dwyer, *The Judicial Assessment of Expert Evidence* (CUP 2008) 135.

[7] Sujit Choudhry, 'So What is the Real Legacy of Oakes? Two Decades of Proportionality Analysis under the Canadian Charter's Section 1' (2006) 34 Supreme Court L Rev 501, 524.

[8] See Jula Hughes and Vanessa MacDonnell, 'Social Science Evidence in Constitutional Rights Cases in Germany and Canada: Some Comparative Observations' (2013) 32 NJCL23, 29–32.

[9] Cora Chan, 'Proportionality and Invariable Baseline Intensity of Review' (2013) 33(1) LS 1, 15; Panaccio (n 3) 121–22. cf Aharon Barak, *Proportionality: Constitutional Rights and their Limitations* (CUP 2012) 436–37.

questions of both law and fact, although analyses of the two questions are not always distinct in court judgments. In theory, discharge of the burden of proof on questions of fact does not necessarily entail discharge of that burden on questions of law. In the rights context, however, questions of law are often dependent on findings of fact,[10] and thus discharge of the burden of proof on the latter often leads to discharge of that on the former as well.

The third device—the standard of review—determines the threshold of error in a prior decision made or view proffered by the defendant that is required for judicial intervention. For example, a court may review a public body defendant's argument that its rights-limiting measure passes the proportionality test using such standards as correctness, reasonableness, or manifest unreasonableness.

The fourth device is the giving of weight to a prior decision or a party's view that the requisite burden and standard of proof and standard of review have been discharged. Assume that the public body defendant bears the burden of demonstrating that a rights limitation is proportionate on a balance of probabilities. The giving of weight represents how easy the court makes it for the public body to discharge that burden. The court defers by allowing deference reasons to add weight to the public body's conclusion, meaning that the latter does not need to proffer as many cogent reasons or as cogent reasons on the merits as it would normally need to in discharging its burden. Those deference reasons reweigh the public body's case on the merits, pre-empt the court's own reasoning on the merits, or override the court's view of the merits in whole or in part, with the result that they render the public body's case more weighty and hence in fulfilment of the requisite burden.

The fifth device is choice of interpretation.[11] When the court defers through this device, it chooses an interpretation of a constitutional provision that affords the primary decision maker more decision-making room for reasons that arise from the comparative institutional positions of the court and the primary decision maker but do not hinge upon the decision maker's adoption of that interpretation. For example, a court may define the right to marry narrowly so that it does not cover same-sex marriage, not for the reason that the primary decision maker has argued for that narrow definition in court or adopted it in its decision-making, but rather for the reason that it believes that such controversial and morally complex issues as whether same-sex marriage ought to be permitted should be left to democratically elected representatives, and that not constitutionalizing same-sex marriage gives such representatives more room to decide the matter.

Because the choice of interpretation is less discussed as a device for deference than the other devices in the proposed schema, further explanation of how it can

[10] See eg Anne Carter, *Proportionality and Facts in Constitutional Adjudication* (Hart 2021) 6.

[11] cf Tom Hickman's, 'standard of legality' in Tom Hickman, *Public Law after the Human Rights Act* (Hart 2010) 99–111.

serve as such a device is in order. The choice of interpretation can serve as a device for deference when the principles that govern constitutional interpretation in a polity sanction the courts to consider deference reasons and to hand down an interpretation that gives the executive or legislature greater scope for action when such reasons call for it, but leave the courts with some leeway as to what the interpretation ought to be in a particular case. Not all considerations of constitutional interpretation that give the original decision maker greater room for action are deference considerations; only those that arise from the comparative institutional positions of the court and the original decision maker are. The choice of interpretation is used as a device for deference when the court hands down an interpretation of a constitutional provision that gives the decision maker more permissible scope of action based on deference considerations that do not hinge upon the decision maker's adoption of that interpretation.

There are many and varied approaches to constitutional interpretation. Following Philip Bobbitt, I group them into textual, structural, historical, doctrinal, ethical, and prudential approaches.[12] Without considering which approach or combination of approaches is normatively warranted, a consideration that depends on the context, I argue that all of these approaches are capable of sanctioning, to varying degrees, reasons for deference. Hence, regardless of which approach or combination of approaches to constitutional interpretation should be adopted, I argue that they are all capable of accommodating deference considerations to varying degrees.

The textual approach examines what the constitutional text means or meant at the time of interpretation or time of drafting, whereas the structural approach infers meaning from the institutional structures established by the provisions of the constitution. The historical approach looks at what the drafters intended the provision in question to mean, whilst the doctrinal approach focuses on what meaning has been established by prior cases. The ethical approach interprets the text in light of the values, traditions, and history of the polity, whilst the prudential approach counsels an overall cost–benefit analysis in choosing amongst various interpretations. The textual, structural, historical, and doctrinal approaches are all in theory capable of accommodating reasons for deference because the sources they point to—namely, the text, structure, original intent, doctrine, fundamental values, and principles of the constitutional order—may well call for deference considerations. For example, the structural approach may reveal a division of powers that calls for deference. The fundamental principle of the separation of powers may demand that the courts give weight to the relative democratic legitimacy of the legislature or executive. As for the prudential approach, the approach itself explicitly calls for the courts to take into account both considerations of legitimacy and strategic

[12] Philip Bobbitt, *Constitutional Fate: Theory of the Constitution* (OUP 1982).

considerations for deference. Examples of the choice of interpretation as a tool for deference are given in sections V–VII.

Accordingly, regardless of which interpretative approach a polity adopts, deference considerations can become relevant in the interpretative process. Nevertheless, whether deference considerations should be taken into account in the interpretation process, and, if so, what kinds of considerations and to what degree they should be taken into account, varies by context. For example, the text and structure of the constitution may point to relative democratic legitimacy considerations or to no deference considerations at all. Also, because the prudential approach to interpretation—alone amongst the various interpretative approaches—necessarily mandates deference considerations, such considerations are more likely to be warranted in situations in which that approach is justified.

The sixth and final device covered by my schema is the choice of remedy, a device that is available to the courts when they decide what remedy should be granted in a particular case. This device is deployed when the court chooses a remedy that gives the primary decision maker more room to fashion a response to the court's ruling based on deference considerations that do not hinge upon whether the decision maker argues for that remedy. An example of such a device at work is when the court chooses a declaration of incompatibility over a remedial interpretation, not because the legislature has argued for the former in court, but because the court believes that democratic legitimacy would be enhanced if the elected legislature were granted more room to respond to the court's ruling. As with the choice of interpretation device, not all considerations of remedial discretion that call for greater policymaking room to be granted are deference considerations; only those that arise from the comparative institutional positions of the court and the original decision maker are. The choice of remedy can serve as a device for deference when the principles that govern remedial choice in a polity sanction the court to take into account deference considerations and to hand down a remedy that gives the executive or legislature greater scope for action when such considerations call for it, but leave the court with leeway to determine the actual remedy in a particular case.

The principles governing the choice of remedy vary by jurisdiction, but often reflect an amalgamation of concerns about democratic legitimacy (ie allowing democratically elected authorities to have sufficient room to fashion a response to a negative court ruling), as well as reasons pertaining to the systemic effects of a court decision. In particular, numerous reasons listed under the third set of grounds identified in Chapter 2 become salient only at the remedial stage, the stage at which the court needs to face head-on the potential impact of the coercive and immediate enforcement of an applicant's rights on the governmental system.[13]

[13] For the potential systemic impact of individual remedies, see eg Ernest J Weinrib, *Corrective Justice* (OUP 2012) 107–15; Kent Roach, 'Remedies for Laws that Violate Human Rights' in John Bell, Mark Elliott, Jason NE Varuhas, and Philip Murray (eds), *Public Law Adjudication in Common Law*

Examples include ensuring the coherence of government policy when it is possible to allow the government to decide all related issues in one go;[14] ensuring that a court decision will not lead to knock-on effects that the court is unable to foresee;[15] giving state institutions the flexibility to respond to new information or circumstances;[16] and respecting inter-institutional comity when another branch of government is considering the issue in question.[17]

III. Comparison of Devices

A detailed comparison of the devices will be conducted in Chapters 4 and 5. For now, it suffices to note the different ways in which the first four devices (ie the burden of proof, standard of proof, standard of review, and giving of weight) and the final two (ie the choice of interpretation and choice of remedy) grant leeway to the primary decision maker. The first four devices concern the approach the court takes to a prior decision made by the primary decision maker or to a view proffered by it in court. They serve to relax the court's scrutiny of such a decision or view, thereby enhancing the likelihood of the decision maker having more policymaking leeway (eg to retain the policy being challenged). When the court lowers the standard of review, reverses the burden of proof so that it falls on the applicant instead of the decision maker, lowers the decision maker's standard of proof, or grants weight to the decision maker's decision or view, it is requiring less from the decision maker to convince the court of its decision or view, thereby increasing the likelihood of the decision maker having more policymaking room.[18] In contrast, the final two devices—choice of interpretation and choice of remedy—are not necessarily tied to the scrutiny of prior decisions or views. When these devices are deployed, the court is choosing a narrower interpretation of a right or a remedy

Systems: Process and Substance (Hart 2016) 269; Robert Leckey, *Bills of Rights in the Common Law* (CUP 2015) 128–69; Aruna Sathanapally, *Beyond Disagreement: Open Remedies in Human Rights Adjudication* (OUP 2012) 26–29, 87–100.

[14] Aileen Kavanagh, *Constitutional Review under the UK Human Rights Act* (CUP 2009) 182–83. A classic example is *Bellinger v Bellinger* [2003] UKHL 21, [2003] 2 AC 467 [39]–[49].

[15] See eg *In Re S (Minors) (Care Order: Implementation of Care Plan)* [2002] UKHL 10, [2002] 2 AC 291 [35]–[44]. See also Michael Taggart, 'Proportionality, Deference, Wednesbury' (2008) NZ L Rev 423, 458.

[16] Jeff King, *Judging Social Rights* (CUP 2012) ch 9; Cass R Sunstein, 'Foreword: Leaving Things Undecided' (1996) 110(4) Harv L Rev 6, 8.

[17] *R (on the application of Nicklinson and another) v Ministry of Justice* [2014] UKSC 38, [2015] 1 AC 657 [116]–[128]; *The Queen on the application of The National Council of Civil Liberties (Liberty) v Secretary of State for the Home Department and another* [2018] EWHC 975 (Admin), [2019] QB 481 [93]; also *Bellinger* (n 14) [37]; cf *R (Steinfeld and another) v Secretary of State for International Development* [2018] UKSC 32, [2020] AC 1 [58].

[18] cf Aileen Kavanagh, *The Collaborative Constitution* (CUP 2023) 272, which views the giving of weight and giving of leeway as separate ways of affording respect to the primary decision maker.

that gives the decision maker more leeway to respond to the court's ruling, and not necessarily because the decision maker has argued for that remedy or interpretation in court or adopted that interpretation in its decision-making. Although in reality the imperatives of the two sets of devices go hand in hand most of the time, it is possible for them to diverge. For example, the remedy that the decision maker prefers may not be the remedy that the court deems as giving the decision-making more policymaking room. In this case, deference using the first four devices may yield a different result from that yielded by use of the final two. This point will be further elaborated upon in section VII. For now, it is sufficient to note that the first four devices operate by relaxing the court's review of a prior decision or view, whereas the final two devices do not. From this point onwards, I refer to the first four devices as 'review devices' whenever I need to distinguish them from the final two devices.

Both kinds of devices may be available to a court for the adjudication of a particular issue. For example, on the issue of what remedy the court should grant, the court could defer via the giving of weight device (a review device), say, by affording extra weight to the primary decision maker's argument in court that a particular remedy should be granted (thereby allowing the decision maker to get away with gaps in its logic), on the ground that the decision maker has more legitimacy than the court to decide what remedy the court should grant. The court could also defer by choosing a declaration of incompatibility over a remedial interpretation because it considers it desirable to give democratically elected representatives more room to respond to a negative court ruling. Courts can and sometimes do utilize both kinds of device with respect to the same issue. For example, the court may grant a declaration of incompatibility both because it has accorded extra weight to the decision maker's preference that such a remedy be granted and because it wants to afford the decision maker more policymaking room.

IV. Methodology and Originality

The overarching aim of this chapter is to distil the available deference devices at a conceptual level, an aim driven by the normative ambition of this book: to determine how the courts should express deference. To achieve that aim, I do not limit myself to devices that have actually been adopted by the courts. The fact that a device has not been used by a court does not preclude it from being a device. At the same time, however, I draw from case law to formulate my schema. How the courts have actually deferred provides inspiration for determining what devices are conceptually available and illustrates how they can be used. This combination of methods is deemed more suitable than a method that draws solely from case law. The latter would be unable to yield devices that are available conceptually and should be adopted in certain circumstances but have not actually been adopted by the courts in practice. The combination of methods is also more suitable than a method that does not draw from case law, and hence risks producing findings that are impracticable.

I adopt a temporal approach to identify the devices for deference that are available to the courts using the three-stage structure of human rights adjudication—definition, limitation, and remedy—as a structural framework for the schema. The four review devices are derived from the nature of human rights adjudication as a forum that involves evaluations of the acceptability of the executive or legislature's decisions or of the adequacy of the arguments and evidence proffered by the litigation parties, and as a forum that requires the courts to make decisions about the law even in circumstances of uncertainty. The two other devices are distilled from two issues that have been used by the courts to grant leeway to the executive or legislature, namely, constitutional interpretation and the selection of an appropriate remedy.

The distinction between the choice of interpretation and the five other devices assumes that constitutional interpretation does not entirely dictate the application of the latter devices. If it did, then all of the devices would be reducible to the choice of interpretation device. This assumption is grounded in the jurisdictions under study, as their constitutional provisions leave considerable room for the courts to determine at least some of the devices of the standard of review, burden of proof, standard of proof, giving of weight, and choice of remedy. The courts in those jurisdictions have also treated the application of at least some of the devices as more than a mere exercise in constitutional interpretation. For example, the 'demonstrably justified' formula in the limitation clauses of the Canadian Charter of Rights and Freedoms[19] and the New Zealand Bill of Rights Act 1990[20] intimates that the state bears the burden of demonstrating the justifiability of a prima facie rights limitation. However, the Canadian and New Zealand courts have not treated that formula as conclusive of the burden and standard of proof, but rather have adjusted it as they deem fit in the circumstances.

The devices identified may also apply to non-human rights adjudication and even non-adjudicative settings, but, as a collection, they are particularly relevant to human rights adjudication. I do not seek to identify an exhaustive list of the devices available in all rights cases, the contexts of which vary widely, but only to identify those available to the courts in a rights adjudication setting regulated by the three-stage framework. The salience of the individual devices varies across cases, and additional devices may well be available in specific rights contexts.

This book is not the first attempt to identify devices for deference in rights adjudication. There are numerous scholarly discussions of the devices that the courts can use or have used to express deference. However, there has hitherto been no in-depth examination of the key devices available conceptually, an

[19] Section 1.
[20] Section 5.

examination that is needed to answer this book's normative inquiries. For example, David Wiseman[21] adopts the same three-stage framework to identify the deference strategies adopted by the Canadian courts, but he does not examine the way in which those strategies relax judicial reasoning at the rights definition and remedial stages. Guy Davidov[22] and Brian Foley[23] highlight the possibility of expressing deference at the rights definition stage, but they do not elaborate on how judicial reasoning can be relaxed at that stage.[24] Mark Elliott,[25] Alison Young,[26] Paul Craig,[27] Richard Edwards,[28] and Rosalind Dixon,[29] amongst others,[30] have identified devices akin to what I call the standard of review and/or giving of weight to views as devices for calibrating the intensity of review at the rights limitation stage, but they stopped short of exploring the possibility of employing those devices at the rights definition or remedial stages. The standard of proof has attracted considerable attention in Canadian jurisprudence, with such scholars as Sujit Choudhry[31] and Kent Roach[32] having analysed it. The burden of proof has attracted relatively less attention, although there is helpful analysis by Julian Rivers,[33] Aharon Barak,[34] Janneke Gerards,[35] Guy Davidov,[36] Brian

[21] Wiseman (n 5).

[22] Guy Davidov, 'Judicial Deference and the Constitutional Protection of Human Rights' (1998) Thesis submitted in conformity with the requirements for the degree of Master of Laws at Faculty of Law of University of Toronto 56.

[23] Brian Foley, *Deference and the Presumption of Constitutionality* (Institute of Public Administration 2008) ch 3.

[24] cf Alison Young, *Democratic Dialogue and the Constitution* (OUP 2017) 228. I have previously highlighted the choice of a narrow interpretation of a right as a possible means of deference at the rights definition stage but have not hitherto explored the application of the other devices at that stage nor analysed deference at the remedial stage. Cora Chan, 'A Preliminary Framework for Measuring Deference in Rights Reasoning' (2016) 14(4) International Journal of Constitutional Law 851, 858–60.

[25] Mark Elliott, 'Proportionality and Deference: the Importance of a Structured Approach' in Christopher Forsyth, Mark Elliott, Swati Jhaveri, Anne Scully-Hill, and Michael Ramsden (eds), *Effective Judicial Review: A Cornerstone of Good Governance* (OUP 2010) 269.

[26] Alison L Young, 'In Defence of Due Deference' (2009) 72(4) MLR 554, 555; Alison L Young, 'Will You, Won't You, Will You Join the Deference Dance?' (2014) 34(2) OJLS 375, 389–90; Young, *Democratic Dialogue* (n 24) 227.

[27] Paul Craig, *Administrative Law* (8th edn, Sweet & Maxwell 2016) 617–27, 652–68.

[28] Richard A Edwards, 'Judicial Deference under the Human Rights Act' (2002) 65(6) MLR 859, 872–82.

[29] Rosalind Dixon, *Responsive Judicial Review: Democracy and Dysfunction in the Modern Age* (OUP 2023) 130–31.

[30] See eg Janneke Gerards, 'Pluralism, Deference and the Margin of Appreciation Doctrine' (2011) 17(1) Eur LJ 80, 88; Kirsty McLean, *Constitutional Deference, Courts and Socio-Economic Rights in South Africa* (Pretoria University Law Press 2009) 144–45.

[31] Choudhry (n 7).

[32] Kent Roach, *The Supreme Court on Trial: Judicial Activism or Democratic Dialogue* (rev edn, Irwin Law Inc 2016) 181–83, 195–96. See also Guy Davidov, 'The Paradox of Judicial Deference' (2000–2001) 12 NJCL 133, 162–63.

[33] Rivers (n 1). For my reply to Rivers, see Cora Chan, 'The Burden of Proof Under the Human Rights Act' [2014] JR 46.

[34] Barak (n 9) ch 16.

[35] Gerards (n 30) 88.

[36] Davidov, 'Judicial Deference' (n 22) 168–73; Davidov, 'The Paradox of Judicial Deference' (n 32) 154, 162–63.

Foley,[37] and David Kenny.[38] My own work has identified the standard of proof, burden of proof, standard of review, and giving of weight as devices for deference but stopped short of applying them at the definition and remedial stages.[39] There is a rich body of literature on constitutional remedies,[40] albeit little analysis of how judicial reasoning can be diluted at the remedial stage. My analysis builds on these works by systematically collating devices into a schema, articulating the methodology for such collation and explaining how the devices can function as devices for deference with illustrations from selected jurisdictions.

One study is particularly systematic in distilling deference devices, and is thus worth mentioning at greater length. As discussed in Chapter 1, Dean Knight identifies four prevalent approaches to calibrating deference in judicial review (including but not limited to human rights cases): scope of review, grounds of review, intensity of review, and contextual review.[41] Knight's project is both descriptive and normative: he traces trends in the use of these approaches across the Commonwealth and evaluates the relative merits of each. He derives the four approaches by examining the doctrine practised in the jurisdictions under study. Knight's work is valuable in offering in-depth analysis of some of the most common ways of expressing deference in judicial review, covering (in the parlance of this book) the devices of burden of proof, standard of proof, standard of review, giving of weight to views, and choice of interpretation. However, as explained in Chapter 1, Knight's study falls short of laying the conceptual foundations needed to achieve this book's normative aims. Insofar as identifying devices for deference in rights cases is concerned, the complementarity between my analysis and Knight's work is valuable for at least two reasons. First, the burden of proof, standard of proof, choice of interpretation, and choice of remedy—all of which are conceptually available and have been used by courts in rights adjudication—are given no consideration (in the case of the choice of remedy) or little consideration (in the case of the other devices) in his scheme. Second, because Knight's study covers judicial review generally, it does not offer an in-depth exposition of how the identified deference methods play out in human rights adjudication; for example, it does not examine how the devices function at the three stages of such adjudication.

[37] Brian Foley, 'The BUPA Ireland Case and Constitutional Litigation' (2010) 45 IJ 230.

[38] Kenny, 'Proportionality, the Burden of Proof' (n 1). See also David Bilchitz, 'Necessity and Proportionality: Towards A Balanced Approach' in Liora Lazarus, Christopher McCrudden, and Nigel Bowles (eds), *Reasoning Rights: Comparative Judicial Engagement* (Hart Publishing 2014) 46–47, which suggests devices akin to the standard of proof, burden of proof, and standard of review.

[39] Chan, 'Proportionality' (n 9) 5–6; Chan, 'A Preliminary Framework' (n 24) 858–60.

[40] See eg Kent Roach, *Constitutional Remedies in Canada* (2nd edn, Thomson Reuters 2019); Sathanapally (n 13); Leckey (n 13); Erin F Delaney, 'Analyzing Avoidance: Judicial Strategy in Comparative Perspective' (2016) 66 Duke LJ 1, 43–57; Dixon, *Responsive Judicial Review* (n 29), 176–80, 204–41; Rosalind Dixon, 'The Forms, Functions, and Varieties of Weak(ened) Judicial Review' (2019) 17(3) ICON 904, 912–14.

[41] Dean R Knight, *Vigilance and Restraint in the Common Law of Judicial Review* (CUP 2018).

This brings us to an analysis of how the six devices introduced in section II can operate at the three stages of adjudication, beginning with the rights definition stage.

V. Rights Definition Stage

Deference appears to be less frequent at the rights definition stage than at the limitation and remedial stages but is nonetheless conceptually possible and has been observed on occasion.[42]

1. Choice of interpretation

The courts may defer by defining a right stipulated in a rights instrument in a way that expands the primary decision maker's scope of legally permissible action for reasons that arise from the comparative institutional positions of the two institutions. This is what occurred in the most significant judgment of the trio of cases known as the Labour Trilogy. In *Reference re Public Service Employee Relations Act (Alta.)*, the Canadian Supreme Court had to decide whether a law that prohibited strikes and mandated arbitration to resolve collective bargaining deadlocks violated freedom of association.[43] Beetz, Le Dain, and La Forest JJ defined that freedom narrowly to preclude the right to strike and collectively bargain for reasons related to expertise. In their view, assessing the propriety of strikes and collective bargaining involved a 'balance of competing interests in a field' that required 'specialized expertise', and hence the freedom in question should be defined narrowly so that the court would not 'becom[e] involved in a review of legislative policy for which it is really not fitted'.[44]

Another example of the choice of interpretation device being deployed at the rights definition stage is the UK case of *Pretty v Director of Public Prosecutions and Secretary of State for the Home Department*, which concerned whether the ban on assisted suicide was compatible with the applicant's right to life and right not to be subjected to inhuman or degrading treatment, amongst other rights under the European Convention on Human Rights.[45] Lord Steyn remarked that such rights could not possibly be interpreted as including the right to commit assisted suicide:

[42] See eg Lorian Hardcastle, 'Proportionality Analysis by the Canadian Supreme Court' (157–62) and Talya Steiner, 'Proportionality Analysis by the Israeli Supreme Court' (312–18) in Mordechai Kremnitzer, Talya Steiner, and Andrej Lang (eds) *Proportionality in Action: Comparative and Empirical Perspectives on the Judicial Practice* (CUP 2020).

[43] [1987] 1 SCR 313.

[44] ibid [144].

[45] [2001] UKHL 61 [2002] 1 AC 800. I thank the reviewer for reminding me of this example.

> [i]n our parliamentary democracy ... such a fundamental change cannot be brought about by judicial creativity. If it is to be considered at all, it requires a detailed and effective regulatory proposal. In these circumstances it is difficult to see how a process of interpretation of convention rights can yield a result with all the necessary in-built protections. Essentially, it must be a matter for democratic debate and decision-making by legislatures.[46]

2. Burden and standard of proof

In addition to using the choice of interpretation device, a court can defer by adjusting the burden and standard of proof at the rights definition stage. In the jurisdictions under study, the burden of proof generally falls on the applicant at the definition stage, who must show that there has been a prima facie limitation of the right concerned. However, a court can increase its degree of deference by raising the standard to which the applicant must demonstrate a proposition. For example, in assessing whether the reduction of a government subsidy affected dignified human subsistence in a welfare right case[47] or whether a given comparator should be used in an equality case, a court could defer by requiring the applicant to demonstrate its legal or factual propositions to a high degree of certainty. A court can also weaken its deference by shifting the burden on all or particular questions of law or fact to the public body defendant, as occurred in *R v Kapp*,[48] in which the Canadian Supreme Court held that a government programme affording aboriginal fishers certain privileges did not violate the right to equality. The majority held that after an applicant has demonstrated that a distinction is being made on a prohibited ground, the burden shifts to the government to demonstrate that the act concerned is ameliorative for a disadvantaged group and that once that burden is discharged there is no need to proceed to rights limitation analysis.[49]

3. Standard of review and giving of weight to views

The courts can adjust the standard of review in assessing the arguments of the original decision maker, a strategy deployed in *Kapp*, in which the majority judges held that the court should assess the state's conclusion that the programme in question would meet its ameliorative goal (and hence was not rights limiting) using a mere rationality standard, a standard that accorded 'significant deference' to the

[46] ibid [57]–[58].
[47] HCJ 366/03 *Commitment to Peace and Social Justice v Minister of Finance*, IsrSC 60(3) 464 [2005], discussed in Steiner (n 42) 314.
[48] 2008 SCC 41, [2008] 2 SCR 483.
[49] ibid [37]–[41].

legislature, in order to give the legislature 'some leeway' to experiment with 'innovative programs' to enhance the 'conditions of a disadvantaged group' even if the effects of those programmes were not yet clear.[50]

The final way in which a court can adjust its degree of deference is by giving more or less weight to the primary decision maker's definition of a constitutional right. This device was used in the Hong Kong Court of First Instance's judgment in *W v Registrar of Marriages*,[51] which held that Hong Kong's then prevailing marriage law, which did not allow post-operative transsexual persons to marry in their post-operative gender, did not violate the right to marry. The court determined that that right should be defined by societal consensus and, notwithstanding evidence showing such consensus to be unclear, accepted the legislature's judgment (as embodied in the existing marriage law) as reflecting it. The court took the view that 'the legislature is in a much better position than the court to determine the relevant contemporary societal consensus'.[52] In other words, the court added decisive weight to the legislature's views on what societal consensus was on the basis of epistemic considerations.

VI. Rights Limitation Stage

Compared with deference at the rights definition and remedial stages, there is considerably more discussion of deference in judicial reasoning at the rights limitation stage. I therefore address the application of each device at that stage in this section at greater length to engage with the existing discourse.

1. Choice of interpretation

At the rights limitation stage, interpretation of the limitation clauses in a rights instrument determines the criteria that prima facie limitations of a right must meet in order to be constitutionally permissible. In the jurisdictions under study, the limitation clauses on qualified rights have in general been interpreted as requiring the four-limb, strict necessity proportionality test laid down in the Canadian case of *R v Oakes*,[53] insofar as the constitutionality of legislation is

[50] ibid [47]–[49].

[51] [2010] HKCFI 827, [2010] 6 HKC 359.

[52] ibid [195].

[53] [1986] 1 SCR 103. For the global spread of the proportionality principle, see eg Alec Stone Sweet and Jud Mathews, *Proportionality Balancing & Constitutional Governance: A Comparative & Global Approach* (OUP 2019); Alec Stone Sweet and Jud Mathews, 'Proportionality Balancing and Global Constitutionalism' (2008–09) 47 Colum J Transnatl L 72; Moshe Cohen-Eliya and Iddo Porat, *Proportionality and Constitutional Culture* (CUP 2013); Barak (n 9); Po Jen Yap and Chien-Chih Lin, *Constitutional Convergence in East Asia* (CUP 2021).

concerned.[54] The four-limb, strict necessity test requires that a rights limitation pursue a legitimate aim, be rationally connected to that aim, and be no more than necessary for achieving the aim and that the harm and benefit of the limitation be fairly balanced. It is also the standard that is generally applicable to administrative acts that prima facie limit rights in the United Kingdom, Israel, and Hong Kong, although the standard for such acts is less clear in Canada,[55] Ireland,[56] and New Zealand.[57] However, the courts have sometimes interpreted a limitation clause as requiring a test that is less demanding than the four-limb, strict necessity test. For example, with respect to social and economic policies that interfere with the right to property under Article 1 of Protocol 1 of the Human Rights Act 1998 (HRA), the UK courts have held that this article requires only that rights limitations be in pursuit of a legitimate aim 'in the public interest' and that there be a 'reasonable relationship of proportionality' between the means and the aim, effectively collapsing the third and fourth limbs of the proportionality test. This less demanding interpretation of the article is appropriate, in their view, to give due respect to a democratic body's determination, in setting socioeconomic policies, of 'the public interest by reference ... to political, economic and social considerations'.[58]

2. Standard of review

As explained above, the standard of review sets the threshold of error in a prior decision or view expressed that is required for judicial intervention. If the court determines that the limitation clause in question should be interpreted as requiring a four-limb, strict necessity test and that the primary decision maker bears the burden of demonstrating that the rights limitation concerned passes that test, then the standard of review constitutes the yardstick by which the court reviews the adequacy of the decision maker's contention that the limitation indeed passes the

[54] Note that the limitation clauses on different rights may be formulated differently. See Steven Greer, 'Constitutionalizing Adjudication under the European Convention on Human Rights' (2003) 23(3) OJLS 405, 414–29. See also Barak (n 9) 133–46, 238–39, which argues that rules of proportionality can be understood as arising from the interpretation of constitutional provisions. cf Andrew S Butler, 'Limiting Rights' (2002) 33 Victoria U Wellington L Rev 113, 140–45, which argues that courts should treat the exercise of distilling the legal test that a rights limitation should pass more seriously as an exercise of constitutional interpretation.

[55] See text to nn 65–69.

[56] Hilary Biehler and Catherine Donnelly, 'Proportionality in the Irish Courts: The Need for Guidance' (2014) 3 EHRLR 272; cf Alan DP Brady, 'Proportionality, Deference and Fundamental Rights in Irish Administrative Law: The Aftermath of Meadows' (2010) 32 Dublin U LJ 136.

[57] Claudia Geiringer, 'Sources of Resistance to Proportionality Review of Administrative Power Under the New Zealand Bill of Rights Act' (2013) 11 NZ J of Public and Intl L 123; Hanna Wilberg, 'The Bill of Rights in Administrative Law Cases: Taking Stock and Suggesting Some Reassessment' (2013) 25 NZ U L Rev 866.

[58] *AXA General Insurance Ltd and others v HM Advocate and others* [2011] UKSC 46, [2012] 1 AC 868 [29]–[33], [83].

test. Courts can adjust the standard of review in at least two ways.[59] First, they can keep the legal test set by constitutional interpretation, for example, a four-limb, strict necessity proportionality test, but review one or more limbs on, say, an unreasonableness standard rather than a correctness standard. If this way of relaxing the standard of review is adopted, the four-limb, strict necessity test still very much figures in the judicial analysis. Second, courts can adjust the standard by reformulating that test.[60] If this way of diluting the standard of review is adopted, the four-limb, strict necessity formula no longer figures in the judicial analysis. Let us examine the two methods in turn.

With respect to the first method, the courts in both the United Kingdom and Hong Kong have accepted that the courts should review rights limitations against the four-limb, strict necessity proportionality test on a correctness standard. Insofar as a review of administrative actions is concerned, the positions in Canada, Ireland, and New Zealand are less clear.[61] The correctness standard can be lowered in relation to questions of law, fact, or mixed questions of law and fact on any of the limbs of the four-limb strict necessity proportionality test. The reduced standards commonly adopted by the courts include reasonableness and manifest unreasonableness.

Numerous jurisdictions have diluted the inquiry on the third limb using the reasonableness filter. For example, the Canadian Supreme Court has taken the position that 'the difficulty of devising legislative solutions to social problems which may be only incompletely understood'[62] should affect the degree of deference accorded. Hence, in cases in which, for example, 'multi-faceted remedial regimes to protect constitutional rights', such as the implementation of pay equity measures,[63] are challenged, as long as the primary decision maker can demonstrate that the steps taken fall within 'a range of reasonable alternatives' the courts should not interfere.[64]

[59] There have been criticisms of the ways in which courts relax the standard of review. See eg Alec Stone Sweet, 'The Necessity of Balancing: Hong Kong's Flawed Approach to Proportionality, and Why it Matters' (2020) 50 Hong Kong LJ 541 for a critique of the 'manifestly without reasonable foundation' formula. My analysis here seeks merely to present examples of how the standard has been relaxed by courts; it should not be read as an endorsement of existing practices.

[60] Admittedly, it is not always easy to tell from the written judgment whether a court has adopted a less demanding proportionality test because it considered such a test to be required as a matter of constitutional interpretation (ie it used the choice of interpretation device) or because it deemed it appropriate to apply the test determined by constitutional interpretation in a less demanding manner (ie it used the standard of review device). The difficulty of distinguishing the use of these two devices in judgments does not affect the key argument being made here, namely, that the two devices are conceptually distinct. The cases I have selected to illustrate the 'choice of interpretation' device are cases in which the courts made it unequivocally clear that they were engaging in a constitutional interpretation exercise, whereas those I have selected to illustrate the review devices are those in which the courts appear not to have engaged in such an exercise.

[61] See nn 56–57, 65–69.

[62] *RJR-MacDonald Inc. v Canada (Attorney General)* [1995] 3 SCR 199 [135] (McLachlin J).

[63] *Centrale des syndicats du Québec v Quebec (Attorney General)*, 2018 SCC 18, [2018] 1 SCR 522 [46].

[64] ibid.

An example of the application of the reasonableness standard on all limbs of the proportionality test can be found in Canadian Charter jurisprudence on administrative law. The Canadian Supreme Court established in *Doré v Barreau du Québec*[65] that the courts should examine administrative actions that prima facie limit rights using the reasonableness standard, although the standard should incorporate elements of proportionality.[66] The reasons given for deference in the case included both epistemic and legitimacy considerations. Administrative bodies possess specialized expertise and are sanctioned by the Parliament of Canada to apply charter rights 'to a specific set of facts and in the context of their enabling legislation'.[67] Nevertheless, post-*Doré* case law is inconsistent in applying the reasonableness standard. In *Loyola High School v Quebec (Attorney General)*,[68] for example, Abella J, in invalidating a ministerial decision to require all aspects of a school's programme to be taught from a religion-neutral perspective, seems to have applied the correctness standard,[69] requiring a proportionate balance to be struck between rights protection and the relevant statutory mandate.

An example of the manifest unreasonableness standard is the UK Supreme Court's application of a 'manifestly without reasonable foundation' lens to one or more limbs of the proportionality test 'in cases concerned with judgments of social and economic policy in the field of welfare benefits and pensions' as a general principle.[70] A standard similar to the 'manifestly' standard has been employed by the Israeli courts. In *Adalah Legal Centre for Arab Minority Rights in Israel v Minister of Interior*, for example, the Supreme Court of Israel had to decide whether certain restrictions on Palestinians entering Israel for family reunion purposes were proportionate limitations of the right to equality and family life on national security grounds.[71] Taking into account the importance of the countervailing right involved—that is, Israelis' right to life—Cheshin VP diluted the standard of review at, inter alia, the fourth limb into an inquiry akin to manifest disproportionality: 'the court will intervene only when the measure chosen significantly deviates from the boundaries of the margin, and it is clearly disproportionate'.[72]

I now turn to the second method of diluting the standard of review, that is, replacing the four-limb, strict necessity formula in its entirety. Useful examples can be gleaned from Irish jurisprudence. Despite *Heaney v Ireland* having established

[65] 2012 SCC 12, [2012] 1 SCR 395.

[66] ibid [57].

[67] ibid [30]–[54].

[68] 2015 SCC 12, [2015] 1 SCR 613.

[69] Paul Daly, 'Struggling Towards Coherence in Canadian Administrative Law? Recent Cases on Standard of Review and Reasonableness' (2016) 62 McGill LJ 527, 553–54.

[70] *R (on the application of SC, CB and 8 children) v Secretary of State for Work and Pensions and others* [2021] UKSC 26, [2022] AC 223 [158]. The court emphasized, however, that such application was not a mechanical rule: the appropriate degree of deference to be accorded in a particular case should be determined by weighing all relevant factors (at [158]–[161]).

[71] HCJ 7052/03, PD 61(2) 202 [2006].

[72] ibid [119] citing HCJ 4769/95 *Menahem v. Minister of Transport*, IsrSC 57(1) 235, 280 [2003].

the multi-limb proportionality test for assessing whether legislation complies with constitutional rights,[73] the Irish courts have from time to time applied less-demanding formulae.[74] For example, in In *Re Article 26 and the Employment Equality Bill 1996*,[75] the court had to determine whether the exemption of certain age groups from the prohibition against age discrimination in employment was discriminatory. The court remarked that where the legislature intended to balance different constitutional values, 'a difficult exercise' that was 'peculiarly within the province of the Oireachtas',[76] the *Tuohy v Courtney*[77] standard applied; that is, the court should not interfere unless, judging 'from an objective stance', 'the impugned legislation is so contrary to reason and fairness as to constitute an unjust attack on some individual's constitutional rights'.[78] The Irish court's deferential posture here appears to have been influenced by the importance of the right concerned because, in assessing whether the impugned law violated the right to due process, it reverted to the four-limb proportionality test.[79] Similarly, although *Meadows v Minister for Justice, Equality, and Law Reform*[80] is considered to have established proportionality as the standard for assessing the compatibility of administrative acts with fundamental rights in Ireland, not all of the Supreme Court judges involved in the case understood proportionality as conveying the *Oakes* formula.[81] Fennelly J, for example, held that an administrative decision could be struck down only if it fell foul of the classic unreasonableness test, that is, if it 'plainly and unambiguously flies in the face of fundamental reason and common sense'.[82]

3. Burden of proof

In all but one of the jurisdictions under study, the general rule is that once an applicant establishes a prima facie rights limitation (at the rights definition stage), the public body defendant bears the burden to establish the legal proposition that the limitation passes the proportionality test and the burden of proving the facts needed to establish the proposition.[83] Ireland is the exception in that the burden of

[73] [1994] 3 IR 593.
[74] Brian Foley, 'The Proportionality Test: Present Problems' (2008) 1 JSIJ 67.
[75] [1997] IESC 6, [1997] 2 IR 321.
[76] ibid 343.
[77] [1994] 3 IR 1.
[78] n 75, 334, 344.
[79] ibid 383.
[80] [2010] IESC 3, [2010] 2 IR 701.
[81] See Paul Daly, 'Standards of Review in Irish Administrative Law After Meadows v Minister for Justice, Equality and Law Reform' (2010) 32 Dublin U LJ 379.
[82] *Meadows* (n 80) [66]–[72]. Biehler and Donnelly (n 56); cf Alan DP Brady, 'Proportionality, Deference and Fundamental Rights in Irish Administrative Law; The Aftermath of Meadows' (2010) 32 Dublin U LJ 136.
[83] For the importance of the burden and standard of proof in proportionality analysis, see Carter (n 10) ch 7.

proof at both the rights definition and limitation stages falls on the applicant: the presumption of constitutionality is assumed to apply at both stages, and the state bears no burden, a situation that Foley describes as placing a 'double onus' on the applicant.[84]

Even if the burden initially falls on the state at the rights limitation stage, the courts may still grant leeway to it by shifting the burden on, inter alia, one or more limbs of the proportionality test.[85] Burden shifting has been observed on all four limbs of the proportionality test. Note that the test for legality on a particular limb becomes a negative test after the burden on that limb is reversed.[86] For example, if the burden of proof is shifted to the applicant at the rights limitation stage, the applicant is required to prove disproportionality (rather than proportionality, as would have been the case had the burden been on the state instead).

British Telecommunications Plc v The Secretary of State for Business, Innovation and Skills[87] offers an example of a court having shifted to the claimants the burden on the legal questions of whether the third and fourth limbs are satisfied. In this case, certain legislative provisions regulating online copyright infringement were challenged on the ground that they violated freedom of expression and the right to privacy. The High Court of England and Wales found that a large degree of deference should be afforded the legislature in this case for various reasons. First, the matter was one of 'social and economic policy' involving 'important and conflicting interests', the balancing of which should be performed by an elected parliament.[88] Second, UK Parliament had consulted the relevant parties and tried out a non-legislative scheme, a process that likely imbued it with regulatory insights that the court lacked.[89] Third, the court lacked the time and processes to determine a matter as complex and polycentric as the one at hand.[90] Finally, the countervailing interest—the right to property—was also a fundamental right, and it was thus right for the court to give the legislature considerable leeway to strike the balance concerned.[91] The court exhibited deference by, inter alia, shifting the burden on the third and fourth limbs to the applicant. It held that 'in order to

[84] Foley, 'The BUPA Ireland case' (n 37) 232. There are dicta suggesting that the burden should shift to the state at the rights limitation stage. For example, in *BUPA Ireland Ltd v Health Insurance Authority* [2006] IEHC 431, McKechnie J suggested that once an applicant has demonstrated a prima facie rights infringement, the burden of justification should be borne by the state ([247]), discussed in Foley, *Deference and the Presumption of Constitutionality* (n 23) 68. See also *Fleming v Ireland* [2013] IEHC 2, discussed in Kenny, 'Proportionality, the Burden of Proof' (n 1). However, that suggestion has not been taken up, and the Irish position remains that the burden is on the applicant at both the rights definition and limitation stages.

[85] See eg Davidov, 'The Paradox of Judicial Deference' (n 32) 162–63.

[86] See eg David Kenny, 'Proportionality and the Inevitably of the Local: A Comparative Localist Analysis of Canada and Ireland' (2018) 66 AJCL 537, 559.

[87] [2011] EWHC 1021 (Admin), [2011] 3 CMLR 5.

[88] ibid [211].

[89] ibid [212].

[90] ibid [213].

[91] ibid [215].

succeed on the proportionality challenge', the claimants 'need[ed] to show ... there was a clearly less intrusive but equally effective means of resolving the relevant problem' and that the 'legislator [had] unlawfully failed to balance the relevant interests at stake'.[92]

Burden shifting has been observed on the first and second limbs of the proportionality test as well. In *Beit Sourik Village Council v The Government of Israel*, the Israeli Supreme Court had to decide whether the seizure of certain plots of land to erect a separation fence was a proportionate limitation of the landowners' rights.[93] The court held that because the first three limbs of proportionality analysis 'raise[d] problems within the realm of military expertise' a large dose of deference was warranted.[94] On the first limb, it placed the burden on the petitioners to 'negate' the 'assumption' that the fence was motivated by security rather than political considerations. The court also held that in addition to the first limb, the second and third limbs also required military professional expertise that the court lacked.[95] It further held that when there was conflicting expert advice on the second and third limbs, as was the situation in this case, the court 'must place the expert opinion of the military commander at the foundation of [its] decision'.[96] On the facts, the petitioners in the case did not discharge their 'heavy burden' to convince the court that their expert advice should be preferred to the state's.[97] The fourth limb, in contrast, involved 'humanitarian considerations' rather than 'military considerations', which the court considered itself to have expertise in, and therefore scrutinized more rigorously.[98]

This example supports two points made earlier on. First, the distinction between the burden of proof on questions of law and that on questions of fact may not be clear from written judgments. For example, which type of burden is meant in the references to 'burdens' in the *Beit Sourik* judgment is unclear. Second, in rights adjudication, proof of the points of facts at issue (in *Beit Sourik*, whether the purpose of constructing the fence was security related, whether the chosen route of the fence could achieve said purpose, and whether another route could achieve it to the same extent) may also discharge proof of the questions of law at issue (ie whether there is a legitimate aim, whether the means are rationally connected to the aim, and whether the means are no more than necessary for achieving the aim).[99]

92 ibid [227], [243].
93 HCJ 2056/04, IsrSC 58(5) 807 [2004].
94 ibid [46].
95 ibid [45]–[46].
96 ibid [47].
97 ibid [47], [56].
98 ibid [48].
99 See Carter (n 10).

4. Standard of proof

The standard of proof is applicable to questions of law and fact at all four stages of the proportionality test. The spectrum of the standard can be represented numerically, with the highest standard requiring 100 per cent certainty, and the lowest close to 0 per cent. The standards of proof that the courts have used or mentioned range from absolute certainty to demonstration of a theoretical possibility. I have grouped the following illustrations into five levels of proof, with decreasing demands on proof.[100]

The first level requires absolute or near certainty. The courts in the jurisdictions under study rarely, if ever, require absolute certainty. In *Adalah Legal Centre for Arab Minority Rights in Israel v Minister of Interior*, for example, the Israeli Supreme Court explained that it did not require absolute certainty that a blanket prohibition on Palestinians of a certain age range entering Israel would achieve the proclaimed security purpose.[101] A 'serious likelihood' rather than 'slight and theoretical possibility' was considered to suffice.[102] However, the near certainty standard, which is akin to the 'beyond reasonable doubt' standard typically adopted in criminal cases, has sometimes been applied by the Israeli courts. Although such application occurred before proportionality was established as a test of legality in Israel, it shows how the near certainty standard can be applied in assessing various limbs of the proportionality test. In *Kol Ha'am Co Ltd v Minister of the Interior*, the Israeli Supreme Court held that it would be justifiable for the Interior Minister to suspend a publication containing material critical of the government if he could show with 'near certain probability' that public peace would be endangered without such suspension.[103] It has been observed that the probability threshold in this and other Israeli cases has been determined by the relative importance of the right and the countervailing interest at stake.[104] Where freedom of speech has conflicted with the right to impartial legal proceedings, for example, the courts have required a lower standard of proof, namely, that there is a 'reasonable likelihood' of harm to the latter right absent the limitation on the former right, a standard that is further discussed below.[105]

The second level of proof requires 'compelling evidence', and is akin to the US standard of 'clear and convincing evidence'. A good example is *R v K.R.J.*, in which the Canadian Supreme Court struck down in part the retrospective application of

[100] cf CMA McCauliff, 'Burdens of Proof: Degrees of Belief, Quanta of Evidence, Or Constitutional Guarantees' (1982) 35 V and L Rev 1293, 1332; Nance (n 2) 58.

[101] *Adalah Legal Centre for Arab Minority Rights in Israel* (n 71).

[102] ibid [66] (Barak P).

[103] HCJ 73/53, PD 7 871, 892 [1953], as discussed in Moshe Cohen-Eliya and Gila Stopler, 'Probability Thresholds as Deontological Constraints in Global Constitutionalism' (2010) 49 Colum J Transnl L 75, 99–100.

[104] ibid 100.

[105] ibid, citing HCJ 696/81 *Azulai v State of Israel*, PD 37(2) 565 [1983].

a more severe punishment against sex offenders on the ground that it was a disproportionate limitation of the constitutional guarantee of entitlement to the 'benefit of ... lesser punishment' when the punishment for an offence is increased after the offence's commission.[106] Abella J, dissenting in part, ruled that because of the significance of that guarantee, the primary decision maker bore the heavy burden of demonstrating through 'compelling evidence' that the retrospective application concerned was needed.[107]

A similar standard was applied in *Ressler and Knesset*, in which the Israeli Supreme Court found a law deferring military service for yeshiva students to be unconstitutional.[108] The court held that because of the importance of the right to equality, there had to be a 'real, significant probability that the means chosen by the Legislature' would attain its purposes of 'promot[ing] compromise and balance among conflicting objectives ... to promote equal distribution of the security burden ... and the integration of hareidi men into the workforce', a standard that was not discharged on the facts of the case.[109] This case arguably also illustrates the influence that the temporal dimension of a case can have on the standard of proof. A court may require a higher standard of proof from the original decision maker as the effects of a policy become more measurable over time,[110] leading to higher expectations that the state will 'provide data to support its claim of effectiveness'.[111] In an earlier challenge to the same law,[112] the Israeli court held back from striking down the law despite finding a lack of any rational connection based on the evidence available at the time. Instead, it deferred because the law had only just been implemented, and the court could not rule out the possibility that the law could, in time, achieve the government's proclaimed effects. It therefore decided to 'wait and see if the Law would bring about the desired social change'.[113] One reading of this judgment is that the government managed to pass constitutional muster merely by proving a theoretical possibility that the means could achieve the aims. Then, ten years into the law's operation, the court held in *Ressler* that 'we have reached a point where we are no longer speaking of conjecture. We are not examining the Law prior to its implementation by the Executive, when the possibilities for realizing its purposes are merely educated guesses'.[114] At this point, the court was able to assess the law using data from an extended implementation period, and would have been able

[106] 2016 SCC 31, [2016] 1 SCR 906 [2].
[107] ibid [126].
[108] HCJ 6298/07 *Ressler v Knesset*, IsrSC 65(3) 1 (2012).
[109] ibid [2], [53].
[110] See Hughes and MacDonnell (n 8) 48–53. cf Mike Redmayne, 'Expert evidence and scientific disagreement' (1996–97) 30 UC Davis L Rev 1027, 1076.
[111] Steiner (n 42) 344.
[112] HCJ 6427/02 *Movement for Quality Government in Israel v The Knesset*, IsrSC 61(1) 619 [2006].
[113] *Ressler v Knesset* (n 108) discussing *Movement for Quality Government in Israel* ibid [11].
[114] *Ressler v Knesset* (n 108) [55].

to uphold it only if there were a real and significant possibility of it achieving the desired effects.

The third level of proof requires proof on a balance or preponderance of evidence or probability, the usual standard in civil proceedings. The Canadian Supreme Court famously laid down in *Oakes* that the state must demonstrate proportionality on a preponderance of probabilities.[115] In *RJR-MacDonald Inc v Canada (Attorney General)*,[116] in determining whether a statutory prohibition on all advertising and promotion of tobacco products and other restrictions on the sale and promotion of tobacco were proportionate limitations of the right to property, McLachlin CJ, whilst acknowledging the difficulty of scientifically proving the impact of tobacco advertising, insisted on the civil standard of proof.[117] The 'serious likelihood' threshold applied by the Israeli Supreme Court in *Adalah Legal Centre* conveys a similar standard.[118]

The fourth level of proof requires a reasonable basis for the primary decision maker's conclusion. The standard of 'reasonable basis for belief' or 'reasoned apprehension of harm' has been observed in Canadian jurisprudence. In *RJR-MacDonald*, La Forest J emphasized that two contextual elements—the nature of the right and nature of the legislation—should determine the standard of proof.[119] On the former, the judge was of the view that the type of expression at stake in the case—the promotion of tobacco—was far from the '"core" of freedom of expression values', and thus entitled to 'a very low degree of protection'.[120] On the latter, he remarked that the case involved legislating for the 'laudable social goal' of protecting public health and vulnerable groups, an area in which the social science evidence is unclear and mediation of competing social interests is involved. In these circumstances, it was best to leave decisions to 'elected representatives, who have at their disposal the resources to undertake them, and who are ultimately accountable to the electorate'.[121] Given that the 'ramifications of legal rules on the social and economic order are not matters capable of precise measurement, and are often "the product of conjecture, fragmentary knowledge, general experience and knowledge of the needs, aspirations and resources of society, and other components"', a mechanistic insistence on the civil standard of proof would 'paralyz[e] the operation of government in the socio-economic sphere'.[122] Hence, the judge concluded the government needed only to demonstrate that it had a reasonable basis for its conclusions on proportionality.

[115] *Oakes* (n 53) 137.
[116] *RJR-MacDonald* (n 62).
[117] ibid [137].
[118] See n 102.
[119] *RJR-MacDonald* (n 62) [64].
[120] ibid [75].
[121] ibid [65]–[70].
[122] ibid [67] (references omitted).

The fifth and lowest level of standard of proof observed in the cases requires proof only to a 'slight and theoretical possibility' or that the realization of an outcome not be mere 'speculation'. As discussed above, the Israeli courts have rejected this standard. However, an example of its application can be found in the UK Supreme Court's judgment on the constitutionality of a ban on assisted suicide in *R (on the application of Nicklinson and another) v Ministry of Justice*.[123] Lord Neuberger seems to have applied a standard akin to mere proof of a slight and theoretical possibility of the ban being proportionate. He took the view that the government's concern about abuses of a system of assisted suicide could not possibly be rejected as 'fanciful or unrealistic'.[124] Despite finding that the limitation on the right to a private life was 'grave', that the arguments for the ban were 'by no means overwhelming', that the 'present official attitude to assisted suicide seems in practice to come close to tolerating it in certain situations', and that the 'rational connection' between the aim and the ban was 'fairly weak',[125] the judge concluded that the court could not yet hold that the ban infringed the right in question.[126] There were 'too many uncertainties' for the court to issue a declaration of incompatibility, he averred.[127] One possible reading of this judgment is that the judge was ready to rule in favour of the government despite it not having demonstrated a reasonable basis for its conclusions. Various reasons were cited for the court's deference, including that it could not be 'properly confident that [it had] the evidence' to conclude that a feasible assisted suicide scheme existed, and hence that the third and fourth limbs of proportionality were satisfied.[128] The judgment suggests that because the public interest in protecting the vulnerable was significant and because it was difficult to obtain direct proof that lifting the ban on assisted suicide would lead to abuse, the court required the government merely to demonstrate a risk of abuse, and hence the passing of the third and fourth limbs, to a low standard of proof.

5. Giving of weight to views

The courts in some of the jurisdictions under study have emphasized that the primary decision maker must discharge its burden at the limitation stage with sufficient cogent and persuasive reasons. However, in reality, the courts have, for deference reasons, generally required less than sufficient or cogent reasons on the merits, correspondingly allowing those deference reasons to add weight to the

[123] *Nicklinson* (n 17).
[124] ibid [88].
[125] ibid [111].
[126] ibid [113].
[127] ibid [127].
[128] ibid [120].

decision maker's judgments, thereby making it easier for the decision maker to discharge its burden.

The use of this device, that is, the giving of weight to views, is prominent in Canadian jurisprudence discussing the need for the courts to allow evidential gaps in the government's case to be filled by logic and common sense,[129] at least according to one reading of the judgments concerned. For example, in *RJR-MacDonald*, the Canadian Supreme Court emphasized that social and economic policies are not always susceptible to scientific proof, and, accordingly, that the courts should sometimes be ready to fill evidential gaps with logic and common sense.[130] These and similar remarks can be read in three ways, the third of which is relevant to the device under discussion. The first is that the court is not deferring in allowing logic and common sense to fill evidential gaps. It is simply reiterating the incontrovertible proposition that courts apply logic and common sense in reasoning about the merits of a case; for example, it is commonplace for courts to take judicial notice of facts that are widely known. Cogent reasons include both scientific evidence and logic and common sense, and, in relying on the latter, a court is not relaxing the cogency of reasons on the merits required of the government decision maker. The second reading is that the remarks suggest that the court is lowering the standard of proof.[131] As noted, however, it is the third possible reading that suggests use of the device of interest. According to this reading, the standard of proof remains the same, but the court is making it easier for the decision maker to discharge that standard. It is allowing deference considerations to add weight to the decision maker's case such that it passes the standard of proof. According to this reading, reference to reliance on logic and common sense is but a euphemism for the court granting the decision maker's case despite the decision maker not having proffered cogent reasons on the merits to discharge its burden.[132]

The use of this giving of weight device is also discernible in two types of cases, at least according to one reading of those cases. The first type is cases in which the court engages in little reasoning on the merits, states that it is giving weight to the primary decision maker's judgment for deference reasons and accepts that judgment. One reading of such cases is that the court's own balance of reasons on the merits does not suggest that the primary decision maker's case meets the requisite standards, but it allows deference reasons to add weight to the decision maker's conclusion anyway, with the result that those standards are met. For example, in *Kwok Cheuk Kin v Secretary for Constitutional and Mainland Affairs*, the Hong

[129] This is also related to the debate on whether the parties need only prove their claims of harms and benefits of a measure to a theoretical level. See eg Colleen M Flood, 'The Evidentiary Burden for Overturning Government's Choice of Regulatory Instrument: The Case of Direct-to-Consumer Advertising of Prescription Drugs' (2010) 60 U Toronto LJ 397, 399–400.

[130] *RJR-MacDonald* (n 62) [66]–[67], [137]–[138], [154], [184].

[131] Hughes and MacDonnell (n 8) remarked that it may be hard to tell whether the court has lowered the standard of proof or allowed the government to satisfy that standard more easily, 32–33.

[132] cf Hardcastle (n 42) 172–73.

Kong Court of Final Appeal held that a law banning legislators from standing in a by-election triggered by their resignation was a proportionate measure to protect the integrity of the Legislative Council.[133] Citing the legislature's legitimacy and expertise in making 'political judgment[s] or prediction[s] [of legislators' behaviour]',[134] the court stated that it would afford great weight to the legislature's judgment in determining whether the ban passed the third limb of the proportionality test, and then accepted said judgment with little reasoning on the merits.[135]

In the second type of cases in which the device's use is discernible, the courts expressly state that they are not persuaded on the merits that the primary decision maker's case fulfils the requisite standards of proof and review but still allow deference considerations to add weight to the decision maker's conclusion, with the result that it meets those standards. For example, in *The Queen on the application of Louis Farrakhan v Secretary of State for the Home Department*, the government had barred the applicant from entering the United Kingdom to address an audience, claiming that non-disclosable evidence suggested that he posed a threat to public order.[136] Despite finding the legal merits of the case to be 'finely balanced' and that 'it would have been better had he [the Home Secretary] been less diffident about explaining the nature of the [undisclosed] information and advice that he had received', the English and Welsh Court of Appeal ruled in favour of the government on several grounds, including that the state was 'far better placed' than the court to come to the correct judgment on the merits.[137] Another example is Lord Mance's judgment in *Nicklinson*, which gave 'considerable weight' to the legislature's 'value judgments of difficulty and delicacy' on the issue of the legalization of assisted suicide, 'even if the evidence appears to a court weaker and less conclusive than it might be'.[138]

VII. Remedial Stage

Deference features prominently at the remedial stage in all of the jurisdictions under study. The judicial reasoning on remedial deference can be conceptualized using all six devices proposed herein, although judicial and academic discussions of the subject have tended to focus on one device alone, that is, the choice of remedy, which is undoubtedly the most prominent device for deference at the remedial stage. In the following, I explain the application of each device in turn.

133 [2017] HKCFA 44, [2017] 5 HKC 242.
134 ibid [55].
135 ibid [55]–[57].
136 [2002] EWCA Civ 606, [2002] QB 1391.
137 ibid [71]–[79].
138 *Nicklinson* (n 17) [189].

1. Choice of interpretation

At the remedial stage, courts sometimes have to engage in constitutional interpretation to discern the meaning of constitutional provisions that regulate the court's remedial discretion. A court can defer to a greater extent by reading such provisions as incorporating more criteria that would allow room to be afforded the primary decision maker to fashion a response to the court's ruling. For example, section 24(1) of the Canadian Charter of Rights and Freedoms grants the courts the authority to hand down a remedy that is 'appropriate and just in the circumstances'. In *Doucet-Boudreau v Nova Scotia (Minister of Education)*,[139] the Canadian Supreme Court held that this provision should be interpreted generously and expansively,[140] and laid down a number of considerations that should guide a court's determination of what remedy is appropriate and just. These considerations include not just that the remedy must be 'one that meaningfully vindicates the rights and freedoms of the claimants'[141] but institutional considerations as well, such as that the remedy 'must strive to respect the ... separation of functions among the legislature, the executive and the judiciary' and not 'depart unduly or unnecessarily from [the courts'] role of adjudicating disputes'.[142] Nor should the court be allowed 'to leap into the kinds of decisions and functions for which its design and expertise are manifestly unsuited. The capacities and competence of courts can be inferred, in part, from the tasks with which they are normally charged....'[143]

Whilst the courts in some of the jurisdictions under study have handed down interpretations of constitutional provisions on remedies, those interpretations are usually stipulated in broad terms, leaving ample discretion for the courts to decide what remedy would satisfy the criteria on the facts,[144] an issue to which we now turn.

2. Choice of remedy

The choice of remedy device relates to determining what remedy would satisfy constitutional requirements. If those requirements are ascertained by interpreting the constitutional provisions that govern remedial discretion, then this device involves application to the facts of the meaning of such provisions, as determined by the constitutional interpretation exercise. The court asks, for example, what remedy would fulfil the aforementioned considerations on an 'appropriate and

[139] 2003 SCC 62, [2003] 3 SCR 3.
[140] ibid [23].
[141] ibid [55].
[142] ibid [56].
[143] ibid [57].
[144] See eg Roach (n 40) [3.100].

just' remedy on the facts of the case. Very often, however, the court does not engage in constitutional interpretation to ascertain the requirements a remedy has to satisfy and instead dives straight into choosing amongst various remedies. Either way—with or without a preceding constitutional interpretation exercise—the court may choose from a range of remedies that give the primary decision maker a greater or narrower scope of permissible action in response to the court's finding of a rights violation. The court defers via the choice of remedy device by choosing a remedy that grants the decision maker a greater scope of permissible action. The exact remedies available to the court depend on the jurisdiction, but, broadly speaking, the typical remedies in the selected jurisdictions can be categorized into four types:[145]

1) the court declares a rights violation, mandates that it be redressed and itself decides how it should be redressed (eg remedial interpretation or coercive orders that the government must take specific actions, such as injunctions or mandamus);
2) the court declares a rights violation and mandates that it be redressed but does not decide how it should be redressed (eg a declaration of invalidity or the remitting of an executive decision);
3) the court declares a rights violation but does not say whether it should be redressed, or if so how (eg a declaration of incompatibility or inconsistency); or
4) the court grants no remedy.

These categories can be considered as being in increasing order of deference, albeit only crudely. How deferential a remedy is depends on the context, how it is used, and whether it is used in conjunction with other ancillary tools. It cannot be determined in the abstract. For example, whilst a declaration of incompatibility (category 3) can be considered more deferential than a declaration of invalidity (category 2) because it apparently leaves the public body with the legal option of not redressing the rights violation, its (non)deferential force may be comparable in jurisdictions in which a court ruling effectively reflects what a supranational court is likely to rule, suggesting that if the public body does not comply with the declaration of incompatibility, it will likely face unfavourable proceedings at the supranational court.[146] Furthermore, the breadth of the remedial order matters: a remedial interpretation (category 1) that introduces a minor change to a small part

[145] On constitutional remedies generally, see ibid; Sathanapally (n 13); Leckey (n 13); Sujit Choudhry and Kent Roach, 'Putting the Past Behind Us? Prospective Judicial and Legislative Constitutional Remedies' (2003) 21 Sup Ct L Rev 205.

[146] Sathanapally (n 13) 77. See also Kavanagh, *The Collaborative Constitution* (n 18) 251–56.

of a regulatory scheme may leave more room for action than a declaration of invalidity (category 2) for the entire scheme.

The deferential force of the remedies in categories 1 and 2 can be adjusted by temporal instruments,[147] such as postponing the date on which the remedy takes effect (the longer the suspension, the wider the executive or legislature's permissible scope of action); restricting the remedy's temporal effect (eg requiring prospective as opposed to retrospective operation or the stipulation of a transition period, and the longer the period of exemption, the wider the executive or legislature's permissible scope of action); and exempting the applicant from the aforementioned temporal strictures. The deferential force of the remedies in categories 2 and 3 (whether deployed with temporal instruments or not) can also be weakened by adding other binding measures, including mandatory remedies in the form of injunction, prohibition, and mandamus, which provide for various degrees of judicial supervision. Examples include the granting of such 'negative' remedies[148] as refusing to protect the government from the consequences of abusing the law or barring prosecution before the impugned act is rectified[149] and such 'affirmative remedies'[150] as setting a timeframe for compliance, imposing reporting requirements, or instructing the government to take into account a list of considerations in rethinking the policy concerned.

The deferential force of the remedies in all four categories can be reduced by a court making exhortatory remarks on what the executive or legislature should do in response to the court's judgment.[151] Although such remarks are non-binding, they nevertheless limit the decision maker's policymaking leeway because if the decision maker does not act in accordance with them it risks having the measure concerned deemed unconstitutional and attracting a remedy in future litigation. Exhortatory remarks therefore suggest actions that may be legally impermissible in future. The extent to which the remarks restrict the decision maker's policymaking leeway depends, inter alia, on their degree of instructiveness[152] (eg detailed vs general guidelines, whether there is an express mention of the possibility of the court viewing a measure negatively in future should the remarks not be heeded) and the likelihood of another round of litigation and of the court acting on previous remarks in a future case.

[147] See eg Choudhry and Roach (n 145); Leckey (n 13) 102–09, 137–44; Rosalind Dixon and Sam Issacharoff, 'Living to Fight another Day: Judicial Deferral in Defense of Democracy' [2016] Wis L Rev 683.

[148] David Kenny, 'Remedial Innovation, Constitutional Culture, and the Supreme Court at a Crossroads' (2017) 40 Dublin U LJ 85, 95.

[149] See Po Jen Yap, 'Remedial Discretion and Dilemmas in Asia' (2019) U Toronto LJ 84.

[150] *Doucet-Boudreau* (n 139) [29].

[151] See Leckey (n 13) 109–15; Kavanagh, *The Collaborative Constitution* (n 18) 312–22. cf Janet McLean, 'Legislative Invalidation, Human Rights Protection and s 4 of the New Zealand Bill of Rights Act' (2001) 2001 NZ L Rev 421, 442

[152] See Kavanagh, *The Collaborative Constitution* (n 18) 314–15

A court's choice of remedy is often deployed as a device for deference. The choice is generally guided by balancing the need to grant an effective remedy to an individual with the need to give effect to legitimacy concerns (which are stronger when eg there is more than one way to remedy the rights violation, the devising of an alternative scheme is needed, or a less deferential remedy would entail radical and controversial reform) and the need to account for other considerations, for example, that a less deferential remedy would harm the coherence of policy in related areas of law, have far-reaching knock-on effects, lead to a legal void that would endanger public safety, or seriously harm inter-institutional comity. The following paragraphs provide examples of the courts deferring by choosing a relatively deferential remedy amongst the options available to it.

The choice of a declaration of incompatibility over remedial interpretation as a means of deference is frequently discussed in UK judgments. In *In Re S (Minors) (Care Order: Implementation of Care Plan)*,[153] for example, the court overturned the lower court's remedial interpretation of a legislative child protection scheme because such an interpretation would lead to an overhaul of legislation and have 'far-reaching practical ramifications' that the court felt unable to evaluate.[154] Similarly, the New Zealand Supreme Court, in choosing between these two remedies, emphasized that judicial interpretation should not be used to legislate, which is the task of the legislature.[155]

Temporal tools are commonly used. In Canada, suspensions 'have become almost routine'.[156] In *Re Manitoba Language Rights*,[157] the first case in which the Canadian Supreme Court deployed suspension as a tool, the court suspended invalidation to allow for the translation and re-enactment of unilingual acts enacted by the Manitoba legislature. The criteria for granting a suspension have expanded over the years, from requiring non-suspension to seriously harm the public interest to covering, inter alia, considerations of the government's legitimacy to reformulate legislation.[158]

The courts have also appended suspensions and declarations with binding measures that attenuate their deferential force to enhance the effectiveness of a remedy for an individual or ensure that the government will indeed rectify the unconstitutionality. In *Carmody v Minister for Justice*, the Irish Supreme Court declared it unconstitutional to deny a defendant in certain criminal proceedings the

[153] *In Re S (Minors)* (n 15).
[154] ibid [43]–[44].
[155] See eg *Paul Rodney Hansen v The Queen* [2007] NZSC 7, [2007] 3 NZ L Rev 1 [156] per Tipping J. Note, however, that the court's finding of legislative inconsistency in this case took the form of an informal declaration embedded in its judicial reasoning (a declaration that has since become known as a 'Hansen declaration'), or of what Petrie calls an 'indication of inconsistency' rather than a formal declaration of inconsistency. See Nicholas Petrie, 'Indications of inconsistency' (2019) 78(3) CLJ 612; Philip A Joseph, *Constitutional and Administrative Law* (Thomson Reuters, 2014) 1287.
[156] Leckey (n 13) 139; Choudhry and Roach (n 145) 228.
[157] [1985] 1 SCR 721.
[158] Leckey (n 13) 138–41.

right to apply for legal aid to obtain legal representation.[159] The court made an order that barred prosecution unless and until the individual defendant in question was granted that right.[160] In *W*, the Hong Kong Court of Final Appeal gave the legislature twelve months to comprehensively reform the current marriage laws to bring them into compliance with transsexual persons' right to marry, but it ordered that remedial interpretation would take effect should the government fail to act by the expiry of that period.[161] In *Doucet-Boudreau*, despite remitting to the executive the decision concerning how to provide school facilities to implement minority language educational rights, the Canadian Supreme Court retained the jurisdiction to supervise such implementation, including by way of hearing reports from the government.[162]

A final example is *Nicklinson*, which is an illustration of the courts not granting a remedy in deference to the government, as well as of the use of exhortatory remarks to reduce deference. Lord Neuberger remarked that even if he were to conclude that the ban on assisted suicide was rights incompatible, he would not issue a declaration of incompatibility at that point in time.[163] The reasons he cited included the need to leave it to the democratically elected parliament to determine a deeply controversial issue, the resolution of which would require legislative input and the fact that UK Parliament was due to consider the issue soon, thereby raising considerations of inter-institutional comity.[164] *Nicklinson* also illustrates how exhortatory remarks can limit a government's policymaking leeway. Lord Neuberger indicated the possibility of a declaration of incompatibility being issued in future if the government took no action and made exhortatory remarks on what Parliament should consider in re-evaluating the ban, although he stopped short of saying that such a declaration would definitely be issued in future or of imposing a timeframe for the government to act.[165]

3. Standard of review and giving of weight to views

Unlike the case at the rights definition and limitation stages, there is no prior decision by the executive or legislature for the courts to review at the remedial stage. However, the parties concerned may still make submissions on what remedies should be granted, and the courts can adjust their degree of deference to those submissions using the review devices. For example, the court may adjust the standard

[159] [2009] IESC 71, [2010] 1 IR 635.
[160] See Kenny, 'Remedial Innovation' (n 148) 94.
[161] *W* (n 51) [150].
[162] *Doucet-Boudreau* (n 139) [60]–[86].
[163] *Nicklinson* (n 17) [113].
[164] ibid [116].
[165] ibid [118], [128]. For subsequent developments on the issue of assisted suicide, see *R (on the application of Conway) v The Secretary of State for Justice & Ors* [2018] EWCA Civ 1431, [2019] 1 All ER 39.

of review and be willing to accept the executive or legislature's proposed remedial order unless it is manifestly inappropriate. The court may also give extra weight to the executive or legislature's views on what the remedy should be.

4. Burden and standard of proof

The court may defer by treating a remedy advocated by a litigating party as the default remedy and granting it unless the court is convinced to a high degree that an alternative remedy would be more just and/or appropriate. The burden and standard of proof seem to be at play in, for example, Irish jurisprudence on suspensions of invalidity.[166] In *PC v Minister for Social Protection*,[167] O'Donnell J emphasized that suspensions, whilst permissible in principle, should be granted only in 'exceptional' circumstances and that immediate invalidation was still the 'normal remedy', 'from which the court should be slow to depart, and against which any other remedy should be measured and justified',[168] suggesting that immediate invalidation was the default remedy and that a heavy burden of justification lay with the side advocating for an alternative remedy.

As mentioned in section III, whilst both a review device and the choice of remedy may point towards the same remedy being adopted by the court, that is not necessarily the case. Unlike the first two stages of adjudication, at which the views of the original decision maker (applicant) on a matter are almost always aligned with an option that grants the decision maker more (less) scope for permissible action (eg the decision maker almost always prefers a narrower interpretation of the constitutional right in question), there seem to be more instances of non-alignment at the remedial stage.[169] The original decision maker may have reasons for preferring a remedy that grants it less room for response, and the applicant may have reasons for preferring a remedy that grants the decision maker more room for response. For example, a government might argue for a remedial interpretation instead of invalidation if the latter would exert a more negative impact on its image,[170] if it wished to save the time needed to revisit the impugned act in order to deal with more urgent bills,[171] or if invalidation would leave a legal void that would seriously endanger public safety. On the other side, an applicant might prefer invalidation over the remedial interpretation of a law that restricted freedoms if such an interpretation would be unable to alleviate the law's chilling effect

[166] See Oran Doyle and Tom Hickey, *Constitutional Law: Text, Cases and Materials* (2nd edn, Clarus Press 2019) 268–72.
[167] [2018] IESC 57.
[168] ibid [21].
[169] Kavanagh, *The Collaborative Constitution* (n 18) 247–50.
[170] Kavanagh, *The Collaborative Constitution* (n 18) 249–50; cf Sathanapally (n 13) 92–93.
[171] The government may not want an item to be forced on its agenda. Sathanapally (n 13) 29; Leckey (n 13) 135.

on freedoms.[172] In circumstances such as these, in which the imperatives of the review devices and those of the choice of remedy device diverge, there is no clear answer as to which remedy is more deferential overall.

VIII. Conclusion

This chapter has introduced six devices for deference: the burden of proof, standard of proof, standard of review, giving of weight, choice of interpretation, and choice of remedy, noting that the first four devices (which I call 'review devices') enable the court to relax its review of the decision being challenged or the view proffered by the primary decision maker in court. It has also illustrated how the devices can be used at the rights definition, limitation, and remedial stages by drawing on case law from Canada, Hong Kong, Ireland, Israel, New Zealand, and the United Kingdom. With both the reasons and devices for deference now explained, we proceed to an exploration of how the court should deploy the six devices to express its reasons for deferring, which is the subject of Chapters 4 and 5.

[172] See Roach, *Constitutional Remedies in Canada* (n 40) 8.50.

4
Choice of Device I: Type of Reasons

I. Introduction

In Chapter 2, I explain that judicial deference occurs when the court grants leeway to the legislature or executive—leeway that it would not have granted if it had merely considered the balance of reasons bearing on the rights issue before it—for reasons that arise from the comparative institutional position of the court, noting that there are three categories of such reasons: those relating to arriving at correct outcomes on the rights issue in question, those relating to respect for constitutional legitimacy, and those relating to other considerations that the court should take into account in adjudication. Chapter 3 then explains that courts have at their disposal six devices for exercising deference, namely, the burden of proof, standard of review, standard of proof, and giving of weight (what I call the 'review devices') and choice of interpretation and choice of remedy.

Building on these ideas, this chapter and Chapter 5 explore what I call the 'internal logic' of deference, that is, how courts should deploy the six devices to express their reasons for deference. The discussion in these chapters does not take into account the considerations of formulating deference methods that are workable for judges and predictable for litigants, which constitute 'external constraints' and are addressed in Chapter 6. This chapter focuses on the qualitative aspect of internal logic analysis: it explores how courts should choose which device to use, or which issue to apply a particular device to, to express their reason for deferring in a given case. Chapter 5 then focuses on the quantitative aspect of such analysis: it explores how courts should choose which device or combination of devices to use, and which stage of adjudication to defer at, to give effect to the strength of their reason for deference, that is, to express the right degree of deference.

Whilst I do not seek to exhaustively identify all situations in which one or more devices should be used, I expound the normative considerations that can be expressed by each device, which will enable us to see when the choice of device matters and how it matters. For example, suppose we find that the burden of proof can express both the reason of arriving at correct outcomes and the reason of democratic legitimacy but that the standard of review can express the latter reason alone. If in a particular case the reason for deference is democratic legitimacy, then the court can in principle (subject to practicability and other considerations) choose either device to fulfil that reason. However, if the reason for deference concerns

Deference in Human Rights Adjudication. Cora Chan, Oxford University Press. © Cora Chan 2024.
DOI: 10.1093/9780198921677.003.0004

arriving at correct outcomes, then it is more appropriate for the court to defer via the burden of proof.

Before we proceed, a word about the use of numerical figures is in order. In this and Chapter 5, I occasionally use such figures to show that the various devices (as well as the different ways of using them) exert different levels of deference. For example, in demonstrating that the 'manifest unreasonableness' and 'unreasonableness simpliciter' standards of review are different, I state that the former standard means that the court will interfere only if it is at least, say, 90 per cent certain that the decision-maker is mistaken, whilst the latter means that it will interfere only if it is at least, say, 60 per cent certain that the decision-maker is mistaken. Figures such as these are used only to show that the deferential force of the various devices (or various ways of using them) differs. They are not meant to illustrate the exact degree of difference or to pinpoint with precision the level of deference a given device exerts, both of which are unnecessary for our purposes. Whilst the ordinal ranking in deference that these illustrations use is not arbitrary, the exact figures are arbitrarily assigned.

The remainder of the chapter is organized as follows. In section II, I survey existing discussions on the topic, and then in section III analyse the choice between the burden and standard of proof on the one hand and the standard of review on the other. Section IV analyses the choice between the giving of weight device and the three aforementioned review devices. Section V proceeds to analyze the choice between the review devices and the choice of interpretation and remedy devices, and section VI examines how courts determine which substantive issues to defer on. Section VII concludes.

II. Existing Discussions

The question of how courts should choose amongst various deference devices is underexplored. There is little discussion of the question in case law, much of which fails even to expressly distinguish the devices in analysing deference. Take the UK House of Lords' judgment in *R (on the application of the Countryside Alliance and others) v Attorney General and others* as an example.[1] In reasoning that a statutory ban on the hunting of wild mammals with dogs was rights-compliant, Lord Hope remarked that a 'close and careful examination of the factual basis' for the government's decision was not required and that it was 'open to' the government to reason and conclude as it did.[2] This remark can be read as relaxing the standard of review, lowering the standard of proof, or giving extra weight to the government's case. Some cases clearly point to a specific device (eg standard of review) being

[1] [2007] UKHL 52, [2008] 1 AC 719.
[2] ibid [78] (Lord Hope).

grounded in particular considerations (eg constitutional legitimacy, expertise, etc.) but do not discuss whether the courts can express these considerations using other devices as well. Examples of such cases are given in sections III.2–3.

An apparent exception to the dearth of discussion on how courts should choose amongst various devices is the Canadian Supreme Court's judgment in *Canada (Minister of Citizenship and Immigration) v Vavilov*,[3] a case that concerned whether the Canadian government's decision to cancel the citizenship granted to the Canadian-born child of parents who were later discovered to be foreign spies was reasonable. Although *Vavilov* was not a human rights case, the court's extensive discussion of the considerations that should determine the standard of review and degree of weight to be given to the original decision-maker in administrative law cases sheds light on the considerations that should determine the use of the various devices in human rights cases as well. The court established that the standard of review should be determined exclusively by the legislative allocation of powers and by rule-of-law considerations,[4] with concerns over relative expertise being deferred to the stage when the court decides how much weight to give to a public authority's view that the standard of review has been met.[5] However, this position is based on the pragmatic consideration of ensuring that the standard of review analysis is predictable and workable—in the court's view, allowing contextual analysis of expertise to determine the standard of review leads to too much uncertainty—rather than on any differences in the normative values that the various devices can express.[6]

There is likewise little discussion in the academic literature on how to choose between the devices. The bulk of the literature does not explicitly discriminate between the devices. For example, in explaining how the seriousness of a rights limitation should affect judicial rigour, Julian Rivers uses wording that suggests that this factor should affect the burden of proof, standard of review, standard of proof, and/or the degree of weight given to the original decision-maker's views.[7] Similarly, in explaining the impact of deference, Aileen Kavanagh uses wording suggestive of the impact on the standard of review, burden of proof, and/or standard of proof.[8] Janneke Gerards argues that a court's degree of deference can be divided into various tiers, with each tier reflecting combinations of the particular locations of the burden of proof, standard of proof, standard of review, and degree of weight to

[3] 2019 SCC 65, [2019] 4 SCR 653.

[4] ibid [16]–[72].

[5] ibid [93]–[125].

[6] ibid [7]–[10], [21]–[29]; Paul Daly, 'The *Vavilov* Framework and the Future of Canadian Administrative Law' (2020) Ottawa Faculty of Law Working Paper No 2020-09, 4–12, 30–32 <https://ssrn.com/abstract=3519681> accessed 20 April 2022.

[7] Julian Rivers, 'Proportionality and Variable Intensity of Review' [2006] CLJ 174, 203–06.

[8] Aileen Kavanagh, 'Defending Deference in Public Law and Constitutional Theory' (2010) 126 LQR 236, 239–40; Aileen Kavanagh, *Constitutional Review under the UK Human Rights Act* (CUP 2009) 169–76, 211–22.

be given to the primary decision-maker's views.[9] In all of these discussions, the authors adopt terminology suggesting that numerous devices are at play, but they do not expressly distinguish amongst them. It is unclear whether they have a view on how courts should choose particular devices to express their reasons for deference or indeed whether they believe there is an important choice to be made at all.

There are a few exceptions, with several authors flagging the possibility of the devices expressing different considerations on deference, and hence the possibility that one rather than another device should be chosen to express a certain consideration. Tom Hickman suggests that the importance of the right concerned should affect the extent to which courts 'adapt their procedures so that they can enhance their own knowledge of the relevant facts', but not the degree of weight afforded the primary decision-maker's views, although he does not explain why this is the case.[10] He observes that, in practice, the courts may instead instantiate considerations regarding the importance of the right at stake through a device that is 'conceptually different' from the aforesaid adaptation of procedures, namely, the standard of review, and remarks that it is 'inevitable that public law will give effect to the same considerations in different ways' and that efforts to achieve a 'perfectly coherent doctrinal and analytical methodology' are 'probably crying for the moon'.[11] Like Hickman, Brian Foley also argues that the importance of the right should not affect the standard of review: the fact that a right is important says nothing about which institution is in a better position to protect it.[12] I evaluate Hickman and Foley's positions as I develop my arguments in the rest of this chapter.

One piece of work explores in relative depth whether the use of the various devices is justified by different ideas, and thus deserves special mention here. Mark Elliott argues that 'intrinsic deference' (which covers, in the parlance of this book, the burden of proof, standard of review and standard of proof)[13] should be determined primarily by the importance of the value compromised by the impugned decision, whereas 'adjudicative deference' (which covers, in the parlance of this book, the degree of weight to be given to the administrator's view that the requisite burden has been discharged) should be determined primarily by the relative expertise and constitutional legitimacy of the court and the administrator in determining the issue.[14] He nevertheless argues that both sets of reasons underlie both intrinsic and adjudicative deference, which share the 'common

[9] Janneke Gerards, 'Pluralism, Deference and the Margin of Appreciation Doctrine' (2011) 17(1) ELJ 80, 87–101.

[10] Tom Hickman, *Public Law after the Human Rights Act* (Hart 2010) 167–68.

[11] ibid 168.

[12] Brian Foley, *Deference and the Presumption of Constitutionality* (Institute of Public Administration 2008) 168–69.

[13] cf Marcus Teo, 'Proportionality as Epistemic Independence' [2022] PL 245, 247–48.

[14] Mark Elliott, 'From Bifurcation to Calibration: Twin-Track Deference and the Culture of Justification' in Hanna Wilberg and Mark Elliott (eds), *The Scope and Intensity of Substantive Review: Traversing Taggart's Rainbow* (Hart 2015) 70–73, 80–82.

concer[n]' of maintaining a distinction between the roles of the court and administrator. Relative expertise and constitutional legitimacy play a secondary, 'backstop' function in determining intrinsic deference in that the standard of review should never be set at a full merits review, whilst the importance of the right plays a subsidiary role in determining adjudicative deference in that the fundamentality of a right may curb the degree of such deference.[15] The proposed mapping, Elliott argues, introduces a division of labour between the devices that enables the court to 'capture the full richness of the considerations' that ought to animate deference.[16] I evaluate Elliott's position later in this chapter and in Chapter 6.

III. Standard of Review Versus Burden and Standard of Proof

Having surveyed the existing discussions on the subject, let us now begin to explore how a court should choose amongst the various devices to express its reasons for deference. This section examines how the choice amongst the standard of review, burden of proof, and standard of proof should be made, assuming that the devices are applied to the same issue in adjudication (eg the issue of how a right should be defined or of whether a government measure is no more than necessary). It makes two key arguments. First, if the court wishes to accord deference to the superior abilities of the public body defendant vis-à-vis the court to arrive at correct outcomes on, and its superior constitutional legitimacy to decide, the rights issue at hand, it sometimes does not matter which of the three devices is chosen because nothing in the nature of the devices bars them from expressing such reasons for deference. However, there are situations in which the choice matters because such reasons can be served only, or to a greater degree, by one device rather than another. Four such situations will be identified. Second, if the court wishes to fulfil considerations regarding prior probability theory, to accommodate the relative difficulties of proof faced by the litigation parties or to minimize the social costs of an erroneous ruling—considerations that involve comparisons between the applicant and the public body defendant rather than between the court and the public body defendant—it should choose the burden and standard of proof rather than the standard of review.

In the following, I first expound the nature and modus operandi of the three aforementioned devices. I then expose some of the justifications underlying each and, finally, assess whether those justifications can underpin any other of the three devices.

15 ibid 83, 85–86.
16 ibid 84–85.

1. Comparison of nature and modus operandi

Let us begin by analysing the nature and modus operandi of the three devices. The practical payoff of this analysis will become clear in section III.4 when we examine when the devices can or cannot be used in lieu of one another to express a normative value.

Two related points must be noted about the nature of these three devices. The first concerns their primary target audience. The standard of review is a device that is primarily directed towards the *court*. It delineates the instances in which the court interferes with a prior decision made by or a view proffered in court by a public body defendant. A direct consequence of lowering the standard of review is a wider range of answers by the public body to the legal question at stake being deemed acceptable or permissible *by the court*,[17] by which I mean a decision or view that the court will not disturb. Hasan Dindjer explains how lowering the standard of review widens the range of permissible answers: the court allows a wider range of weights to be accorded to considerations for and against the decision and sanctions any decision that is 'taken for reasons which are, from the perspective of ... [such weightings,] undefeated – not outweighed, excluded, and so on'.[18] The wider the range of weights accorded to the relevant considerations, the broader the range of permissible answers. Lowering the standard of review also results in the public body having to proffer less proof, albeit only indirectly as a result of the range of acceptable answers being expanded.[19]

In contrast, the burden and standard of proof are rules of adjudication directed towards the *parties to litigation*, in particular towards the party that bears the burden of proof, which, at the rights limitation stage, is often the public body. A direct consequence of lowering the standard of proof or reversing the burden of proof is the public body having to prove less vis-à-vis the applicant. Such lowering or reversal also leads to a wider range of answers being deemed permissible by the court, albeit only indirectly as a result of the need for the public body to proffer less proof.

The second, related, point concerns the relationship that the devices seek to regulate. The standard of review directly—and exclusively—regulates the relationship between the court and the public body defendant, that is, the party whose decision is to be reviewed.[20] It does not so regulate the relationship between, say, the applicant and the public body defendant. In contrast, the burden and standard of

[17] This is not predicated upon the court determining that there is more than one correct answer. The court may be of the view that there is only one correct answer but nonetheless deems a range of answers to be acceptable.

[18] Hasan Dindjer, 'What Makes an Administrative Decision Unreasonable?' (2021) 84(2) MLR 265, 267.

[19] cf ibid 292.

[20] cf Paul Craig, 'Varying Intensity of Judicial Review: A Conceptual Analysis' [2022] PL 442, 443.

proof directly regulate the relationship between the applicant and the defendant, a relationship that is mediated by the court.

These differences will become clearer as we examine the different ways in which the standard of review operates. There are two common ways of deciding whether a decision has been taken outside the permissible range, corresponding to two conceptions of the standard of review. The first, what I call the 'epistemic threshold conception',[21] understands the various standards of review as conveying the differing levels of confidence the court must have that the primary decision-maker's factual proposition is wrong before rejecting the latter's decision. According to this conception, a manifest unreasonableness standard means that the court will deem a decision as being outside the permissible range only if the court is at least, say, 90 per cent certain that the primary decision-maker is mistaken; the unreasonableness simpliciter standard means that the court will interfere only if it is at least, say, 60 per cent certain that the decision-maker is wrong; and the correctness standard means that the court will intervene as long as it is at least, say, 30 per cent certain that the decision-maker is wrong.[22] If this conception of the standard of review is adopted, then the standard operates in a very similar manner to the standard of proof, which measures the level of confidence that a court must have that the primary decision-maker's factual proposition is correct before accepting it. The aforesaid manifest unreasonableness standard, for example, corresponds to a requirement for the defendant to convince the court of a proposition to a minimum of more than 10 per cent certainty. This conception is adopted by Stephen Perry, who observes that:

> [a]fter all, what else could it mean to say that a person regards a person as wrong but reasonable than that she believes the decision is mistaken but recognizes that there is at least a nonnegligible possibility that *she* might be wrong and the tribunal right? An unreasonable decision, on the other hand, is one which she convinced to some relatively strong degree of uncertainty could not be right.[23]

The conception can also be found in several judicial remarks. For example, the observation in *Law Society of New Brunswick v Ryan* that the patent unreasonableness standard can be distinguished from the unreasonableness simpliciter standard in that the former requires there to be 'no real possibility of doubting that the decision is defective'[24] can be read as manifesting the epistemic threshold conception. It must be noted, however, that even if the epistemic threshold conception is

[21] Borrowing from Perry's wording in Stephen Perry, 'Second-order Reasons, Uncertainty and Legal Theory' (1988–89) 62 S Cal L Rev 913, 934.

[22] As explained in section I, the exact percentages are arbitrarily assigned and used only to show that the various standards are different.

[23] Perry (n 21) 938–39, emphasis in original.

[24] 2003 SCC 20, [2003] 1 SCR 247 [52]–[53].

adopted, the standard of review and standard of proof have different emphases: the former denotes the level of confidence that the court must have that the primary decision-maker is *wrong*, whereas the latter denotes that which the court must have that the decision-maker is *correct*. The distinction follows from the differences in the nature of the two devices. The standard of review is a court-centric device denoting when the court will interfere with a decision-maker's decision, whereas the standard of proof is a device directed primarily at the party that bears the burden of proof, denoting how much it needs to prove before its proposition will be accepted.

The second conception, what I call the 'type of error conception', understands different standards of review as delineating different ranges of error that trigger court intervention. The broader the list of errors, the narrower the permissible range of answers. For example, the correctness standard can be understood as connoting that the court will intervene upon finding any error; the reasonableness standard as catching only, say, logical errors in the decision-maker's reasoning process, discriminatory conduct and the taking into account of irrelevant considerations; and the manifest unreasonableness standard as catching only decisions that are, say, 'unsupported by relevant reasoning and evidence'.[25] A decision is deemed outside the permissible range if it is tainted by any of the covered errors. This conception can be found in case law. For example, Lord Neuberger's remarks in *The Queen on the Application of Sinclair Collis Limited v The Secretary of State for Health*[26] suggest such a conception. In reasoning that certain anti-tobacco measures are not manifestly unreasonable, he suggested that the decision in question should be allowed to stand unless a narrow category of errors was found to be involved, namely, an 'ulterior motive' or a justification 'so weak ... [or] so illogical as to justify' court interference.[27] References in judgments to the 'obviousness', 'immediacy',[28] or 'materiality'[29] of an error can also be read as indicative of the type of error conception: the courts can be read as saying that easy-to-detect errors, or errors with a tight causal connection to the decision in question, are types of error that trigger intervention.

This conception is also found in the literature. Paul Daly's indicia of unreasonableness, for example, which encompasses 'illogicality', 'disproportionality', 'inconsistency with statute', and 'unexplained changes in policy', is suggestive of it.[30] David Dyzenhaus's definition of reasonableness as requiring the court to start by examining the public authority's reasoning process to determine whether it leads

[25] This was the test for manifest unreasonableness proposed in Paul Daly, *A Theory of Deference in Administrative Law: Basis, Application and Scope* (CUP 2012) 179–81.
[26] [2011] EWCA Civ 437, [2012] QB 394.
[27] ibid [231], [237] (Master of the Rolls).
[28] *Canada (Director of Investigation and Research) v Southam Inc* [1997] 1 SCR 748 [57].
[29] *Vavilov* (n 3) [300] (Abella and Karakatsanis JJ).
[30] Daly, *A Theory of Deference* (n 25) 143–51.

to the given outcome rather than making a decision afresh and then assessing whether the public authority's decision coincides with the court's,[31] can also be understood as manifesting a type of error conception: only errors in the primary decision-making process are caught by the reasonableness standard of review.

If the type of error conception is adopted, the modi operandi of the standard of review and standard of proof become less similar. The two conceptions of the standard of review may overlap, in that types of error (such as those that refer to the magnitude or obviousness of the error) can and may be taken to function as indicators of the court having a high level of confidence that the primary decision is mistaken. If the types of error map onto the court's expertise, that is, the court interferes only with respect to mistakes it has the expertise to determine, then types of error can function as indicators of the court's level of confidence that the primary decision-maker is wrong. Nevertheless, the type of error conception is not reducible to the epistemic threshold conception because it is possible for the delineation of types of error to not map onto the court's expertise; for example, the court may carve out areas in which the primary decision-maker has more democratic legitimacy, but not more expertise, to handle.

With the differences in the nature and operation of the standard of review and burden and standard of proof clarified, we are now ready to examine the reasons that can justify the use of these devices.

2. Some considerations that can justify modifying the standard of review

As a device that directly regulates how interventionist a court is in the primary decision-maker's decision, the standard of review is naturally determined by the relative abilities of the two institutions to arrive at correct outcomes on, and their relative constitutional legitimacy to decide, the rights issue at hand. If the primary decision-maker has more expertise and legitimacy to decide the issue, then the court may require itself to be extremely certain that a mistake has been committed before intervening (applying the epistemic threshold conception of the standard of review) or leave certain kinds of error undisturbed (applying the type of error conception of the standard of review).

[31] David Dyzenhaus, 'Dignity in Administrative Law: Judicial Deference in a Culture of Justification' (2012) 17(1) Review of Constitutional Studies 87, 113; David Dyzenhaus 'The Politics of Deference: Judicial Review and Democracy' in Michael Taggart (ed), *The Province of Administrative Law* (Hart 1997) 303–07. Compare Jerry L Mashaw, *Reasoned Administration and Democratic Legitimacy: How Administrative Law Supports Democratic Government* (CUP 2018) 116–24. For different ways of understanding 'process', see Timothy Endicott, *Administrative Law* (3rd edn, OUP 2015), s 6.9; Aileen Kavanagh, 'Reasoning About Proportionality Under the Human Rights Act 1998: Outcomes, Substance and Process' (2014) 130 LQR 235, 246–49.

Courts frequently relax the standard of review for such reasons. In *Doré v Barreau du Québec*, for example, the Canadian Supreme Court held that the reasonableness rather than correctness standard of review should apply when the court is assessing the proportionality of a rights-limiting decision by an administrator, who has 'by virtue of expertise and specialization, particular familiarity with the competing considerations at play in weighing *Charter* values'.[32] In *Hysan Development v Town Planning Board*, the Hong Kong Court of Final Appeal established that the courts should examine, inter alia, whether the primary decision-maker has special competence on or expertise in the matter in question in deciding whether to apply the 'manifestly without reasonable foundation' standard.[33]

In addition to considerations of relative expertise and legitimacy, it is also worth examining the role that the importance of the right at stake plays in determining the standard of review because this factor features prominently in the few scholarly discussions on the justificatory bases for use of that device. There is disagreement in the literature over whether such importance should influence the standard of review. Hickman argues that the standard should be defined exclusively by the constitutional allocation of powers (as part of constitutional legitimacy), which, in the context of the UK Human Rights Act 1998, dictates that the correctness standard be applied to 'bring rights home'.[34] In particular, he emphasizes that the importance of the right should not affect the standard of review, although, as mentioned above,[35] he does not explain why. Foley argues that the importance of a right should not affect the standard of review because it does not tell us whether the court or the legislature is in a better position to protect the right.[36] To the contrary, Elliott argues that the importance of the right should be the primary consideration determining the standard of review.[37] In dissecting this issue, it should first be noted that the importance of the right is a factor rather than a ground for deference, to use the distinction drawn in Chapter 2. Such importance can suggest multiple grounds for deference, one being that the more important a right is, the stronger the constitutional imperative for the courts to scrutinize any act that limits it. Once this link between a factor and ground is brought to light, it becomes clear that Elliott's position that the importance of a right is relevant in determining the standard of review is more tenable than that of Hickman and Foley. As explained in this subsection, the standard of review can be justified by the relative legitimacy of the court and primary decision-maker in determining the issue at hand. The importance of a right, being a factor that affects the relative legitimacy of the court in scrutinizing the limitation thereon, can therefore be relevant in determining the standard of review.

32 2012 SCC 12, [2012] 1 SCR 395 [47].
33 [2016] HKCFA 66, (2016) 19 HKCFAR 372 [114]–[118].
34 Hickman (n 10) 111.
35 Text to nn 10 and 11.
36 Text to n 12.
37 Text to nn 14–16.

3. Some considerations that can justify modifying the burden and standard of proof

The burden and standard of proof are determined at least in part by considerations concerning arriving at correct outcomes. The criminal and evidence law literature is instructive in this respect. Commentators from these areas of law have argued that the burden of proof should be determined in part by 'prior probability theory', whereby the party that advances a position that is less likely to be correct prior to the proffering of evidence bears the responsibility of proving its position.[38] Applying this theory to the human rights context, if, in a particular case, the government's track record shows it to be highly unlikely to unjustifiably limit a right, then there are reasons for placing the burden of demonstrating the unjustifiability of the prima facie rights limitation on the applicant. Nevertheless, given that evidence of the likelihood of the primary decision-maker being correct is unlikely to be available in rights cases, prior probability theory, whilst valid as a justificatory basis for the burden of proof in rights cases in theory, is unlikely to offer such a basis in practice.

In addition, together with the standard of proof, the burden of proof can be deployed to alleviate concerns over the primary decision-maker's difficulties of proof,[39] a consideration that is also relevant to arriving at correct outcomes. In rights adjudication, it is sometimes difficult for the decision-maker to demonstrate that a chosen measure is the least restrictive alternative, for example, in situations turning on 'arbitrary, but unavoidable, distinctions of degree'.[40] If it is substantially easier for the applicant to prove that there is a less restrictive but equally effective alternative, then it may be justified, as Rivers argues, for the court to reverse the burden of proof.[41]

Furthermore, the burden and standard of proof can be used as tools to minimize the social costs of an erroneous ruling in situations of uncertainty.[42] There has been extensive discussion in evidence law on how the burden and standard of proof can be deployed to minimize the cost of errors.[43] Applying those insights, the costs of an erroneous ruling against an applicant are a function of the importance of the right at stake, the seriousness of the limitation thereon, and the probability that harm to the right will materialize if an erroneous ruling is handed down,

[38] See eg David Hamer, 'Presumptions, Standards and Burdens: Managing the Cost of Error' (2014) 13 Law, Probability and Risk 221, 223–24; Mike Redmayne, 'Standards of Proof in Civil Litigation' (1999) 62(2) MLR 167, 184.

[39] See eg David Hamer, 'The Presumption of Innocence and Reverse Burdens: A Balancing Act' (2007) 66(1) CLJ 142, 158–70.

[40] Julian Rivers, 'The Presumption of Proportionality' (2014) 77(3) MLR 409, 428–29.

[41] ibid 429.

[42] ibid 418–19.

[43] See eg Alex Stein, *Foundations of Evidence Law* (OUP 2005); Hamer, 'The Presumption of Innocence' (n 39); CMA McCauliff, 'Burdens of Proof: Degrees of Belief, Quanta of Evidence, Or Constitutional Guarantees' (1982) 35 V and L Rev 1293, 1318–23.

whilst the costs of an erroneous ruling against the primary decision-maker are a function of the importance of the countervailing right or interest, the seriousness of the possible harm thereto and the probability that such harm will materialize if an erroneous ruling is handed down.[44] If the latter costs significantly outweigh the former, then it makes sense to err on the primary decision-maker's side. That can be achieved by applying a standard of proof lower than a balance of probabilities, which skews the risk of erroneous rulings against the decision-maker.

There has been some discussion in the literature of the last-mentioned rationale for adjusting the burden and standard of proof in rights cases. Rivers argues that one of the main functions of the burden of proof is to allocate the risks of error. Two situations that he considers to warrant a reversal of that burden—conflicts of rights and 'minor limitations of rights in pursuit of important but diffuse public goods'—involve the countervailing interest or right possibly trumping the applicant's rights.[45] Colleen Flood has raised the concern that if the courts insist upon a stringent standard of proof in realms in which there are 'inherent methodological difficulties' in proving the 'relative benefits of different policy approaches', then the government 'may be hindered in their ability to develop innovative policy or to respond to emerging risks to safety'.[46] Likewise, Sujit Choudhry argues that it is not sensible to insist upon stringent evidential proof in cases in which 'it is impossible to prove with scientific certainty' the proportionality of a measure.[47]

This rationale for adjusting the standard of proof, namely, to lower the cost of an erroneous ruling, is also widely reflected in case law, particularly in cases in which the original decision-maker sought to limit rights in order to protect vulnerable groups. In *R v KRJ*, for example, Brown J argued that given the inherent difficulty of proving the effect of a measure in reducing recidivism, holding 'Parliament to an exacting standard of proof' would deny 'Parliament the room necessary to perform its legislative policy-development role when addressing' the 'chronic social problem' of 'recidivism in cases of sexual offences against children'.[48] The court should therefore apply a lower standard of proof to enable Parliament to 'innovate in finding a solution to chronic harms'.[49] In *R (on the application of Nicklinson and another) v Ministry of Justice*, Lord Neuberger's application of a lower standard of proof was motivated by a precautionary attitude: 'given the reasonable concerns expressed by the Secretary of State (particularly the concern to protect the

[44] cf Aharon Barak, *Proportionality: Constitutional Rights and Their Limitations* (CUP 2012) 348.

[45] Rivers, 'The Presumption of Proportionality' (n 40) 428–30.

[46] Colleen Flood, 'The Evidentiary Burden for Overturning Government's Choice of Regulatory Instrument: The Case of Direct-to-Consumer Advertising of Prescription Drugs' (2010) 60 U Toronto LJ 397, 399, 411.

[47] Sujit Choudhry, 'So What Is the Real Legacy of Oakes? Two Decades of Proportionality Analysis under the Canadian *Charter*'s Section 1' (2006) 34 SCLR (2d) 501, 524–25. See also the precautionary principle in scientific disputes eg Caroline E Foster, *Science and the Precautionary Principle in International Courts and Tribunals: Expert Evidence, Burden of Proof and Finality* (CUP 2011).

[48] 2016 SCC 31, [2016] 1 SCR 906 [135] (Brown J).

[49] ibid [154] (Brown J).

weak and vulnerable)', there are 'too many uncertainties' over the feasibility of a system of assisted suicide to justify issuing a declaration of incompatibility.[50] In *Sinclair Collis*, Arden LJ expressly applied a precautionary principle, holding that the government 'is not prevented from making a decision by reason of the fact that the effectiveness of the ban on [tobacco vending machines] in reducing underage tobacco purchases is not capable of clear proof...'.[51] She placed the burden of adducing evidence to show that the proposed alternative of a voluntary code would be equally effective on the claimants.[52]

This section has thus far examined three normative considerations that regulate the burden and standard of proof: prior probability theory, the relative difficulties of proof, and minimizing the social costs of an erroneous ruling. It is convenient to note at this juncture that these three considerations are not reasons for deference as defined in Chapter 2, that is, reasons that arise as a result of the comparative institutional positions of the *court* and the public body defendant. The comparisons that give rise to these three considerations are comparisons between the positions of the *applicant* and the public body defendant—the relative probability of the applicant and public body being correct, the relative difficulties they face in proving a proposition, and what is at stake for the applicant and the wider public interest represented by the public body. They are not comparisons between the institutional positions of the public body and the *court*. Therefore, they are not strictly speaking reasons for deference as defined in this book. Lord Kerr seems to recognize that difficulties of proof and a comparison of what is at stake for the applicant and the public are not reasons for deference, as can be seen from his remarks in *Nicklinson*. He stated that requiring less proof when

> the need for a particular measure may not be susceptible of categorical proof ... should not be confused ... with deference to the so-called institutional competence of the legislature. The court's ... more generous attitude [in lowering the standard of proof] is not based on the view that Parliament is better placed to make a judgment ... Rather, it reflects the reality that choices in these areas [ie 'between fiercely competing and apparently equally tenable opinions'[53]] are difficult to make and that it may not be easy to prove that the right choice has been made.[54]

Nevertheless, because the three aforementioned normative considerations are possible justifications for adjusting the burden and standard of proof, it is useful to include them in the present assessment of whether the various devices can be justified by the same normative considerations.

[50] [2014] UKSC 38, [2015] 1 AC 657 [120], [127] (Lord Neuberger).
[51] *Sinclair Collis* (n 26) [141]–[143] (Arden LJ).
[52] ibid [164] (Arden LJ).
[53] *Nicklinson* (n 50) [348] (Lord Kerr).
[54] ibid [348] (Lord Kerr).

4. Choosing amongst the devices

The foregoing discussion has established that use of the standard of review as a device can be justified by the respective abilities of the court and public body defendant to arrive at the correct outcome on, and their relative constitutional legitimacy to decide, the rights issue in question, and the burden and standard of proof by considerations of prior probability, minimizing the harm of an erroneous ruling and the relative difficulties of proof. This subsection assesses whether these three devices can be justified by the considerations that underlie one another. If a consideration can justify the use of two or all three of the devices, then it does not matter which of the devices is used to express that consideration because both or all three can express it. Conversely, if a consideration can justify the use of one of the devices but not the other two, then the court must choose that device to express it.

Let us first examine whether the burden and standard of proof can be justified by the relative expertise and legitimacy of the court and primary decision-maker to determine the rights issue in question, before evaluating whether the standard of review can be justified by the aforesaid considerations underlying the burden and standard of proof.

At first glance, the standard and burden of proof by nature cannot be justified by the relative abilities and legitimacy of the court and the primary decision-maker in determining an issue. It appears that when such reasons for deference are involved, the court should choose the standard of review rather than the standard and burden of proof to express them. As explained in section III.1, these latter devices primarily regulate the relationship between the applicant and the primary decision-maker and, correspondingly, that between the applicant's right and the countervailing public interest or right. That the public body has more expertise than the court in deciding an issue shows only that the public body is more likely than the court to get the issue right; it does not show that the public body is more likely than the applicant to get it right, and it is not obvious why the public body should be allowed to prove less (or even nothing at all) vis-à-vis the applicant when it is more likely than the court to get it right. Likewise, that the public body has more legitimacy than the court in deciding an issue says nothing about the relative positions of the applicant and public body, and it is not apparent why the public body should be allowed to prove less vis-à-vis the applicant when it has more such legitimacy.

Deeper reflection, however, reveals that the normative bases for adjusting the standard and burden of proof can encompass considerations of the relative competence of the court and original decision-maker. It is true that, unlike the standard of review, which is concerned exclusively with the court–defendant relationship, the burden and standard of proof are concerned primarily with the applicant–defendant relationship. However, the latter devices are ultimately enforced by the court, and so the relationship that they regulate is in fact a three-way one involving the applicant, the public body defendant, and the court. In setting the burden and standard of proof, whilst it would make no sense for the court to consider the relative expertise of the court and public body without regard for the applicant's position, it makes perfect sense for the court to consider comparative expertise by incorporating the applicant's expertise into the equation. If the court decides that the public body has more expertise concerning a given issue *than the court and the applicant combined*, then it makes sense for the court to lighten or even reverse the burden of proof. For example, assume that the two sides to litigation proffer conflicting, yet equally compelling, expert evidence on whether a Covid-19 vaccine pass as opposed to a health pass (ie a requirement to demonstrate vaccination rather than just a negative Covid-19 test result to enter stipulated premises) is no more than necessary to halt the spread of the virus. The court has no expertise in this area, whilst the government's expert has better credentials and more experience than the applicant's. In this case, the government apparently has more expertise than the court and applicant combined, and the court has grounds to give some default weight to the government's judgment, requiring it to prove less, or, if the government's expertise is extremely compelling, to even start from the default position of accepting the government's judgment, requiring the applicant to disprove it. The same holds for the relative legitimacy of the court and public body. If the latter's legitimacy to determine an issue is greater than that of the court and applicant combined, then it makes sense to give effect to such superior legitimacy by lowering or even reversing the burden of proof.

That the relative legitimacy and abilities of the court and public body defendant to determine an issue can justify variance in the burden and standard of proof finds support in the literature. For example, Guy Davidov argues that where a decision is 'based on a deliberated and considerate policy'—and hence is imbued with greater legitimacy—'there should be a strong presumption in favour of' the decision, and the burden should shift to the applicant at the fourth limb of proportionality.[55] Similarly, Rivers proposes that 'procedurally-rigorous judgements of proportionality by well-qualified public bodies' should attract a reverse burden at the third and fourth limbs of proportionality,[56] suggesting that, in his view, if the original decision-maker is more likely than the applicant to be correct and adopts legitimate decision-making processes, then its judgment deserves some default weight.

This proposition is also reflected in case law. In *Beit Sourik Village Council v The Government of Israel*, the Israeli Supreme Court was faced with conflicting expert opinions on whether the seizure of certain plots of land to erect a separation fence was rational and no more than necessary.[57] The court held that

[55] Guy Davidov, 'Judicial Deference and the Constitutional Protection of Rights' (1998) Thesis submitted in conformity with the requirements for the degree of LLM at University of Toronto 170 <https://tspace.library.utoronto.ca/handle/1807/16154> accessed 20 April 2022.
[56] Rivers, 'The Presumption of Proportionality' (n 40) 430–31.
[57] HCJ 2056/04, IsrSC 58(5) 807 [2004].

because the government had professional military expertise, the court should place the government's expert opinion 'at the foundation of [its] decision', with the petitioners bearing the 'heavy burden' of convincing the court that their expert view was to be preferred to the state's, a burden that was not discharged on the facts.[58]

It is not uncommon for the courts to justify lowering the standard of proof with considerations of *both* minimizing the cost of an erroneous ruling *and* relative expertise and legitimacy. In *RJR-MacDonald Inc v Canada (Attorney General)*, La Forest J did not insist upon a '"rigorous" civil standard of proof'[59] for a combination of both considerations. On the one hand, given the 'detrimental social effects of tobacco consumption', the relatively peripheral aspect of freedom of expression at stake (ie commercial advertisement) and the unavailability of definitive scientific proof of the connection between advertising and tobacco consumption,[60] the court should not insist upon a strict civil standard of proof, which 'could have the effect of virtually paralyzing the operation of government in the socio-economic sphere'.[61] On the other hand, difficult choices involving 'conflicting scientific evidence' and diverging 'demands on scarce resources' should be made by elected representatives rather than the courts, which 'are not specialists in the realm of policy-making, [and] nor should they be'.[62]

The reasoning in this judgment reinforces the point made in Chapter 2 that the factors that affect the level of judicial scrutiny can be indicative of more than one ground for relaxing such scrutiny. For example, uncertainty in light of conflicting scientific evidence can suggest outcome and constitutional legitimacy grounds for deference but also a basis for lowering the standard of proof to minimize the social costs of an erroneous ruling. That a less serious aspect of freedom of expression is involved is indicative of a weaker constitutional imperative on the part of the courts to scrutinize the limitation thereon. When combined with highly important countervailing public interests, however, it also suggests that the stakes for the applicant are lower than those for society, a state of affairs that justifies lowering the standard of proof to minimize the social costs of an erroneous ruling. Hence, remarks such as Steven Greer's claiming that the importance of the right at stake should affect the burden and standard of proof[63] can be read as indicating that relative constitutional legitimacy (ie the court has a stronger constitutional imperative to intervene when more important rights are involved) and/or the minimization of the social costs of an erroneous ruling (ie the burden should be made heavier to

[58] ibid [47], [56].

[59] [1995] 3 SCR 199 [64] (La Forest J).

[60] ibid [66]–[67].

[61] ibid [67].

[62] ibid [68], quoting from *Irwin Toy Ltd v Quebec (Attorney General)* [1989] 1 SCR 927, 993–94.

[63] Steven Greer, '"Balancing" and the European Court of Human Rights: A Contribution to the Habermas-Alexy Debate' (2004) 63(2) CLJ 412, 431–33.

minimize those costs when an important right is at stake for the applicant) should underpin these devices.

Although the nature of the burden and standard of proof poses no impediments to giving effect to the primary decision-maker's superior ability and greater legitimacy vis-à-vis the court to determine the rights issue in question (the reasons for deference that underpin the standard of review), those reasons may in concrete situations be realized, or realized to a greater extent, only if one rather than the other device(s) is used. In these situations, the court should pick the device(s) that better realizes those reasons. Four examples are in order.

First, if the court's lack of expertise and legitimacy to adjudge an issue relates only to certain types of error, then the values of arriving at correct outcomes and respect for constitutional legitimacy are better served by carving out the errors in question from its purview (ie using the type of error conception of the standard of review) than by reversing the burden of proof or lowering the standard of proof across all aspects of the issue.

Second, there may be instances in which the court's ability to adjudicate an issue is so weak that the court cannot even determine whether the primary decision-maker's case meets the epistemic threshold set by the standard of proof, however low that threshold may be. As Perry argues, a judgment on whether an epistemic threshold is met 'always requires at least *some* familiarity with the underlying reasoning and will often be compatible with, or even demand, a very extensive familiarity'.[64] In situations in which the court's ability to adjudge an issue is too weak to allow it to determine with any level of confidence whether the decision-maker is correct, the value of arriving at correct outcomes might be better served by excluding certain types of error from its purview (ie lowering the type of error conception of the standard of review) than by lowering the standard of proof.

Third, it is possible for the court to be in a better position to assess whether the primary decision-maker is *wrong* than to assess whether it is *correct*, by virtue of the fact that it is easier to prove an existential than a universal claim.[65] For example, a court may find it easier to be at least 90 per cent certain that a decision is wrong than to be at least 10 per cent certain that it is correct. In this case, the court's relative lack of ability to adjudicate an issue is more appropriately addressed through the epistemic threshold conception of standard of review than the standard of proof device.

A fourth and final example relates to the different relationships that the three devices regulate, a point explained in section III.1. To recap, the standard of review exclusively regulates the court–defendant relationship, whereas the burden and standard of proof regulate the three-way relationship involving the applicant

[64] Perry (n 21) 943–44, emphasis in original.

[65] KW Saunders, 'The Mythic Difficulty of Proving a Negative' (1985) 15 Seton Hall L Rev 276; Hamer, 'The Presumption of Innocence' (n 39) 160.

as well. In situations in which the applicant is very much part of the picture concerning the court's comparative expertise and legitimacy, such as when, for example, the court is faced with conflicting expert opinions (as in *Beit Sourik Village Council*, discussed above[66]), the burden and standard of proof would be more suitable devices than the standard of review for expressing the considerations of relative expertise and legitimacy.

We now turn to the issue of whether the standard of review can be justified by the normative considerations that justify the burden and standard of proof, as established in section III.3, namely, prior probability theory, the relative difficulties of proof and minimizing the social costs of erroneous rulings. My answer is 'no' for all three considerations. Hence, where the court needs to give effect to such considerations, it should use the burden and standard of proof instead of the standard of review to do so.

Regarding prior probability theory, it cannot provide a justificatory basis for adjusting the standard of review. A judgment that the public body's position is more likely to be correct than the applicant's says nothing about the relative abilities of the public body and *court* to get an issue right. That the public body is more likely than the applicant to get an issue right does not mean that the public body is more likely than the court to do so. Because the standard of review is a device that directly regulates the court–defendant relationship alone, it cannot be based on the relative likelihood of the parties getting an issue right. Therefore, if the court wants to lighten the burden of the party that is more likely to be correct prior to proof, it should adjust the burden and standard of proof instead of the standard of review.

We now move on to examine the applicant and public body defendant's relative ease of proof. Because lowering the standard of review, like lowering the standard of proof, can achieve the effect of the court demanding fewer arguments or less evidence from the public body, it is possible to alleviate the difficulties of proof faced by the public body by lowering either standard. However, because the standard of review is directly concerned with the court–defendant relationship alone, it is not an appropriate device for accommodating the relative difficulties of proof faced by the two litigation parties. There is no reason for the court to deem a wider range of answers by the public body permissible just because it is more difficult for the public body than the applicant to prove a proposition. Thus, if the court wants to make the job easier for the party that faces relative difficulties of proof, it should lower that party's standard of proof or not require it to bear the burden of proof rather than lower the standard of review.

Finally, before leaving this section, let us examine whether the standard of review can be justified by the need to minimize the social costs of an erroneous ruling. To recap, the burden and standard of proof can minimize such costs by

[66] Text to nn 57 and 58.

skewing the risk of an erroneous ruling towards the party to which less harm would likely materialize should an erroneous ruling against it occur. When the harm of an erroneous ruling against the public body exceeds that of an erroneous ruling against the applicant, the social costs of an erroneous ruling can be reduced by lowering the standard of proof on the public body. Whether the standard of review can skew the results in a similar way depends on which conception of the standard of review is adopted and what the normative basis for adjusting that standard is. Let us first look at the type of error conception. If the types of error are *not* delineated by the relative expertise of the court and public body (ie the types of error identified as triggering intervention are not necessarily those that the court is better at assessing), then by exempting more types of error from triggering judicial intervention, a lowered standard of review reduces the likelihood of a ruling against the public body, but not necessarily the likelihood of an *erroneous* ruling against the public body. If, in contrast, the types of error carved out correspond to the court's expertise, then the lower the standard of review, the lower the risk of an erroneous ruling against the public body, meaning that relaxing the standard of review can achieve the effect of minimizing the social costs of an erroneous ruling. If the epistemic threshold conception of the standard of review is adopted, then the results can be skewed in much the same way as the standard of proof. However, because the standard of review directly regulates the court–defendant relationship exclusively, it is not an appropriate tool for minimizing the social costs of an erroneous ruling, a consideration that does not arise from comparison of the positions of the court and public body defendant. Hence, if the court needs to minimize the social costs of an erroneous ruling, it should use the burden and standard of proof rather than the standard of review.

To conclude, two guidelines for how the court should choose amongst the burden of proof, standard of proof, and standard of review can be distilled. The first is that when the court wishes to accord deference to the superior abilities of the primary decision-maker to arrive at correct outcomes on, or to its superior constitutional legitimacy to decide, the rights issue at stake, it can in principle do so through all three devices, that is, the burden of proof, standard of proof, and standard of review. However, it should choose one over the others when such values can be better served by that device. Four examples serve to illustrate. First, if the court's relative lack of expertise and legitimacy to determine an issue relates only to certain types of error, it should defer by lowering the type of error conception of the standard of review rather than by reversing the burden of proof or lowering the standard of proof across all aspects of the issue. Second, if the court's ability to determine an issue is too weak to allow it to determine with any level of confidence whether the primary decision-maker is correct, it should defer by lowering the type of error conception of the standard of review rather than by lowering the standard of proof. Third, if the court is in a better position to assess whether the decision-maker is wrong than to assess whether it is correct, then the court should give effect to relative expertise concerns through the epistemic threshold conception of the standard of review rather than through the standard of proof device. Fourth, if the court needs to take into account the relative expertise or legitimacy of the applicant (vis-à-vis the primary decision-maker or the court), then the burden and standard of proof would be more suitable devices than the standard of review for expressing those considerations.

The second guideline is that if the court needs to give effect to the prior probability theory, address the relative difficulties of proof or minimize the social costs of an erroneous ruling, then it should adjust the burden and standard of proof rather than the standard of review.

IV. Giving of Weight Versus Other Review Devices

We now move on to an examination of how courts should choose between the giving of weight device and the three devices examined above, namely, the burden of proof, standard of proof, and standard of review, assuming that the devices apply to the same issue in adjudication. I make three key arguments. First, courts can sometimes use the giving of weight device in lieu of the burden and standard of proof to express the normative considerations underlying the latter devices. However, there are situations in which doing so is unsuitable, for example, where placation of the public is the reason for deference and the public prefers that deference be exercised through a particular device. In that case, the court should express its reason for deference through the public's preferred device. Second, courts can sometimes use the giving of weight device in lieu of the standard of review to express the normative considerations underlying the latter, if the epistemic threshold conception of the standard of review is adopted. If the type of error conception is adopted instead, then the court should use the standard of review instead of the giving of weight device if the reasons for deference are better served by excluding certain types of errors from the court's review. Third, because of the temporal sequence of the devices, a court can use the giving of weight device to fulfil deference considerations that were not apparent to it at earlier stages of adjudication.

Let us begin by analysing the nature of the giving of weight device, which is necessary to understand the reasons for deference it is capable of expressing. The giving of weight can be understood in either its movable or static sense. In its movable sense, it is a basic idea that underlies both the burden and standard of proof, as well as the epistemic threshold conception of the standard of review, all of which can be expressed in terms of giving the original decision-maker varying degrees of presumptive weight.[67] However, the giving of weight can also be understood

[67] The difficulty of distinguishing a use of the standard of proof and of the giving of weight device has been highlighted in Jula Hughes and Vanessa MacDonnell, 'Social Science Evidence in Constitutional

in its static sense to refer to the court's giving of weight to a party's proposition that the requisite burden and standard of proof and standard of review have been discharged.

As should be clear from Chapter 3, this book understands the giving of weight device in its static sense, that is, as referring to the giving of weight to a party's propositions concerning whether the burden and standard of proof and standard of review have been met, and it is on this static sense that the book relies when it refers to the giving of weight as an individual device for deference. However, because adjustment of the burden and standard of proof and the epistemic threshold conception of the standard of review effectively equates to the giving of varying degrees of presumptive weight to one or both litigation parties, the reasons that justify each of these devices can in principle be expressed using the giving of weight device. Nevertheless, there are situations in which the facts necessitate discrimination amongst the devices. For example, where placation of the public is the reason for deference and the public wants deference to be exhibited through a particular device (eg the standard of proof), the court should choose the public's preferred device.

Contrary to the burden and standard of proof and the epistemic threshold conception of the standard of review, the type of error conception of the standard of review cannot be reduced to the giving of weight concept. Carving out certain types of error from the court's jurisdiction does not equate to giving weight to the primary decision-maker's views on the exempted error types; rather, it equates to the court not examining those errors at all. If the type of error conception of the standard of review is adopted, then the court should defer by lowering the standard of review rather than using the giving of weight device in situations in which outcome, legitimacy, or other reasons for deference are better served by carving out certain types of error from the court's purview than by allowing the court to review them.

Furthermore, there are workability and legal certainty concerns that dictate the choice of one device rather than another. I explore this issue further in Chapter 6. For now, it suffices to highlight that it is only *after* the court has settled the question of what the standard of review and burden and standard of proof are that it decides how much weight to accord to the primary decision-maker's view that the requisite standards and burden have been met. Thus, whilst the burden of proof, standard of review and standard of proof have to be determined before the merits of the case are closely examined, the giving of weight device enters the stage only when the court embarks on such examination.

Rights Cases in Germany and Canada: Some Comparative Observations' (2013) 32 NJCL 23, 32–34 and Foster (n 47) 233–34. Foley goes so far as to argue that '[r]educed to its most basic form, the deference question concerns the weight which courts should attribute to the decisions of non-judicial institutions': Foley, *Deference and the Presumption of Constitutionality* (n 12) 256.

The implication is that whilst the burden of proof, standard of proof, and standard of review can reflect only relatively abstract considerations that are salient to the court before the merits of the case are closely examined (eg the nature of the right, seriousness of the rights violation, and countervailing interest, whether the original decision-maker is democratically returned), the giving of weight device can reflect considerations that become salient only when the merits of the case are closely examined (eg when the court is assessing the specific question of, say, whether the government has superior expertise to assess whether a Covid-19 vaccine pass as opposed to a health pass is no more than necessary to protect public health). The giving of weight device can thus serve as a residual device, accommodating normative considerations on deference that were not apparent to the court when it determined the burden of proof, standard of proof and standard of review. A ground for deference or a factor that suggests that ground may become clear only once the court begins to examine the merits of the case closely, in which case that ground/factor can be accommodated only through the giving of weight device. *If* the court *had known* of the existence of the ground or factor *before* it closely engaged with the merits of the case at hand, then it could have chosen to express it earlier through the burden and standard of proof or standard of review. In practice, however, courts do not always have such foresight, and thus have to resort to the more ad hoc device of the giving of weight.

To recap the arguments made in this section so far: first, courts can sometimes use the giving of weight device to give effect to the normative considerations that underlie the burden and standard of proof and epistemic threshold conception of the standard of review. In some situations, however, the use of one device is more appropriate than that of another. Second, courts should defer via the type of error conception rather than the giving of weight device if the reasons for deference are better fulfilled by carving out certain types of error from the court's review. Third, if a court needs to defer for reasons that were not apparent to it when it determined the burden and standard of proof and standard of review, then it can rely on the giving of weight device at a later stage of adjudication.

Before departing this section, let us evaluate Elliott's position on the justifications for using the various devices, which, like my arguments in this section, is also based in part on the temporal dimension of the devices. As section II explains, Elliott examines two sets of considerations governing the devices for deference, namely, the importance of the right harmed by the impugned act and the relative expertise and legitimacy of the court and administrator. He makes three points that are crucial for present purposes. First, both sets of considerations play a part in determining what he calls 'intrinsic deference' (which covers the devices of standard of review, and burden and standard of proof) and 'adjudicative deference' (which covers the device of giving of weight).[68] Second, only one of the two sets plays a

[68] Elliott (n 14) 83–86.

primary role in determining intrinsic or adjudicative deference: the importance of the right is the primary consideration determining the former, whilst relative expertise and legitimacy are the primary considerations determining the latter.[69] Third, Elliott denies the relevance of the extent of the rights limitation and seriousness of the harm to the countervailing interest to the determination of intrinsic deference.[70] The analysis in section III.4 and in the present section supports his first point, and I will thus focus on evaluating his second and third points here. I argue that although his second point is not entirely accurate, there is an important grain of truth in it, and that his third point is not sound.

Elliott justifies his second point by arguing that the temporal dimension of the deference devices dictates that intrinsic deference can be determined only by relatively abstract considerations that are salient even before the court decides whether the burden of proof has been discharged, whilst adjudicative deference can take into account considerations that arise 'on-the-ground' when the court assesses the 'quality of the justification actually offered' to discharge the burden.[71] This is an important insight, and, as can be seen from the discussions above, one that informs my arguments in this section. It explains Elliott's position that intrinsic deference can be determined by the importance of the right at stake, and adjudicative deference by the court and administrator's relative expertise and legitimacy. But it is not obvious why primary and secondary weight must be attached to the two sets of considerations for the determination of intrinsic and adjudicative deference, respectively. As section III.4 and the present section have established, considerations of the relative expertise and legitimacy of the court and primary decision-maker, which are factors that suggest the values of arriving at correct outcomes and respecting constitutional legitimacy, are relevant to the determination of both intrinsic deference and adjudicative deference. Such considerations do not necessarily take on a secondary role in setting intrinsic deference, and thus it is not accurate to say that relative expertise and legitimacy assume primary and secondary importance in establishing adjudicative and intrinsic deference, respectively. However, because intrinsic deference has to be determined in the abstract, it must be determined by factors that suggest relative expertise and legitimacy *and* can be ascertained by the court even before its close examination of the merits of the case. As explained above, the importance of the right is one such factor.[72] How much adjudicative deference to accord, in contrast, is determined on the ground; the court does not necessarily have to rely on abstract factors. Thus, there is a grain of truth in Elliott's argument that the importance of the right plays a significant role in setting intrinsic deference: the court needs to rely on abstract factors such as

[69] ibid 73–82.
[70] ibid 81 esp at fn 95.
[71] ibid 71, 81.
[72] Section III.2 and the preceding discussion in the present section.

the importance of the right to discern relative expertise and legitimacy to a greater extent when determining intrinsic deference than when determining adjudicative deference.

Nevertheless, Elliott's third point is not justified. It is unclear why the extent of the rights limitation and the seriousness of the harm to the countervailing interest (which, like the importance of the right, are also factors that can be discerned in abstract, and, as explained in Chapter 2,[73] are suggestive of such grounds for deference as relative constitutional legitimacy) cannot play a part in determining intrinsic deference as well. Elliott posits that because the devices relating to intrinsic deference determine the heaviness of the defendant's burden of justification that should 'ideally obtain without reference to factors, particular to the more specific features of the case', they should be 'informed primarily by reference to the normative significance of the at-risk value'.[74] However, this is an assertion rather than an explanation. Why should intrinsic deference not also be principally informed by other considerations that both relate to the specific features of the case and *can* be ascertained by the court in the abstract, such as the extent of interference with the right?

Hence, whilst Elliott's insight that intrinsic deference must be determined by relatively abstract considerations by virtue of its temporal framework is valuable, his conclusion about ruling out specific considerations cannot be justified by the internal logic of deference.

V. Choice of Interpretation and Choice of Remedy Versus Review Devices

Having examined how courts should choose amongst the review devices, let us now evaluate how they should choose between a review device on the one hand and the choice of interpretation and choice of remedy devices on the other. Sometimes it does not matter which set of devices is used. Assume, for example, that the public is strongly pro-government and anti-court because of institutional differences between the court and the government. The public will be placated, and the court judgment better received, if the court grants leeway to the government during adjudication regardless of how that leeway is granted. Assume further that these facts give rise to a reason for deference that is listed under the residual category of grounds in Chapter 2, namely, enhancement of a judgment's efficacy. That reason can be served by any device on any issue, and hence the court may choose any device to fulfil it.

[73] See section V of Chapter 2.
[74] Elliott (n 14) 81, 85, emphasis omitted.

However, there are times when it matters whether the court selects a review device on the one hand or the choice of remedy and interpretation devices on the other. Let us first consider the choice of remedy device vis-à-vis the review devices before assessing the choice of interpretation device vis-à-vis those devices. From the facts of *Bellinger*, assume that the court needs to determine what remedy to grant after finding that a law prohibiting post-operative transsexual persons from marrying in their post-operative gender violates their constitutional rights. Assume further that the devices for deference available to the court for deciding the issue are the choice of remedy and a review device (say, the standard of review), and, for simplicity's sake, let us focus on constitutional legitimacy reasons for deference. The facts that would trigger use of the choice of remedy device would be that allowing the legislature to decide how to bring marriage laws into line with the court ruling would enhance democratic legitimacy. If such facts exist, then democratic legitimacy would be enhanced if the court, say, granted a declaration of incompatibility rather than adopting a remedial interpretation, thereby giving the legislature more remedial discretion.

The facts justifying use of the choice of remedy device in this example are different from the facts that would have justified the use of a review device, that is, that the executive or legislature has greater democratic legitimacy than the court to decide the question of what remedy should be granted by the court. When the latter facts exist, democratic legitimacy would be enhanced if the court deferred to the executive or legislature's preference (as expressed in court) concerning what remedy should be granted (which, as explained in Chapter 3, may or may not be a remedy that grants the government more room to fashion a response to the court's ruling). The facts that allow the value of constitutional legitimacy to be served are different in relation to a review device and the choice of remedy device. The court's decision about which device to use should depend on which set of facts exists. To demonstrate that the two sets of facts are different, we can imagine a situation in which democratic legitimacy would be enhanced by using one device but not the other. Assume that at the time of the litigation in question, the executive and legislature were unelected but that elections were expected to be introduced soon. In this case, democratic legitimacy could not be enhanced by the court giving weight to the government's view on what remedy to grant, but could be enhanced by the court allowing the government future room to formulate marriage policies (assuming that the government is an elected one when such formulation takes place).

Of course, it may be the case that in most circumstances democratic legitimacy can be enhanced by using both the choice of remedy device and a review device. In that case, in situations where facts calling for deference using both devices exist, the court should defer by using both.[75] Deference that is due on one device cannot be compensated by deference using another.

[75] Unless the use of one renders that of the other otiose, as happens when, say, the court gives 100 per cent weight to the government's preference on what remedy should be granted (using the giving

Let us now turn to comparison of the choice of interpretation device and the review devices. From the facts of *Labour Trilogy*, assume that the court needs to decide whether the right to association includes a right to strike. Assume also that the devices for deference available to the court for deciding the issue are the choice of interpretation device and a review device (say, the standard of review), and, again for simplicity's sake, let us focus on the constitutional legitimacy reasons for deference. The facts that call for the use of choice of interpretation are that defining the right to association to exclude the right to strike would give the government greater room to fashion labour policies, thereby serving the value of constitutional legitimacy. These facts, which justify a narrower interpretation of the right to association, differ from the facts that would justify the use of a review device, that is, that the government has greater democratic legitimacy than the court to decide how the right to association should be defined. When the latter facts exist, democratic legitimacy would be enhanced if the court deferred to the government's preference (as expressed in the impugned law) for defining the right to association narrowly. The court needs to decide whether to use the choice of interpretation device and/or a review device depending on which set of facts exists. If both sets exist, the court should defer using both the choice of interpretation device and the review device.[76] Again, deference that is due on one device cannot be compensated by deference using another.

To conclude, sometimes it does not matter whether a review device or the choice of interpretation or remedy device is used. However, where the facts giving rise to the reasons for deference differ in relation to the two sets of devices, the court should determine which to use according to which set of facts exists. If both sets of facts exist, the court should defer using both sets of devices.

VI. Deference Across Issues

This section considers how courts should determine the substantive issue on which to defer (and hence also the stage of adjudication at which to defer). Sometimes this determination does not matter. The first example given in section V, namely, the public being placated regardless of how deference is accorded, provides one illustration of when the court's choice of issues on which to defer does not matter.

of weight device), leaving no room for the court to use the choice of remedy device. If the court has reached a conclusion in favour of the government using one device, then it is not expected to explain that it might have reached the same conclusion using another device.

[76] Echoing the observation in n 75, this would be the case unless the use of one renders that of the other otiose, as happens when, say, the court gives 100 per cent weight to the government's preferred interpretation of the right (using the giving of weight device), leaving no room for the court to use the choice of remedy device.

Sometimes, however, the institutional facts that give rise to reasons for deference differ between issues, in which case the court should defer on—and only on—the issues to which those facts apply. For example, if the government has expertise at the rights limitation stage but not at the definition stage, the court should defer at the former stage but not at the latter to serve the value of arriving at correct outcomes in the case in question. If the government has expertise on the rational connection and minimal impairment limbs of the proportionality test, but not on the legitimate aim and fair balance limbs, then deference should be accorded on the former but not on the latter to serve that value. The court should choose which issue to defer on according to what expertise and legitimacy the original decision-maker has. Deference that is due on one issue cannot be compensated by deference on another, and deference that is due on two issues cannot be compensated by deference on only one.

Consider, for example, a situation where the review devices at the rights definition and limitation stages cannot be used in lieu of the choice of remedy device, and vice versa. If the government has not thought through the impugned policy but is expected to do so in future, then the value of arriving at correct outcomes in the case in question cannot be served by deferring to a view expressed by the government at the definition and limitation stages. However, the value of achieving a correct policy *in future* (which is classified under the residual category of grounds in Chapter 2) can be achieved if a deferential remedy is granted. The institutional facts that give rise to reasons for deference discriminate between deference at the definition and limitation stages on the one hand and deference at the remedial stage on the other.

Even when certain substantive issues appear to arise at more than one stage of adjudication, it may still matter which stage the court defers at. It is possible, for example, for the issue of how the public interest and the right at stake should be balanced to arise at both the limitation and definitional stages, as occurs when definitional balancing is mandated by the text of the constitution (consider eg the wording of rights with 'internal qualifiers'[77] such as the 'right to peaceful assembly'). In these cases, although the balancing issue arises twice, it ultimately speaks to different questions: once to the question of the right's scope and once to the question of whether the limitation on the right, as defined at the definition stage, is justified. If the government has superior expertise to the court on the issue of balancing in relation to the former, the latter, or both issues, the court should defer on the former, latter, or both, respectively. Deference that is warranted on definitional issues cannot be compensated by deference on limitation issues, and deference warranted on both sets of issues cannot be compensated by deference

[77] Barak (n 44) 32–34. See also Stephen Gardbaum, 'Limiting Constitutional Rights' (2007) 54 UCLA L Rev 789, 801–10.

on just one.[78] Chapter 5 examines the implications of definitional balancing on the issue of double counting.

To conclude, sometimes it does not matter which issue the court defers on. At other times, however, the facts that give rise to reasons for deference discriminate between different issues, in which case the court should determine which issue to defer on according to which set of facts exists.

VII. Conclusion

This chapter has examined how courts should choose amongst the deference devices and decide which issues to defer on to give effect to the reasons for deference. The following guidelines on deference can be distilled:

1) When the court needs to accord deference to the superior abilities or legitimacy of the primary decision-maker to determine the rights issue in question, it can in principle do so by adjusting the burden of proof, standard of proof, or standard of review.[79] However, it should choose one device rather than another when such reasons for deference can be better served by that device. Four examples serve to illustrate:[80]
    a) First, if the court's lack of expertise and legitimacy to determine an issue relates only to certain types of error, it should defer by carving out those types of error (ie by lowering the type of error conception of the standard of review) rather than by reversing the burden of proof or lowering the standard of proof across all aspects of the issue.
    b) Second, when the court's ability to determine an issue is too weak to allow it to determine with any level of confidence whether the primary decision-maker is correct, it should defer by excluding certain types of error from its purview (ie by lowering the type of error conception of the standard of review) rather than by lowering the standard of proof.
    c) Third, if the court is in a better position to assess whether the decision-maker is wrong than to assess whether it is correct, then the court should give effect to relative expertise concerns by lowering the level of confidence needed to determine that the decision-maker is wrong before rejecting its decision (ie lowering the epistemic threshold conception of the standard of review) rather than by lowering the standard of proof that the decision-maker must bear.

[78] Note, however, that deference at an earlier stage may leave no room for deference at a later stage, as happens when deference at the rights definition stage has resolved the case in favour of the government, and hence the court need not proceed to the limitation stage.

[79] Section III.1–4.

[80] Section III.4.

d) Fourth, when the court needs to take into account the relative expertise and legitimacy of the applicant (vis-à-vis the primary decision-maker and/or the court), as occurs when the court is faced with conflicting expert opinions, then it should express considerations of relative expertise and legitimacy through the burden and standard of proof devices rather than through the standard of review device.

2) If the court needs to give effect to prior probability theory, address the relative difficulties of proof, or minimize the social costs of an erroneous ruling, it should adjust the burden and standard of proof rather than the standard of review.[81]
3) In general, the court can use the giving of weight device to give effect to the normative considerations that underlie the burden and standard of proof and epistemic conception of the standard of review.[82]
4) The court should defer via the type of error conception of the standard of review instead of the giving of weight device if the reasons for deference are better fulfilled by carving out certain types of error from the court's review. This is the case when, for example, the court's ability to adjudge certain types of error is so weak vis-à-vis that of the primary decision-maker that the value of arriving at correct outcomes would be better served by excluding those errors from the court's purview than by allowing it to review them.[83]
5) If the court needs to defer for reasons that were not apparent to it when it determined the burden and standard of proof and standard of review, it can rely on the giving of weight device.[84]
6) Sometimes it does not matter whether a review device or the choice of interpretation or remedy device is used: for example, where placation of the public is the reason for deference and the public will be placated regardless of which device is used. When the facts that give rise to the reasons for deference discriminate between the two sets of devices, however, the court needs to determine which set to use according to which set of facts exists. For example, if the government advocating for a certain remedy in court is not democratically elected but elections will be introduced immediately after the litigation in question, then the court should choose a remedy that affords the government more room to respond to the court's ruling rather than give weight to the government's view on what the remedy should be if it wishes to enhance democratic legitimacy.[85]
7) Sometimes it does not matter on which issue the court defers. This is the case where, for example, placation of the public is the reason for deference

[81] Section III.3–4.
[82] Section IV.
[83] ibid.
[84] ibid.
[85] Section V.

> and the public will be placated regardless of the issue on which the court defers. At other times, however, the facts that give rise to the reasons for deference discriminate amongst issues, in which case the court should determine which issue to defer on according to which set of facts exists. For example, if the government has superior expertise on the third limb of the proportionality test but not on the second limb, the court should defer on the former but not on the latter to give effect to the expertise reason for deference.[86]

To comply with the reason for deference concerned, the court should decide how to defer by considering not only the type of reason but also the strength of that reason. The latter issue is the subject of Chapter 5.

[86] Section VI.

5

Choice of Device II: Strength of Reasons

I. Introduction

This chapter is the second of the two chapters in this book examining what I call the 'internal logic' of deference, that is, how courts should deploy the six deference devices to fulfil the reasons for deference. Chapter 4 focuses on the qualitative aspect of the internal logic analysis: it explores how the choice of device is affected by the court's reason for deferring. This chapter focuses on the quantitative aspect of such analysis: it explores how the choice of device is affected by the strength of the court's reason for deferring, that is, the degree of deference due. It compares the degrees of deference expressible by particular devices and at various stages of adjudication and analyses what constitutes the double counting of deference. Such analysis will facilitate court decisions about which device or combination of devices to use and at which stage of adjudication to defer to exert the right degree of deference in a particular case.

The remainder of the chapter is organized as follows. In section II, I compare what I call the range and granularity of deference expressible by the six devices. That comparison paves the way for section III, which first explains how the degrees of deference expressible by various devices can be compared, and then compares the degrees expressible at the three stages of adjudication. This analysis does not cover all possible ways of using the devices or their application to all issues but only some of the more common uses and applications. Sections IV–VI then examine the issue of double counting. The analysis in these sections begins by defining the double counting of deference, and then identifies situations that raise suspicions of double counting.

II. Range and Granularity of Deference

This section compares two quantitative aspects of the deference devices: the range of deference that a device can express (as determined by the minimum and maximum degrees of deference it can express) and how fine-grained the deference expressed is. The comparison is based on the assumption that the devices apply to the same substantive issue in litigation. My key argument is that if the court wishes to express a significant degree of deference or multiple degrees of deference, it cannot rely on the burden of proof alone.

Deference in Human Rights Adjudication. Cora Chan, Oxford University Press. © Cora Chan 2024.
DOI: 10.1093/9780198921677.003.0005

1. Range of deference

Let us begin by comparing the range of deference exemplifiable by the burden and standard of proof, standard of review, and giving of weight. As explained in Chapter 4, the burden of proof, standard of proof, and epistemic threshold conception of the standard of review (ie the conception that understands the various standards of review as conveying the differing levels of confidence that the court must have that the primary decision-maker's factual proposition is wrong before rejecting its decision)[1] can all be conceived of as the affording of varying degrees of presumptive weight to the primary decision-maker's case.[2] Leaving aside the burden of proof for the moment, if the epistemic threshold conception of the standard of review is adopted, then the standard of proof, standard of review, and giving of weight all allow the same possible range of deference: ranging from giving the primary decision-maker's case slightly more than 0 per cent weight to giving it 100 per cent weight. In practice, however, the standard of review and standard of proof are likely to be limited to a small number of standards, with the range of deference expressible limited to that which can be expressed by the standards available.

The burden of proof stands in a different position. Although the common perception seems to be that the burden of proof is an important device,[3] in fact shifting that burden without, for example, adjusting the standard of proof generally exerts very little deference. Some commentaries that suggest the significance of shifting the burden of proof actually presume that the heaviness of the burden (as determined by the standard of proof) for the party bearing it post-shift is correspondingly increased as well. For example, in their analyses of the legal burden in rights adjudication, Aharon Barak[4] and Julian Rivers[5] assume that said burden carries an in-built standard of proof of at least a balance of probabilities (>50 per cent). Accordingly, when the burden at, say, the limitation stage is shifted from, say, the public authority to the applicant, the standard of proof for the latter correspondingly increases from proving that it is at most 50 per cent certain that the measure is proportionate to proving to more than 50 per cent certainty that the measure is disproportionate (for heuristic purposes, let us assume that the standard has

[1] See text to n 21 in Chapter 4.

[2] See section IV of Chapter 4.

[3] See sources in nn 4–7. However, as will be explained, these sources appear to assume that the shifting of the burden of proof is always accompanied by a corresponding change in the standard of proof.

[4] Aharon Barak, *Proportionality: Constitutional Rights and Their Limitations* (CUP 2012) 437, 442–43, which understands the shifting of the burden of proof as the shifting of which party the court would rule in favour of when both sides of the case are equally strong.

[5] Julian Rivers, 'The Presumption of Proportionality' (2014) 77(3) MLR 409, 412, which understands the shifting of the burden of proof as the shifting of the party to whom the court would grant the benefit of the doubt.

increased from 50 to 51 per cent).[6] Similarly, in Jenneke Gerards' triadic scheme of deference, the shifting of the legal burden of proof is accompanied by an increase in the level of proof that the party bearing the post-shift burden needs to meet. For example, for a 'marginal review', the applicant bears the burden of 'adduc[ing] *clear and uncontested* evidence to show that the measure will not and cannot have the desired effects', whilst for 'strict scrutiny', the primary decision-maker bears the burden of showing the adequacy of the measure 'by adducing *conclusive* evidence'.[7] In these discussions, what is doing the real work on deference is not the shifting of the burden per se, but rather the change in the standard of proof that accompanies the shift.[8]

In general, shifting the burden of proof without correspondingly changing the standard of proof exerts trivial deferential force. Assume that the government originally bears the burden of proving the proportionality of an impugned measure on 'clear and convincing evidence' and that this translates into a standard of proof of >60 per cent. Assume further that the burden of proof is shifted onto the applicant whilst the standard of proof remains the same; that is, it is ≤60 per cent for the applicant both pre- and post-shift. In this case, the shift merely alters the rebuttable presumption of who wins on the issue in question 'in the absence of any evidence'.[9] After the shift, the level of proof that the parties strive to proffer in order to win remains the same. The applicant will still try to prove that the proposition is correct to no more than 60 per cent, whereas the government will try to prove that it is correct to more than 60 per cent. The shifting of the burden per se relieves the government to some extent by granting its case some presumptive weight, and it may[10] cause the applicant rather than the government to 'begin calling evidence'[11] in the litigation. In other words, the shift may cause the applicant to bear 'the initial burden of production', a burden that is needed because 'inevitably one of the

[6] Eg Cora Chan, 'The Burden of Proof under the Human Rights Act' [2014] JR 46, 47; Andrew S Butler, 'Limiting Rights' (2002) 33 Victoria U Wellington L Rev 113, 126; these understandings of the burden of proof are at one with the understanding in the evidence law literature. See eg Roderick Munday, *Cross and Tapper on Evidence* (13th edn, OUP 2018) 124; David Hamer, 'Presumptions, Standards and Burdens: Managing the Cost of Error' (2014) 13 Law, Probability and Risk 221, 230, 233. However, as Chapter 3 shows, in the constitutional rights context, the courts have sometimes reduced the standard of proof to below a balance of probabilities, so it is possible for a burden to carry a standard of less than a balance of probabilities.

[7] Janneke Gerards, 'Pluralism, Deference and the Margin of Appreciation Doctrine' (2011) 17(1) ELJ 80, 88, 117 (emphasis added).

[8] cf Mike Redmayne, 'Standards of Proof in Civil Litigation' (1999) 62(2) MLR 167, 172.

[9] Quoted phrase borrowed from Nigel Bridge, 'Presumptions and Burdens' (1949) 12(3) MLR 273, 282. See Rivers (n 5) 416; Hamer (n 6) 221, 226. See also Munday (n 6) 134, in which the author remarks that sometimes the terminology of presumption is used to express or explain the allocation of the burden of proof.

[10] It is not necessarily the case that after the shift the applicant must make the first move. If the 'background information' or 'prior odds' support(s) the applicant rather than the defendant's case, the initial burden might fall on the latter to rebut such evidence instead. Dale A Nance, *The Burdens of Proof: Discriminatory Power, Weight of Evidence, and Tenacity of Belief* (CUP 2016) 95, 210.

[11] Munday (n 6) 122.

parties must start the process'.[12] However, such relief is insignificant in most cases. It has a non-trivial deferential effect in cases in which no information in support of or against either side exists at the start of the litigation, and it is extremely difficult for both the government and the applicant to adduce 'some evidence',[13] although such cases are exceptional.

To date, there has been little scholarly analysis of the isolated impact of shifting the burden of proof, although there is some support in the literature for the position that such an impact is insignificant. Dale Nance, for example, observes that the allocation of the legal burden of proving a proposition to one party is 'essentially meaningless' if the standard of proof is set at a negligible level because 'for all practical purposes' the other party needs to 'eliminate the possibility' of that proposition.[14]

The foregoing analysis establishes that the burden of proof has to work hand in hand with the heaviness of that burden—which is determined first and foremost by the standard of proof—in order to have significant deferential force.[15] The maximum degree of deference that can be exemplified by the burden of proof is therefore lower than that which can be exemplified by the other devices, and coincides with the minimum degree of deference exemplifiable by such burden, a point that will be explained in section II.2.

If the type-of-error conception of the standard of review is adopted (ie the different standards of review are understood as delineating different ranges of error that trigger court intervention),[16] then the minimum degree of deference exemplifiable by the standard of review device is the extent to which the primary decision-maker's burden is eased by the court excluding jurisdiction over a minimal level of error. Meanwhile, the maximum degree is non-justiciability, which has the effect of giving 100 per cent presumptive weight to the primary decision-maker. It should, however, be noted that as explained in Chapter 4, the idea of carving out decisions as unreviewable and affording weight to the decision-maker while reviewing them are conceptually different.[17]

We now turn to a comparison of the devices of the choice of interpretation and choice of remedy. Both devices are in theory capable of giving varying degrees of leeway to the executive or legislature's policy formulation, ranging from slightly over 0 per cent to 100 per cent. In practice, however, the interpretations and remedies available to the court are likely to be limited, and the range of policymaking leeway

[12] Nance (n 10) 4 (emphasis omitted). See also Caroline E Foster, *Science and the Precautionary Principle in International Courts and Tribunals: Expert Evidence, Burden of Proof and Finality* (CUP 2011) 203–04; Redmayne, 'Standards of Proof' (n 8) 172; Bridge (n 9) 286.

[13] Bridge (n 9) 282.

[14] Nance (n 10) 29.

[15] The cases cited in Chapter 3 to illustrate how the burden of proof can be deployed should be understood as exemplifying a corresponding change in the standard of proof or review.

[16] See text to nn 25–31 of Chapter 4.

[17] See section IV of Chapter 4.

that can be accorded is limited to that which can be expressed by the options available. For example, a court may in a particular instance have at its disposal only two remedies—remedial interpretation and a declaration of incompatibility—with no other options (eg suspensions, prospective application, declaration of invalidity).

2. Granularity of deference

The discussion thus far compares the range of deference expressible by the various devices. Let us now compare the granularity of deference expressible thereby. The standard of review, standard of proof and giving of weight are conceptually equally fine-grained. It is conceptually possible to develop infinite standards of review and standards of proof in order to reflect the infinite gradations of weight that can be accorded to the primary decision-maker. However, in practice, the courts in the jurisdictions under study consider the standard of review and standard of proof to be doctrinal tools and have developed only a 'small set of alternative' standards.[18] In contrast, the giving of weight is viewed less as a doctrinal tool in those jurisdictions, hence giving rise to the impression that the deference that device can exemplify ranges 'from a gram to a tonne'[19] and that it is more fine-grained than the other two devices. This is not to say, however, that doctrinal categories cannot be developed around the giving of weight device, or that the standards of review and proof must be limited to a few, merely that this has been the case in practice. Chapter 6 explores the question of whether, given the cognitive limitations of judges and applicants, it is desirable and possible to develop quantum categories[20] (eg low, moderate, and high degrees of weight) around the giving of weight device.[21]

Similarly, it is also conceptually possible to develop interpretations of constitutional provisions and remedial options to match the infinite possible degrees of policymaking leeway to be accorded to the executive or legislature. However, in practice, the courts are likely to be confined to only a few options. Again, this is not to say that more options are not desirable or possible. The analysis in Chapter 6 will shed light on such desirability and possibility.

The burden of proof stands in a different position from the aforementioned devices. It is *binary* in that a party either bears the burden or does not.[22] It operates like an on–off light switch with no dimmer;[23] that is, it functions in an all-or-nothing

[18] Quoted phrase borrowed from Nance (n 10) 59. See also Tom Hickman, *Public Law after the Human Rights Act* (Hart 2010) 137.

[19] Hickman (n 18) 138.

[20] Nance (n 10) 58.

[21] See Hickman (n 18) 138.

[22] Foster (n 12) 274 fn 160.

[23] Gersen and Vermeule used the same analogy in distinguishing *Chevron* as a doctrinal solution (akin to a traditional light switch) from *Chevron* as a voting rule (akin to a dimmer). Jacob E Gersen and Adrian Vermeule, '*Chevron* as a voting rule' (2007) 116(4) Yale LJ 676, 702.

fashion with no gradations in between. Harking back to a point I briefly touched upon in section II.1, the minimum and maximum degrees of deference expressible by the burden of proof are therefore the same: it is the degree of deference that can be conveyed by changing the presumption of who would win in the absence of any evidence in the litigation, a degree that in most cases would be meagre. Hence, to express a significant degree of deference or multiple degrees of deference, the court cannot rely on the burden of proof alone.

With this comparison of range and granularity in mind, let us now turn to a comparison of the degrees of deference exemplified by specific devices.

III. Comparison of Degrees of Deference

The focus here is on comparing the degrees of deference exemplified by adjusting the standards of review and proof and the giving of weight, as well as the degrees that can be exemplified by deferring at the three stages of adjudication. I make two arguments. First, the degrees of deference exemplified by the standard of proof, standard of review, and giving of weight can be compared by assessing how much additional presumptive weight the court affords the public body defendant's proposition. Second, in the polities covered by this study, when deference at the definition and limitation stages is exercised in ways that lead to favourable outcomes for the public body at those stages, the degrees of deference exemplified at the three stages (ie definition, limitation, remedy) are in decreasing order. Hence, if all three stages of adjudication are capable of expressing the reason for deference concerned, the court should choose to defer at the stage that is best able to exemplify the degree of deference due.

We begin with a comparison of the common ways of diluting the standards of review and proof and the giving of weight. If we adopt the epistemic threshold conception of the standard of review, then the degree of deference expressible by adjusting the standard of review, standard of proof, and giving of weight can be compared in a straightforward manner by examining the degree to which they reduce the required level of certainty in the primary decision-maker's proposition and, correspondingly, how much additional presumptive weight is afforded that proposition. Assume that the public authority originally bears the burden of showing the proportionality of a measure to the 'balance of probabilities' standard of proof and that doing so requires proof to >50 per cent certainty (for heuristic purposes, let us deem that standard to be at least 51 per cent). If the standard of review adopted by the court is correctness, then the level of certainty that the court must have before accepting that the measure is proportionate is at least 51 per cent. Whether lowering the standard of review from correctness to reasonableness expresses more deference than lowering the standard of proof to 'a slight and theoretical possibility' depends on the levels of certainty that the lowered standards represent. If the reasonableness standard equates to 30 per cent certainty and the slight and theoretical possibility standard to 1 per cent certainty, then the amount of additional presumptive weight expressed by lowering the standard of review to reasonableness is 51 per cent – 30 per cent = 21 per cent, whereas that expressed by lowering the standard of proof from a balance of probabilities to a slight and theoretical possibility is 51 per cent – 1 per cent = 50 per cent.[24] The latter method therefore expresses a greater degree of deference than the former.

These two methods of granting deference can in turn be compared with the giving of weight device by examining how much additional weight the court grants to the public authority's views through that device. If that additional weight is, say, 40 per cent, then the giving of such weight is more deferential than lowering the standard of review to reasonableness but less deferential than lowering the standard of proof to a slight and theoretical possibility, assuming that the levels of certainty the lowered standards represent are as defined in the preceding paragraph.

If the type-of-error conception of the standard of review is adopted, then the comparison of the degrees of deference exemplifiable by lowering the standard of review, standard of proof, and giving of weight becomes less straightforward. It now depends on the extent to which the public authority's burden is relieved by the exclusion of particular types of error from the court's review in the circumstances.

We now move on to a comparison of the degrees of deference that can be exemplified at the three stages of adjudication. David Wiseman suggests that the degrees of deference that can be expressed at the three stages are in decreasing order. He posits that in the Canadian context if a challenged measure infringes the rights of vulnerable groups, then less deference is warranted, and it would be justifiable for the court to consider expressing its competence concerns through deference at the remedial or limitation stage rather than at the definition stage.[25] Wiseman also argues that concerns about judicial competence at the remedial stage should not be 'fed into' the 'earlier stages of' review under the Canadian Charter of Rights and Freedoms, 'thereby blunting the scope of protection attainable by anti-poverty claimants'.[26] These remarks can be read in two ways. The stronger reading is that the degrees of deference expressed at the rights definition, limitation, and remedial stages are in decreasing order regardless of how deference is expressed. The weaker

[24] As explained in section I of Chapter 4, these percentages are used only to show that the various devices can differ in deferential force. They are not meant to illustrate the exact degree of difference or to pinpoint with precision the level of deference a given device can exert, neither of which is necessary for our purposes. Whilst the ordinal ranking in deference that the illustrations use is not arbitrary, the exact percentages are arbitrarily assigned. Also, given the limits of human cognition, it may be difficult to ascertain the difference between two close standards. Chapter 6 deals with the question of how deference can be made more practicable given human fallibility.

[25] David Wiseman, 'Managing the Burden of Doubt: Social Science Evidence, the Institutional Competence of Courts and the Prospects for Anti-Poverty Charter Claims' (2014) 33 NJCL 1, 13–14.

[26] ibid 30–31.

reading is that when deference at the definition and limitation stages is exercised in ways that lead to favourable outcomes for the primary decision-maker at those stages, deference at the three stages is in decreasing order. The stronger proposition is not plausible given that the level of deference that can be expressed at the three stages depends on the way in which deference is exerted. The weaker proposition is, however, plausible. The rest of this section tests it by comparing three specific methods of deference:

Method 1. Deference at the rights definition stage: defining the constitutional right narrowly to exclude the applicant's activity from the scope of the right so that no prima facie limitation of the right will be found.

Method 2. Deference at the rights limitation stage: finding a prima facie rights limitation, but giving 100 per cent weight to the primary decision-maker's view that the limitation is proportionate.

Method 3. Deference at the remedial stage: finding a prima facie rights limitation and holding it to be disproportionate but granting a declaration of incompatibility (or even declining to grant a remedy) rather than adopting a remedial interpretation, thereby allowing the legislature to decide how to respond to the negative court ruling.

Two illustrations suffice to demonstrate that the degree of deference that can be exemplified by these three methods depends on the social, political, and legal context, although in the jurisdictions under study it is likely to decrease in order.

Illustration 1. In *Bellinger v Bellinger*,[27] the applicant argued that the marriage law at issue violated the right to marry insofar as it made no provision for the right of those who had undergone gender reassignment surgery to marry in their post-operative gender. The government announced its intention to review both the marriage law and the laws on such related issues as gender recognition. Assuming that such an intention gives rise to an inter-institutional comity reason for deference: deference as opposed to non-deference would give Parliament more room to deliberate on the issue of the right of post-operative transsexual persons to marry, as well as on related issues. Defining the right to marry so as to limit it to two parties born biologically male and female (method 1), giving 100 per cent weight to the government's view that the law is proportionate (method 2), and simply declaring the law to be incompatible with the right without dictating a solution or declining to grant a remedy (method 3) can all express the inter-institutional comity reason for deference to some extent. However, whether they are able to express it to the same extent depends on the legal, social, and political significance of the three methods of deference.

[27] [2003] UKHL 21, [2003] 2 AC 467.

Let us compare the first two methods first. The deferential force of both depends on the legal, social, and political significance of the court's reasoning at the definition and limitation stages. If the court's reasoning exerts a strong precedential effect, and the legislature generally takes such reasoning into account in deliberating laws, as is the case in the polities covered by this book, then method 1 is more deferential than method 2 because the former leaves the government with wider permissible scope for action. If the right is defined narrowly to cover only heterosexual marriage between persons born male and female, then in reformulating laws on the right of transsexual persons to marry and same-sex marriage, the legislature need not consider whether those laws are proportionate. In contrast, if the right is defined broadly, then even if the impugned law is found to be proportionate this time around, the legislature still needs to ensure that both the reformulated law and related laws are proportionate. It will be bound by more constraints in its deliberation.

We now move on to compare methods 2 and 3. The extent to which they can express comity depends on the legal, political, and social significance of, on the one hand, a positive legal ruling at the rights limitation stage (method 2) and, on the other, a negative legal ruling at the rights limitation stage coupled with the deferential remedy of a declaration of incompatibility or even no remedy (method 3). If a negative court ruling, even in the absence of an immediate remedy for the individual concerned, exerts political pressure on the legislature to take the ruling into account in reforming the law, as is the case in the polities covered by this book, then method 2 is more deferential than method 3, as it leaves the legislature with wider permissible scope of action. If method 2 is adopted, then the legislature can keep the impugned law in place without worrying that it will be found disproportionate in the near future. In contrast, if method 3 is adopted, although the legislature is technically legally free to retain the impugned law, the negative ruling at the limitation stage may impose social and political pressure on the legislature to reform it, and the risk of a future negative ruling (coupled with the possibility of more intrusive remedies at that point) will likely provide an incentive to think carefully before endorsing the same law. Hence, method 3 imposes more constraints on the legislature's deliberation than does method 2.

Illustration 2. Assume that there is considerable empirical uncertainty over the necessity of a policy that bans all air travel to control the spread of Covid-19. New empirical evidence is expected to soon be available, and the elected executive is expected to review the policy in light of said evidence in the near future.[28] In a present challenge against the ban for violating freedom of movement and the right to privacy, the court is, based on the evidence currently available, 51 per cent sure that the government is wrong, that is, on balance sure that the ban does not pass

[28] cf Mike Redmayne, 'Expert Evidence and Scientific Disagreement' (1996–97) 30 UC Davis L Rev 1027, 1075–76.

the proportionality test. Accordingly, if it has to make a decision now, it will find that the ban is disproportionate. However, if the executive reconsiders the decision in light of the forthcoming information, the resulting decision by the government is likely to be 70 per cent correct. This situation gives rise to a reason for granting the government more room to respond to the court's ruling, namely, to afford the government sufficient flexibility to respond to new information, thereby enabling it to arrive at appropriate policies in future.[29] This ground for deference can potentially be served by defining freedom of movement and the right to privacy narrowly to exclude the right to air travel (method 1), giving 100 per cent weight to the government's views at the limitation stage (method 2) and granting a declaration of incompatibility, leaving it to the government to decide how to respond to a negative court ruling (method 3). In all of these situations, the government is technically legally free to keep the impugned law in place. However, the deferential force of the three methods depends on their legal, social, and political significance.

If the court's reasoning has a strong precedential effect and the government generally takes such reasoning into account in its deliberations, then the three methods decrease in deferential force. Method 1 imposes no constraints on the executive's redeliberation of the ban: the government can keep the ban without considering its proportionality. In contrast, if method 2 is adopted, then even though the ban is found to be proportionate in light of the information available to the court this time around, there is no guarantee that the ban will be so found subsequently in light of the new information. Hence, method 2 imposes pressure on the executive to consider the proportionality of any attempt to impinge upon air travel. Method 3 is the least deferential of the three methods because the court rules out the impugned ban in light of current information. Hence, unless the newly available information clearly demonstrates the proportionality of the ban, the executive will face pressure not to re-enact it. The constraints that the executive faces in redeliberation increase, and, correspondingly, its permissible scope of action decreases as the adjudication proceeds through the three stages.

The above analysis confirms that in polities in which the reasoning of the courts exerts a strong precedential effect and is generally taken seriously by the legislature in its deliberations, even in the absence of an immediate remedy for the individual applicant concerned, methods 1 to 3 decrease in deferential force, and the weaker reading of Wiseman's argument is vindicated.

It is worth mentioning at this juncture a point that seems obvious but is important nonetheless. In situations in which different methods exemplify different degrees of deference, the choice of method should depend on, inter alia, which

[29] I have categorized this reason for deference as falling into the third (or residual) category of grounds defined in Chapter 2. It is different from the first set of grounds for deference, which states that deference will more likely enable the court to arrive at the correct outcome on the rights issue *in the case before it* (given the information at hand). See section IV of Chapter 2.

method expresses a degree of deference that is closer to that warranted by the circumstances, assuming that the methods can all satisfy the reason for deference in the case concerned. In illustration 2, for example, whether deference should be granted at the limitation or remedial stage should depend on which stage of adjudication exerts the level of pressure closest to the optimal level needed to induce the government to deliberate sufficiently to arrive at the appropriate policy on air travel, other things being equal.

This concludes our comparison of the degrees of deference expressed by particular devices and at various stages of adjudication, and leads us to the issue of whether the devices can be used in combination.

IV. Double Counting of Deference

Two general observations that have bearing on the combinability of devices can be drawn from the foregoing discussion. First, as per the discussion in Chapter 4, there are situations in which more than one device is capable of expressing a reason for deference. Second, as per the discussion in this chapter so far, the degree to which such a reason is expressed depends on which devices are used and how, and there may be situations in which the use of a device does not suffice to express the degree of deference that is due. These observations raise the question of whether the devices can be combined to express a particular reason for deference to the right degree. The rest of this chapter focuses on a commonly raised issue in relation to this question: when does the double counting of deference occur?

The risk of double counting deference when multiple devices are used has been highlighted by numerous scholars. Trevor Allan argues that because deference considerations are 'already embodied in traditional doctrine' on, inter alia, distinguishing appeal from review, which rules out a standard of review that calls for the substitution of full merits (manifesting what Kavanagh calls 'minimal deference'), to defer over and above such doctrine (exercising what Kavanagh calls 'substantive deference')[30] 'restates what is already implicit in the ordinary mechanisms of judicial review'.[31] Daly similarly argues that there would be 'unnecessary duplication', resulting in 'inappropriate deference being accorded', if the factors that were 'taken into account in determining unreasonableness [rather than correctness] to be the appropriate standard of review' were 'taken further into account in determining that a "high degree" of unreasonableness would have to be demonstrated before the impugned decision could be struck down'.[32] Alison Young highlights

[30] Aileen Kavanagh, *Constitutional Review under the UK Human Rights Act* (CUP 2009) 227–28.

[31] TRS Allan 'Human Rights and Judicial Review: a Critique of "Due Deference"' (2006) 65 CLJ 671, 679–80.

[32] Paul Daly, *A Theory of Deference in Administrative Law: Basis, Application and Scope* (CUP 2012) 173–74.

three possible forms of double counting. First, if the democratic legitimacy of the legislature is used 'both to justify a test of proportionality, as opposed to substitution', and 'to grant specific weight to the opinion of the executive or legislature when applying the test of proportionality', double counting may result.[33] Second, a 'logical error' may be committed when 'complex social policy issues' are used as a reason 'both to provide a narrow definition of a right' and to adopt a deferential remedy.[34] Third, double counting may occur when the democratic features of the original decision-maker are 'used to justify deference both because the legislature or executive is more likely to reach the right answer… and because this means that the legislature or executive have greater authority to decide the issue'.[35]

Courts have also recognized the possibility of double counting. For example, in *R (on the application DA and others) v Secretary of State for Work and Pensions*, Lord Wilson remarked that the 'same … concept of institutional propriety' underlies deference at both the limitation stage and the remedial stage, and it is 'therefore at [the limitation] stage that, in relation to [a socio-economic measure that differentiates amongst groups], that the concept will usually play its part.'[36] The majority judges in *Canada (Minister of Citizenship and Immigration) v Vavilov* similarly observed that the choice of remedy and the choice of the standard of review are guided by the same rationale, including that 'the legislature has entrusted the matter to the administrative decision-maker'.[37]

The remainder of the chapter dissects the issue of double counting. It offers a definition of double counting, and then, applying that definition, draws the following observations. First, the issue of whether double counting has occurred is highly context dependent, hinging upon, inter alia, how a device is used. Hence, deference using more than one device is neither a necessary nor sufficient condition for double counting. Second, double counting does not occur merely because the court takes into account a factor suggesting deference more than once or defers for the same kind of reason more than once in a case. Finally, courts should be alert to the possibility of double counting in three non-exhaustive situations.

V. Defining Double Counting

Despite the prevalence of concerns over double counting of deference in rights adjudication, no definition of such double counting has yet been offered. I therefore begin the discussion here by offering such a definition: *double counting occurs when the court gives undue additional weight to a normative value (ie a ground as*

[33] Alison Young, 'In Defence of Due Deference' (2009) 72(4) MLR 554, 570.
[34] ibid 578.
[35] ibid 578. See also Alison L Young, *Democratic Dialogue and the Constitution* (OUP 2017) 231–33.
[36] [2019] UKSC 21, [2020] 1 All ER 573 [90].
[37] 2019 SCC 65, [2019] 4 SCR 653 [140].

defined in Chapter 2) *served by deference*. Three preliminary points are in order before I unpack this definition. First, I use the term 'double counting' to refer to all instances in which a value served by deference is given more than its due weight, not to instances in which the weight given is merely double that due. It would therefore be more accurate to use the term 'overcounting'. As double counting is more commonly used, however, I adopt that term instead. Second, what is being double counted can be understood as the weight of the value served by deference. Third, although the focus of this section is the combinability of the devices, and hence the issue of whether a value served by deference is given more weight than warranted, some of its observations are also applicable to the issue of 'undercounting', that is, to giving a value less weight than warranted. For example, if a value can be fully instantiated only by *both* relaxing the standard of review from correctness to manifestly without reasonable foundation *and* giving weight to the public authority's view that that standard has been met, the court would be giving the value unduly little weight if it deferred via the former means alone.

With these preliminary remarks in mind, let us now unpack the proposed definition. Two features of double counting must be noted. First, for double counting to occur, the additional weight accorded by the use of an extra device must be *undue*. Additional weight is undue when the court gives a value more credit than the strength of the value warrants. Suppose, for example, that the UK government mandates the closure of pubs to tackle Covid-19 but allows schools to remain open. Suppose further that there has been very little public consultation on the issue and no debate in Parliament and that the scientific evidence suggests that the impact on the spread of Covid-19 of keeping pubs open and keeping schools open is roughly the same. The fact that the executive, as a general matter, enjoys some indirect democratic legitimacy and has been tasked with policy formulation may call for some degree of respect to be accorded to its decision to close pubs but not schools. If the force of such legitimacy is 'completely exhausted'[38] by the court's application of a standard of review that falls short of the substitution of full merits (ie exercising minimal deference)[39] but the court displays additional deference (ie exercises substantive deference) by, say, giving weight to the executive's view that the decision to close pubs meets the requisite standard of review, then double counting has occurred.

Whether the force of a value has been fully exhausted by the use of a device in a particular way or requires instantiation by other ways or additional devices, is a highly context-dependent issue. It depends, inter alia, on the strength of the value in the circumstances. For example, the legitimacy of the aforesaid hypothetical

[38] Joseph Raz, *The Morality of Freedom* (OUP 1986) 59.

[39] Kavanagh's arguments must be understood as assuming that the standard of review so formulated is clearly distinct from the substitution of full merits, ie that the reduction in the standard of review that comes with recognition of the appeal versus review distinction manifests a non-negligible degree of deference. Otherwise, that reduction would be unable to express any meaningful degree of deference.

decision to close pubs but not schools would be stronger if the decision had been made after extensive consultation with stakeholders and the general public. Had that been the case, the government would not only enjoy legitimacy as a *general* matter by virtue of the way in which it is constituted and its constitutional role, but also enjoy legitimacy *specific* to the decision in question. In other words, the process of making *that* decision would also be imbued with procedural legitimacy. In this case, it may well be justified for the courts to exhibit both minimal and substantive deference. I do not seek to offer a comprehensive methodology for gauging when a particular way of expressing deference sufficiently accounts for a particular value, only to highlight that instantiating the same value through more than one device does not necessarily lead to double counting. Young is therefore correct to observe that Allan's objection that any substantive deference amounts to double counting is predicated upon

> an argument justifying why minimal deference is sufficient to ensure that the courts perform their proper constitutional function of protecting rights, whilst enabling a proper degree of autonomy to the legislature and the executive, such that substantive deference, even if based on institutional features and earned only in specific situations, would undermine the proper constitutional function of the court.[40]

Young rightly observes that this is an argument that Allan has not offered.

Whether the force of a value has been fully exhausted by the use of a device also depends on how the device is used. For example, relaxing the standard of review from correctness to manifestly without reasonable foundation expresses a degree of deference that is greater than that of relaxing it to unreasonableness simpliciter. Hence, using a single device for deference does not necessarily mean that there has been no double counting. If the way in which a device is used expresses the reason for deference to a degree greater than that due, then double counting has occurred despite only one device being used. Conversely, using more than one device for deference does not necessarily equate to double counting.

The second feature of the concept of double counting is that double counting occurs only when the court gives the *same normative value* for deference—a ground as defined in Chapter 2—more than its due weight. As explained in Chapter 2, the value served by deference is to be distinguished from the factors that suggest the value's existence. A factor may be suggestive of more than one value. If a factor suggests two grounds for deference, then taking that factor into account twice to instantiate the two grounds does not per se lead to double counting. Hence, the worry that deference for democratic reasons may lead to double counting because

[40] Young, 'In Defence of Due Deference' (n 33) 576.

the same feature of the original decision-maker—that is, that it is democratically elected—may be counted for both democratic legitimacy grounds and outcome grounds[41] is misplaced. That a decision-maker is democratically elected is a factor, not a ground, for deference. If this factor suggests the existence of two grounds—1) deference is likelier than non-deference to lead to correct outcomes on the rights issue in question and 2) deference is likelier than non-deference to enhance constitutional legitimacy—then taking it into account twice to cover both grounds does not in itself amount to double counting.

Furthermore, there is no double counting merely by reason of the court giving weight to the same *kind* of value (eg expertise, democratic legitimacy) on different issues within a case. For example, if the executive has superior expertise to determine both the second and third limbs of the proportionality test, then deferring on both limbs does not necessarily equate to double counting. The expertise reasons for deferring at the two limbs relate to two separate issues: one to whether there is a rational connection between the aim and the measure, and the other to whether the measure is no more than necessary. Thus, double counting does not occur merely by reason of the court deferring on more than one limb of the proportionality test to serve the same kind of value. Nor is there double counting merely because the same kind of value is given credit in the proportionality analysis of two different issues in the same case.

By the same logic, there is no double counting merely by reason of the court giving weight to the same kind of value on different issues that arise at different stages of adjudication. For example, double counting does not occur simply because democratic legitimacy is given weight once when the court relaxes the standard of review at the limitation stage and then again when the court chooses a declaration of incompatibility over remedial interpretation at the remedial stage. This is the case because deference may be accorded on the basis of two different issues, one on whether the prima facie limitation is justified, and the other on how the rights violation should be remedied. The aforementioned judicial statements in *Vavilov* and *DA* may therefore be misleading. Even if the court cites a similar kind of reason for deference at both the limitation and remedial stages—for example, that the executive or legislature has more constitutional authority than the court to decide the matter—the rationale for deference is not the same when it relates to different issues raised in the two stages of adjudication because one rationale goes to the issue of limitation, and the other to the issue of remedial discretion.[42] The discussion in this paragraph should nonetheless be subject to the analysis in section VI on the risk of over-deference when the court needs to deal with the same sub-issue of balancing at both the definition and limitation stages.

[41] ibid 578.
[42] See section VI of Chapter 4.

VI. Suspect Categories

Identification of instances of double counting involves judgments of the degree of deference warranted in the circumstances and of the degree that can be explicated by the use of the devices in specific ways, judgments that are highly context dependent. This section highlights three non-exhaustive situations that raise suspicions of double counting, and that should therefore trigger closer examination by commentators and litigants and reflection by the courts concerning whether too much credit has been given to the values being served by deference.

1. According substantive deference in the absence of evidence of a rigorous decision-making process

If, in the absence of evidence of a rigorous decision-making process, the court defers to the executive or legislature for democratic legitimacy reasons both by recognizing the appeal versus review distinction (ie by not applying a standard of review that amounts to substitution of full merits)[43] and by other means (eg by giving weight to the original decision-maker's view that the standard of review is fulfilled), there will be suspicions of double counting. As Kavanagh argues, the legitimacy that the legislature and executive enjoy by virtue of their direct or indirect political accountability to the public applies 'across the board to all legislative and executive decisions, no matter what their content'.[44] It appears that such legitimacy is sufficiently accounted for through recognition of the review versus appeal distinction and that something more that demonstrates the legitimacy of the specific decision in question, such as a rigorous decision-making procedure involving public consultation, is needed for deference over and above such recognition.

2. Use of two devices in highly deferential ways within the same limb of the proportionality test for the same spatial reason

The captioned use occurred in *Kwok Cheuk Kin v Secretary for Constitutional and Mainland Affairs*[45] when the Hong Kong Court of Final Appeal both diluted the standard of review at the third limb of the proportionality test to manifestly without reasonable foundation and gave conclusive weight to the legislature in

[43] As explained in n 39, the assumption here is that the reduction in the standard of review that comes with the recognition of the appeal versus review distinction manifests a non-negligible degree of deference. Otherwise, that reduction will not be able to express any meaningful degree of deference.

[44] Aileen Kavanagh, 'Defending Deference in Public Law and Constitutional Theory' (2010) 126 LQR 222, 227–28.

[45] [2017] HKCFA 44, [2017] 5 HKC 242.

determining whether that standard had been met. In both instances of deference, the reason given for deference was that the courts were unequipped to decide 'matters of political judgment or prediction'.[46] This raises suspicion that the grounds for deference arising from the involvement of political matters were given more than their due weight.[47] The court cited the same brief, spatial justification—'matters of political judgment or prediction'—for both lowering the standard of review and giving weight to the legislature in applying that standard without explaining why the reasons for deference arising from political judgments being involved had not been completely exhausted by lowering the standard of review alone. If the court had given more specific reasons for using each device—first explaining why the court lacked the competence to decide whether the impugned decision was no more than necessary, and then explaining why it was still ill-equipped to assess whether the decision met the lower threshold of manifestly without reasonable foundation—then there would be fewer suspicions that the court deferred twice to achieve the same normative value.

3. Deference on issues of proportionality at the rights definition stage

As mentioned in Chapter 4, the same substantive issue sometimes appears to arise at more than one stage of adjudication. For example, when definitional balancing is mandated by a constitutional text, the issue of whether a fair balance has been struck between a given right and the public interest may appear to arise at both the definition and limitation stages. As I previously explained, although the issue may appear to arise twice, the analyses ultimately pertain to different issues: first to what the scope of the right is, and second to whether the limitation on that right, as defined at the definition stage, is justified. Hence, the issue of overlap is more accurately characterized as a *sub-issue* that arises twice, once in relation to the issue of definition and once in relation to the issue of limitation.

As will become clear from the analysis in section V, deference on the same sub-issue that ultimately pertains to two separate issues does not necessarily lead to double counting. However, that the same sub-issue is involved leads to a greater risk of the court according a degree of deference that is greater than that due. This is the case because in contemplating how much deference to accord on the sub-issue at one stage, the court might inadvertently take into account deference that is due only at the other stage, thereby granting an undue additional degree of deference at one or both stages. To grant the right degree of deference at each stage, the

[46] ibid [55]–[57].

[47] Contrast this case with *Kong Yunming v The Director of Social Welfare* [2013] HKCFA 107, (2013) 16 HKCFAR 950 in which the same court gave weight to the grounds for deference arising from the fact that socio-economic policies were involved by diluting the standard of review to 'manifestly without reasonable foundation' without resorting to any additional devices ([41]–[145]).

court must demarcate deference on the sub-issue that pertains exclusively to each stage. The challenge of this exercise can be illustrated by two examples.

The first example concerns rights on which a constitutional text explicitly mandates definitional balancing. In *Hunter et al v Southam Inc*,[48] the Supreme Court of Canada had to decide whether a scheme for authorizing investigation officers to search business premises complied with section 8 of the Canadian Charter of Rights and Freedoms, which guarantees the 'right to be secure against *unreasonable* search or seizure' (emphasis added). The court held that this wording 'indicates that an assessment must be made as to whether in a particular situation the public's interest in being left alone by government must give way to the government's interest in intruding on the individual's privacy in order to advance its goals, notably those of law enforcement'.[49] The court held that to be reasonable, the authorization procedure must be, inter alia, neutral and impartial and be based on 'reasonable and probable grounds, established upon oath, to believe that an offence [had] been committed and that there [was] evidence to be found at the place of the search'.[50] In arriving at that conclusion, the court engaged in a balancing exercise that is typical of proportionality analysis. It is unclear which portion of its considerations belonged to demarcation of the boundaries of the right at the constitutional level and which to an evaluation of whether the right as defined could be limited at the sub-constitutional level.[51] Assume that there were expertise reasons for deferring to the government on the issue of balancing. To avoid over-deference at the rights definition stage, the court had to grant precisely the right degree of deference that pertained exclusively to the balancing exercise for delineating the scope of the right, and no more, a task that is difficult for even the most capable of judges. The difficulty of delineating the balancing considerations that pertain to the respective stages was recognized by the New Zealand Court of Appeal in *Simpson v Attorney-General*, which remarked that it would be 'paradoxical ... that a search unreasonable within the meaning of s 21 [which, like section 8 of the Canadian Charter, guarantees the right against unreasonable search and seizure] can be reasonably exempted from actionability by invoking s 5 [the limitation clause].'[52]

The difficulty of demarcating the considerations of balancing between the definitional stage and limitation stage has also been recognized in the literature. Barak argues that an advantage of relegating public interest considerations to the limitation stage is that '[t]he different considerations will be presented clearly and most precisely, and the weight each is given will be evident—and thus easier to evaluate and criticize'.[53] Van der Schyff seems to recognize the danger of definitional

[48] [1984] 2 SCR 145.
[49] ibid 159–60.
[50] ibid 162–68.
[51] See Barak (n 4) 33.
[52] *Simpson v Attorney-General* [1994] 3 NZLR 667, 677 (Cooke P).
[53] Barak (n 4) 78–79.

balancing leading to over-deference in arguing that definitional balancing may 'pre-empt' the limitation stage.[54]

In short, given judicial fallibility, deference that is due at the limitation stage may mistakenly find its way into the definitional stage, and vice versa, leading to an overdose of deference.

The foregoing analysis has implications for such debates as whether there should be definitional generosity in rights adjudication or whether internal qualifiers on rights are desirable.[55] Whilst I do not seek to take a stance on such a debate, which hinges on issues beyond the scope of this book, my analysis thus far highlights that one downside of incorporating considerations of balancing between a right and the public interest at the definition stage is that doing so increases the risk of over-deference.

The second example relates to courts incorporating issues of balancing into the definitional stage in the absence of an explicit textual mandate to do so, as happens when, say, the court defers 1) once at the rights definition stage by defining the right narrowly for the reason that if the right were defined broadly, the court would have to adjudicate questions of proportionality that it lacked the expertise and legitimacy to decide, and 2) again at the limitation stage for the reason that it lacks the expertise and legitimacy to conduct the proportionality analysis in the case before it.[56] In *Reference re Public Service Employee Relations Act (Alta.)*,[57] McIntyre J of the Canadian Supreme Court refused to interpret freedom of association to include the rights to strike and collectively bargain, partly because of its belief that if it did so, the courts would be inundated with proportionality questions on labour relations that they were generally institutionally and constitutionally incompetent to assess.[58]

The approach of taking into account the court's lack of competence to assess the proportionality of a measure at the rights definition stage may lead to too much deference. Here is why. The court's reasons for deference at that stage can be categorized into two types: 1) grounds relating to arriving at correct outcomes and enhancing constitutional legitimacy *in the case in question*, that is, to avoid having to deal with proportionality analysis that it lacks the expertise and legitimacy to conduct in the case in question;[59] 2) the ground of ensuring correct outcomes and

[54] Gerhard van der Schyff, *Limitation of Rights: A Study of the European Convention and the South African Bill of Rights* (Willem-Jan van der Wolf 2005) 51.

[55] On those issues, see eg Barak (n 4) 33–37, 76–77, 154; van der Schyff (n 54) 29–124; Butler (n 6); Peter W Hogg, 'Interpreting the Charter of Rights: Generosity and Justification' (1990) 28(4) Osgoode Hall LJ 817; Grégoire CN Webber, *The Negotiable Constitution: On the Limitation of Rights* (CUP 2009); Kai Möller, *The Global Model of Constitutional Rights* (OUP 2012).

[56] For examples of how resource allocation considerations may arise at the various stages of adjudication, see Lawrence David, 'Resource Allocation and Judicial Deference on Charter Review: The Price of Rights Protection According to the McLachlin Court' (2015) 73(1) U Toronto Faculty of L Rev 35.

[57] [1987] 1 SCR 313.

[58] ibid [184]–[185].

[59] I categorize these grounds as falling into the first and second sets of grounds for deference defined in section IV of Chapter 2.

legitimate decisions *in future*, that is, minimizing situations in future in which the courts have to decide questions of proportionality that they lack the expertise and legitimacy to decide.[60] Type 1 grounds are precisely the kind of grounds for deference that would arise at the limitation stage had the court proceeded to that stage. In assessing how much deference to accord on type 1 grounds at the definition stage, the court may inadvertently grant a degree of deference that is due only on the issue of proportionality at the limitation stage. To avoid doing so, the court has to delineate and grant the degree of deference that is due on the issue of the proportionality of the impugned measure at the rights definition stage alone, an exercise that puts the cognitive abilities of the courts to the test. Instances in which the court defers on the issue of the proportionality of the impugned measure at the definitional stage thus call for closer examination of whether there has been too much deference.

VII. Conclusion

This chapter has explored the device(s) that courts should use and the stage(s) of adjudication at which they should defer to express the degree of deference due. The following guidelines can be extracted:

1) To express a significant degree or multiple degrees of deference, the court cannot rely on the burden of proof alone.[61]
2) The degrees of deference exerted by the standard of proof, standard of review, and giving of weight can be compared by assessing how much additional presumptive weight the court affords the primary decision-maker's proposition.[62]
3) In the polities covered by this study, when deference at the definition and limitation stages is exercised in ways that lead to favourable outcomes for the primary decision-maker at those stages, the degrees of deference exemplified at the three stages (ie definition, limitation, remedy) are in decreasing order. Hence, if all three stages of adjudication are capable of expressing the reason for deference concerned, the court should choose to defer at the stage that is most able to exemplify the degree of deference due.[63]
4) According to the definition offered in this chapter, double counting occurs when the court gives undue additional weight to a ground (as defined in

[60] I categorize this ground as falling into the third set of grounds for deference defined in section IV of Chapter 2.
[61] Section II.
[62] Section III.
[63] Section III.

Chapter 2) served by deference. Understood as such, deference using more than one device, taking into account more than once a factor suggesting deference, or deferring for the same kind of reason more than once in a case does not necessarily lead to double counting.[64]

5) Courts should be alert to the possibility of double counting in three non-exhaustive categories of cases, namely, when deference over and above the appeal versus review distinction is given in the absence of evidence of a rigorous decision-making process; when more than one device is used in highly deferential ways within the same limb of the proportionality test for the same spatial reason; and when deference is given on proportionality issues at the rights definition stage.[65]

This chapter completes the analysis of internal logic. Together with Chapter 4, it establishes how courts should defer to accord reasons for deference the appropriate level of instantiation. The stage is now set for Chapter 6, which explores the ways in which the principles of internal logic developed in this book can be condensed into methods that are workable for courts and predictable for litigants.

[64] Section V.

[65] Section VI.

6
Choice of Device III: Practicability

I. Introduction

Chapters 4 and 5 explore how courts should use the six devices—namely, the burden of proof, standard of proof, standard of review, giving of weight, choice of interpretation, and choice of remedy—according to the internal logic of deference, that is, to appropriately instantiate the reasons for deference. Chapter 4 focuses on the qualitative aspect of the internal logic analysis: it explores how courts should choose which device to use and which issue to defer on to express a particular reason for deference. Chapter 5 then analyses the quantitative aspect of that analysis: it explores how courts should choose which device or combination of devices to use, and at which stage of adjudication to defer, to express the appropriate degree of deference.

The book has not thus far considered how methods of deference can be made more practicable in light of human fallibility and resource constraints. If a method for determining when, how, and how much to defer is overly complex or vague, it cannot guide judges to arrive at correct assessments of or consistent judgments on deference across cases, and nor can it allow litigants to reasonably foresee how deference will play out in a particular case, even if the method would result in a perfect degree of deference if applied by an omniscient being. As explained in Chapter 1, these workability and legal certainty concerns are 'external constraints' because they are external to courts' reasons for deferring in the first place. Broadly speaking, whilst such concerns determine the extent to which the court should rely on bright-line rules to determine whether, how and how much to defer (and such rules may or may not point towards deference), reasons for deference speak to whether the court should defer to the executive or legislature's judgment on a substantive issue. Different considerations are involved in determining whether the court should use more bright-line rules on deference and whether it should defer. For example, focusing on court competence as a consideration, the former question depends on the court's competence to decide whether, how and how much to defer, whilst the latter depends on the court's competence to decide a substantive issue.[1]

[1] Although this latter competence is relevant to the former question as well.

Deference in Human Rights Adjudication. Cora Chan, Oxford University Press. © Cora Chan 2024.
DOI: 10.1093/9780198921677.003.0006

An illustration is helpful here. Suppose that the court has to decide whether the executive's decision to ban a terrorist suspect from entering the country is necessary to protect national security. The relative competence of the court and the primary decision-maker to determine whether the ban in question is necessary to protect national security goes to whether the court has reasons to defer to the executive's view that the ban is necessary. In contrast, the concerns of workability and legal certainty, such as whether the court is able to come to consistent judgments on deference across cases, determine whether the court should, in deciding whether to defer to the executive's view, follow a rule stating, for example, 'defer to the primary decision-maker in all national security cases' or 'don't defer to the primary decision-maker in any national security cases'. The two kinds of competence—competence to decide questions of deference and competence to decide a substantive issue—are distinct. A court that is highly competent to decide the latter may be incompetent to decide the former.[2] In those circumstances, there is no competence reason for the court to defer to the primary decision-maker's judgment on the substantive issue in question, but there may be good reasons for asking the court to rely to a greater extent on bright-lines rules to guide its deference judgments.

A perennial issue in the deference discourse is how to ensure that methods of deference are, on the one hand, sufficiently clear and simple to address the external constraints upon them and, on the other, sufficiently nuanced and flexible to reflect the internal logic of deference.[3] Prevalent methods either just meet the former criterion, in which case they are criticized for being too crude to reflect the normative justifications for deference in the case in question, or just meet the latter, in which case they are criticized for being too complex to be practicable. The need for a balanced method is summarized well by the Canadian Supreme Court in *Dunsmuir v New Brunswick*: 'What is needed is a test that offers guidance, is not formalistic or artificial, and permits review where justice requires it, but not otherwise. A simpler test is needed.'[4] In Michael Taggart's words, the search is on for 'a map of the rainbow of review' that is both 'reliable and helpful, and we need willing cartographers'.[5]

This chapter is an attempt at such cartography. It introduces several techniques that can be used to strike a balance between the demands of internal logic and external constraints, and illustrates how they can be put into practice. In what follows, I first explain the inevitable trade-off between the practicability of methods of deference and their flexibility in meeting the normative justifications for deference in a particular case. Sections III–VI then introduce four sets of techniques

[2] An example of this will be given in text to nn 1–10 in Chapter 7.

[3] cf Ernest Lim and Cora Chan, 'Problems with *Wednesbury* Unreasonableness in Contract Law: Lessons from Public Law' (2019) 135 LQR 88, 106.

[4] 2008 SCC 9, [2008] 1 SCR 190 [43].

[5] Michael Taggart, 'Proportionality, Deference, Wednesbury' (2008) 2008 NZ L Rev 423, 454.

for balancing the two considerations: the use of rules, presumptions, and factorial analysis; division of work amongst the deference devices; clear and reliable indicators; and gradating and bundling up of deference devices. Methods adopted by judges or proposed by scholars to accommodate practicability concerns are evaluated in the discussion of the four sets of techniques. Section VII concludes.

II. Trade-Off Between Practicability and Flexibility

Let us begin by introducing the trade-off between (1) making methods of deference more workable and predictable and (2) making them more flexible to account for variations in the degree and means of deference across contexts. The tension between them can alternatively be described as tension between enhancing the ability of deference methods to meet external constraints and increasing their flexibility to meet the demands of internal logic in individual contexts. Such tension is inevitable in a non-ideal world in which judges and litigants are fallible, and is an instance of the familiar tension between predictability and flexibility in deciding whether to adopt rule-based decision-making in adjudication. Let me explain.

To fulfil the requirements of internal logic, courts need to accurately distil the reasons for deference that are applicable to a particular issue, balance them to find an optimal level of deference, and express it using the available deference devices according to the principles set out in Chapters 4 and 5. I call this exercise a 'balancing exercise' in this chapter. Its proper performance requires judges to possess the necessary information to achieve the desired balance and the cognitive abilities to properly process that information, as well as freedom from bias and ill will.[6] To be able to predict what the exercise will yield, litigants also need strong cognitive abilities. In an ideal world in which information is perfect and judges and litigants alike have such abilities, the issue of practicability would not arise: judges would face no difficulty consistently discerning the right amount and means of deference via a case-by-case balancing approach, and litigants would have no difficulty predicting what judges would do. However, in a non-ideal world in which information is imperfect and the cognitive and motivational aspects of judges and litigants' capacities are limited, practicability is an issue, and ways to make the balancing exercise more workable and certain must be found.

To increase workability for judges and certainty for litigants, we inevitably need to rely more on prescriptions stated in the form of 'If X (the trigger), then Y (the consequence in relation to a certain device(s) for deference)', where X and Y are based on categories and distinctions that are clear. What constitutes a clear

[6] Adrian Vermeule, *Judging Under Uncertainty: An Institutional Theory of Legal Interpretation* (HUP 2006) 74–79; Neil K Komesar, *Imperfect Alternatives: Choosing Institutions in Law, Economics and Public Policy* (University of Chicago Press 1994) 124–50.

category or distinction will be further explained in section V.1. I use the term 'formalism' as shorthand for methods that rely on such prescriptions.[7] An example of such a prescription would be 'if the decision being challenged in court is a policy governing entitlement to social welfare benefits (the X), then the standard of review should be diluted to "manifestly without reasonable foundation" (the Y)'.[8] I will refer to this example time and again in this chapter.

The formalist character of a prescription is a matter of degree. It depends on whether the prescription is stated in the form of a rule, presumption, or factorial analysis (a point explored in section III) and on the clarity of the X and Y in the prescription (a point explored in sections V.1 and section VI). For now, I wish only to emphasize that the more formalist a prescription is, the less flexible it is.

To understand why that is the case, we need to delve further into the nature of formalist decision-making. In such decision-making, the X in the prescription relies on categories or distinctions (eg 'policies governing entitlement to social welfare benefits') that are taken as indicators of the presence of a normative justification for the Y.[9] X is taken by, say, judges trying to determine how to defer as a 'factual predicate' that stands 'in a relationship of probabilistic causation to the justification' for consequence Y.[10] The normative justification for Y is deemed more likely to exist in a situation where the factual predicate X is present than in a situation where it is absent, other things being equal.[11] To use the distinction drawn in Chapter 2, X is taken as a factor that indicates that there are grounds for Y, and, where the prescription is normatively justified, X is indeed a factor that indicates such grounds. For example, if the aforementioned prescription on social welfare benefits is normatively justified, then the fact that the decision being challenged is an eligibility criterion for a welfare benefit is an indicator that the balance of expertise, legitimacy, and other reasons for deference points towards a high degree of deference (expressible via dilution of the standard of review from correctness to manifestly without reasonable foundation). The prescription is based on

[7] For the importance of legal categorization, see eg Jason NE Varuhas, 'Taxonomy and Public Law' in Mark Elliott, Jason NE Varuhas, and Shona Wilson Stark (eds) *The Unity of Public Law?: Doctrinal, Theoretical and Comparative Perspectives* (Hart 2018). The word 'formalism' has been used in different ways, see eg Cass R Sunstein and Adrian Vermeule, 'Interpretation and Institutions' (2003) 101 Mich L Rev 885, 920–21; Jeff King, 'Institutional Approaches to Judicial Restraint' (2008) 28(3) OJLS 409, 414 and fn 19. I use 'formalism' here merely as shorthand.

[8] This example is adapted from *R (on the application of DA and others) v Secretary of State for Work and Pensions* [2019] UKSC 21, [2020] 1 All ER 573 [65], [113]–[118]. Note that in a subsequent case, the UK Supreme Court emphasized that the fact that 'judgments of social and economic policy in the field of welfare benefits and pensions' are being challenged is only one factor to be considered by the court in deciding the degree of deference to be accorded in the case in question. That factor needs to be weighed against other factors, including whether suspect grounds of discrimination, which call for less deference, are involved: *R (on the application of SC, CB and 8 children) v Secretary of State for Work and Pensions and others* [2021] UKSC 26, [2022] AC 223 [157]–[161].

[9] See Pierre Schlag, 'Rules and Standards' (1985) 33 UCLA L Rev 378, 381–82.

[10] Frederick Schauer, *Playing by the Rules: A Philosophical Examination of Rule-Based Decision-Making in Law and in Life* (OUP 1991) 29, emphasis omitted.

[11] ibid.

the generalization that where the state needs to determine who is entitled to social welfare benefits, strong deference in the standard of review is warranted. It spares judges from having to engage in a balancing exercise on deference each and every time a social welfare distributive policy is challenged, and thus renders the deference enterprise more workable and predictable.

Nonetheless, reliance on such prescriptions is 'necessarily suboptimal' from the viewpoint of attaining correct deference methods in every case[12] because they are based on generalizations, which by nature are not always true. The generalizations in question may already be known to be over- or under-inclusive at the time of rule formulation.[13] For example, even if the balance of expertise, legitimacy, and other considerations points towards a high degree of deference in many or even most cases involving the allocation of social welfare benefits, when such allocation affects an important right (eg when there is discrimination on a suspect ground), the legitimacy reason for deference may pull towards stronger judicial supervision and hence less deference. The inaptness of a generalization may also be occasioned by subsequent 'discoveries or events that ... falsify' generalizations that had hitherto been thought to be true.[14] For example, the revelation of constant blunders in the resource allocation judgments made by a government department, or the replacement of competent with incompetent personnel thereat, may falsify the previous generalization that the department possesses superior expertise and is hence more likely than the court to be correct on social welfare allocation matters. Imposing strict rules on deference requires judges to resist engaging in the balancing exercise themselves[15] and will as a result yield wrong results in cases in which the generalizations are inapt: '[T]he factual predicate may at times not so much further the justification for the rule as impede it.'[16] As David Dyzenhaus remarks in an oft-cited passage:

> [F]ormalism is formal in that it requires judges to operate with categories and distinctions that determine results without the judges having to deploy the substantive arguments that underpin the categories and distinctions. Since those categories and distinctions must take on a life of their own in order to operate in this detached way, they are capable of determining results that contradict the very arguments for these categories and distinctions.[17]

Hence, the more formalist a prescription on deference is, the less flexible it is for attaining a state of deference that suits a particular context.

[12] ibid 100–01, emphasis omitted; Vermeule, *Judging Under Uncertainty* (n 6) 147.

[13] Schauer (n 10) 37.

[14] ibid 34–37.

[15] ibid 76–85.

[16] ibid 34.

[17] David Dyzenhaus, 'Constituting the Rule of Law: Fundamental Values in Administrative Law' (2002) 27 Queen's LJ 445, 450, internal references omitted.

How much formalism on deference is appropriate for a legal system depends on whether more or less of it would better attain the system's goals, as well as the relative weight of those goals.[18] Typical goals in designing a system of rights adjudication are: 1) justice/correct outcomes for the individual before the court; 2) maximization of justice/correct outcomes in adjudication overall; 3) legal certainty and consistency; and 4) optimal use of scarce public resources. The relative weight of these goals, as well as whether more formalist decision-making would better serve them, depends on the following key variables:

1. The information available to and the cognition and motivation of judges.[19] In general, the more competent and well-informed judges are, the less the need for formalist methods because they are likely to be able to discern the optimal level of deference even without relying on bright-line rules. Conversely, the less competent and informed judges are, the greater the need for bright-line rules to maximize correct judgments on deference (provided that those rules are reliable). A decision-making procedure may be optimal because it maximizes correct outcomes overall even if it is not 'aimed at producing the best result for each case'.[20] Note that competence here refers to the court's competence to make correct assessments about whether—and, if so, how and how much—to defer rather than to its competence to answer the substantive question of, say, whether a measure is proportionate. Even if both sides of the litigation proffer evidence on questions of deference, it may still be desirable for a court that lacks the competence to assess such questions to be guided by bright-line rules on deference.
2. The reliability of the generalizations involved. The higher the probability that the presence of the X indicates a justification for the consequence for the deference device(s) (Y), the more reliable the prescription is and the likelier that reliance on it will lead to the right assessment on deference.
3. The relative competence of the rule-setter and rule-applier,[21] which is related to the two foregoing variables. If the rule-setter (say, supreme court judges) is highly capable of identifying reliable indicators of deference, whereas the rule-applier (say, lower court judges) is generally mediocre and expected to yield high error rates if required to engage in the balancing exercise on deference afresh each time, then the greater the use of bright-line rules on deference would be justified.
4. The ease and likelihood with which judicial errors can be rectified.[22] The easier it is to rectify judicial errors, the less need there is for formalist methods

[18] cf King, 'Institutional Approaches' (n 7) 431–32, on the spectrum between what he calls restrictive institutionalism and contextual institutionalism.
[19] Vermeule, *Judging Under Uncertainty* (n 6) 77–78.
[20] Schauer (n 10) 101.
[21] Vermeule, *Judging Under Uncertainty* (n 6) 69.
[22] ibid 78; Sunstein and Vermeule (n 7) 917.

for judges, assuming the rectifiers are less likely to make errors than the original judges.

5. The cost of a judicial error should it not be rectified. This is a function of the importance of the right at stake, the degree of the rights violation, the importance of the countervailing interest at stake, and the magnitude of the harm to that interest should an erroneous ruling be handed down, and it affects the importance of the goal of maximizing correct outcomes overall. The higher the cost of judicial errors, the more important it is to maximize correct outcomes. In addition, in jurisdictions in which the courts have a special constitutional role in guarding individual rights, the more serious the rights violation, the weightier the goal of ensuring that the court does justice to the individual at stake,[23] and hence the greater the need for flexibility to deviate from prescriptions in individual cases. If the seriousness of the rights violation adds more weight to the goal of ensuring individual justice than to the goal of maximizing correct outcomes, then less-formalist methods may be more appropriate in cases involving important rights than in those involving less important rights, other things being equal.
6. Litigants' competence. The more competent litigants are, the less need there is for formalist methods on deference to enable predictability for them.
7. The resources available to the court.[24] If more time and human resources can be afforded for detailed case-by-case balancing exercises by the courts, then the less need there is for formalist methods on deference.

These variables may vary both across jurisdictions and across contexts of human rights adjudication. Accordingly, more formalism may be justified in one area of human rights adjudication than in another, and in some jurisdictions more than in others. The suitability of formalism is 'not a conceptual issue', but rather a 'contingent and empirical issue that can only be assessed relative to the facts about our legal institutions, given their actual capacities and systemic interactions'.[25]

Having introduced the trade-off between practicability and flexibility and clarified the terminology, let us now examine four sets of techniques for striking a balance between the two. The first set explores the use of rules, presumptions, and factorial analysis, which are distinguished by the different *relationships* between X and Y in their prescriptions. The other three sets look at how the balance between practicability and flexibility could be struck in the formulation of these prescriptions. The second set proposes a method that reduces the chances of having to balance conflicting normative considerations and provides a structure for judicial reasoning, thereby increasing workability. The third set looks at how the X in the

[23] See eg Julian Rivers, 'Proportionality and Variable Intensity of Review' [2006] CLJ 174, 205.
[24] Sunstein and Vermeule (n 7) 918, 922; Komesar (n 6) 147–49.
[25] Vermeule, *Judging Under Uncertainty* (n 6) 75. See also Schauer (n 10) 140–41.

prescription can be made clearer, whereas the final set examines how the Y can be made clearer.

III. Rules, Presumptions, and Factorial Analysis

The first set of techniques for striking a balance between practicability and flexibility includes the use of rules (including rules with exceptions), presumptions, or factorial analysis or a combination thereof. Courts are familiar with the use of such tools, and the purpose of this section is to explain how they strike the aforesaid balance in the deference context. Holding the X (the trigger) and Y (the consequence on certain deference device(s)) in these techniques constant,[26] the techniques can be placed on a spectrum of how the balance is struck, with factorial analysis lying on the end with the most flexibility (least formalist) and decision-making based on rules lying on the end with the least flexibility (most formalist), and rules with exceptions and presumptions lying in between.[27] Hence, where more formalism is appropriate, courts should rely more heavily on techniques towards the rule-based end of the spectrum. Let us now examine the techniques one by one.

Factorial analysis asks the courts to balance multiple factors in determining whether deference is due. Each factor embodies one or more principles[28] that, like rules, can be entered into the formula of 'If X, then Y'. For example, the factor of 'the importance of the right' embodies the principle that the more important the right, the less deference that should be accorded.[29] However, unlike rules, the trigger in each principle merely pulls towards or away from the stated consequence of the device, but is not decisive.[30] Whether the court should yield the consequence ultimately depends on the balancing of all relevant factors. In contrast, in rules analysis, the court treats the presence of the trigger as decisive for rendering the consequence. Factors set 'standards of argumentation' and structure 'how the

[26] This proviso is needed because a rule with a Y that relates to, say, only one of numerous available deference devices may not offer more predictability than a presumption with a Y that relates to, say, all available deference devices in the case.

[27] For discussions of rule-based and standard-based judicial decision-making in rights adjudication, see eg Adrienne Stone, 'Proportionality and Its Alternatives' (2020) 48(1) FL Rev 123, 148–53, Adrienne Stone, 'The Limits of Constitutional Text and Structure: Standards of Review and the Freedom of Political Communication' (1999) 23 Melb U L Rev 668, 687–707.

[28] For the use of factors and principles in the deference context, see Jeff King, *Judging Social Rights* (CUP 2012) 143–44. For principles more generally, see eg Ronald Dworkin, *Taking Rights Seriously* (first published 1977, Duckworth 2005) 22–28.

[29] One factor may embody more than one principle. Eg the factor of 'the identity of the decision-maker' may embody the principle that more deference should be accorded to the legislature than to the executive. However, it may also embody the principle that when a decision-maker has professional expertise (eg is a regulator of a self-regulating legal profession), it should be granted more deference.

[30] King, *Judging Social Rights* (n 28) 144; Dworkin (n 28) 26.

courts ought to deliberate on the depth of scrutiny', whilst rules set 'standards of conduct' and 'dictate particular depths of scrutiny'.[31]

Take the oft-cited multifactorial analysis advanced by Laws LJ in *International Transport Roth GmbH & Ors v Secretary of State For the Home Department*[32] as an example. He put forward four principles of deference: 1) more deference paid to an act of Parliament than to an executive decision; 2) more deference where the European Convention on Human Rights states a right in qualified than when it states a right in unqualified terms; 3) more deference due to the democratically elected branches when the subject matter is particularly within their constitutional responsibility; and 4) more deference due when 'the subject matter lies more readily within the actual or potential expertise of the democratic powers'.[33] These four principles essentially ask the courts to weigh and balance the following factors in determining the degree of deference: the identity of the decision-maker (principles 1 and 2), the nature of the act (principle 1), the nature of the right (principle 2), relative constitutional legitimacy (principle 3), and relative expertise (principle 4). Each principle exerts a pull on deference in a particular direction, but the courts still need to weigh the four principles before deciding how and to what degree to defer in the case in question.[34] Factorial analysis hence differs from rules analysis in that it requires the courts to weigh and balance the individual factors. The process can be especially difficult when the factors pull in different directions. As Michael Taggart remarks: '[A]ll factorial tests are ultimately indeterminate, because the result is not determined necessarily by a majority of factors pointing one way. Some factors in some circumstances count for more in the balancing. There are no rules, and sometimes precious little guidance or certainty.'[35]

Factorial analysis is a common juridical tool in the jurisdictions under study. The Supreme Court of Israel held in *Adalah Legal Centre for Arab Minority Rights in Israel v Minister of Interior* that the degree of deference depends on 'the subject-matter of the law[,] the degree of expertise of the court in the field', and the cost of judicial error.[36] The Hong Kong Court of Final Appeal held in *Hysan Development Co Ltd and others v Town Planning Board* that the degree of deference warranted in rights cases depends on 'the significance of and degree of interference with the right in question', '[t]he content and features of the impugned measure, the identity and constitutional role of its originator and any special competence possessed by such person.'[37] The 'functional and pragmatic approach' adopted by the

[31] Torstein Eckhoff, 'Guiding Standards in Legal Reasoning' (1976) 29(1) CLP 205, 207; Dean R Knight, *Vigilance and Restraint in the Common Law of Judicial Review* (CUP 2018) 183, emphasis omitted.

[32] [2002] EWCA Civ 158, [2003] QB 728.

[33] ibid [83]–[87] (Laws LJ).

[34] Aileen Kavanagh, *The Collaborative Constitution* (CUP 2023) 279–81.

[35] Taggart (n 5) 458.

[36] HCJ 7052/03 [7]–[8] (Justice Grunis).

[37] [2016] HKCFA 84, (2016) 19 HKCFAR 635 [107], [114].

Canadian Supreme Court before the revamp in *Canada (Minister of Citizenship and Immigration) v Vavilov*[38] requires the courts to balance the following factors in deciding the standard of review in administrative law: whether there is a privative clause, relative expertise, purpose of the statute, and nature of the question.[39] In the rights context, the Canadian courts have suggested the following non-exhaustive list of factors: 'the vulnerability of the group that the legislator seeks to protect'; 'that group's own subjective fears and apprehension of harm'; 'the inability to measure scientifically a particular harm'; 'the efficaciousness of a remedy';[40] the nature of the individual interest affected; the degree of complexity and polycentricity; democratic pedigree of the rule; and 'role of moral judgments in setting social policy'.[41] Despite the prevalence of factorial analysis, the Canadian courts recognize that the flexibility it entails comes at the price of certainty and workability. It was this recognition that prompted the Canadian Supreme Court in *Vavilov* to replace the functional and pragmatic analysis with a more rule-based approach.[42]

Factorial analysis has also been advocated by numerous scholars, most prominently by 'due deference' theorists, who prefer flexible, context-specific approaches to deference.[43] For example, Aileen Kavanagh highlighted several factors for 'calibrating' the degree of deference, including the nature of the right, the degree of the rights limitation, the impact of the rights-limiting measure on the applicant, the subject matter of the dispute, relative expertise, and the heightened need for democratically legitimate decision-making on controversial policy issues.[44] Murray Hunt's proposed factorial test includes the nature of the right in question, relative expertise and institutional competence, democratic accountability, and the degree to which other accountability avenues are available.[45] Richard Edwards put forward the following factors: the importance of the right in question, whether mediation between competing groups is involved, whether the legislature has carefully weighted the competing interests, the complexity of the subject matter, the origin of the impugned measure, and whether moral judgments are being made in deciding social policy.[46] Jeff King's proposal focuses on four factors: democratic legitimacy, polycentricity, expertise, and the degree to which flexibility is required

[38] *Canada (Minister of Citizenship and Immigration) v Vavilov* 2019 SCC 65, [2019] 4 SCR 653.

[39] See *Pushpanathan v Canada (Minister of Citizenship and Immigration)* [1998] 1 SCR 982 [29]–[38].

[40] *Thomson Newspapers Co v Canada (Attorney General)* [1998] 1 SCR 877 [90]–[91].

[41] *M v H* [1999] 2 SCR 3 [305]–[321] (Bastarache J); see David Wiseman, 'Managing the Burden of Doubt: Social Science Evidence, the Institutional Competence of Courts and the Prospects for Anti-Poverty Charter Claims' (2014) 33 NJCL 1, 12–13.

[42] *Vavilov* (n 38) [7]–[10].

[43] In addition to nn 45–47, see also Alison L Young, 'In Defence of Due Deference' (2009) 72(4) MLR 554.

[44] Kavanagh, *The Collaborative Constitution* (n 34) 277–79.

[45] Murray Hunt, 'Sovereignty's Blight: Why Public Law Needs "Due Deference"' in Nicholas Bamforth and Peter Leyland (eds), *Public Law in a Multi-Layered Constitution* (Hart 2003) 353–54.

[46] Richard A Edwards, 'Judicial Deference under the Human Rights Act' (2002) 65(6) MLR 859, 874–77.

for the decision in question.[47] King provides by far the most instructive account of how courts can assess each of these factors.[48] His suggestions go a long way towards rendering factorial analysis more workable and predictable. However, the challenge of assigning a weight to each factor and balancing them remains. King himself recognizes that factorial analysis may be difficult to implement and proposes a solution to such difficulty, a point I return to later in this section. It suffices to say for now that factorial analysis finds favour with scholars who advocate for more context-sensitive approaches, reflecting its ability to accommodate context but also correspondingly its relative lack of ability to guide judges and litigants.

Examples of commonly cited factors have already been highlighted in Chapter 2. As that chapter explains, some factors (eg expertise) are more 'proximate' to the grounds for deference than others.[49] The more distant factors may suggest the existence of factors that are closer to the grounds. For example, both the nature of the act and expertise are factors, and the former may suggest the existence of the latter (eg that the act is a factual question may suggest that the original decision-maker has superior expertise to the courts).

Factorial analysis for determining deference is to be contrasted with rule-based decision-making. For the latter, once the relevant facts for ascertaining the presence of the trigger (X) are found, the device-specific consequences (Y) should follow.[50] When the courts determine whether, how, and how much to defer according to rules, they need not balance the underlying normative considerations for deference all over again. Holding X and Y constant for both rule-based and factorial analysis, the former achieves a greater degree of workability and certainty.

Whilst rules seem to be less commonly adopted and advocated for than factorial analysis in the jurisdictions under study, there are nonetheless scholars who favour rules for reasons of certainty.[51] Adrian Vermeule, for example, favours a bright-line rule for statutory and constitutional interpretation in the United States. He argues that whenever statutory or constitutional text is unclear, judges should defer to the interpretation thereof by administrative agencies and legislatures respectively.[52] Rules on deference have also been adopted in case law. In Hong Kong, for example, it has been established that suspect grounds of discrimination attract the 'no more than necessary' formula of the proportionality test coupled with the correctness standard of review, whereas the 'implementation of ... socio-economic

[47] King, *Judging Social Rights* (n 28) part II. See also Vicki C Jackson, 'Thayer, Holmes, Brandeis: Conceptions of Judicial Review, Factfinding, and Proportionality' (2017) 130 Harv L Rev 2348, 2388–94, which proposes a list of factors for determining the degree of judicial deference to legislative fact-finding in the US context.

[48] See also Rosalind Dixon, *Responsive Judicial Review: Democracy and Dysfunction in the Modern Age* (OUP 2023) 131–40, which proposes an elaborate scheme for identifying triggers of various levels of review in cases concerning freedom of expression and positive discrimination.

[49] See section V of Chapter 2.

[50] cf Eckhoff (n 31) 208.

[51] cf Schauer (n 10) 85.

[52] Vermeule, *Judging Under Uncertainty* (n 6).

policy choices regarding the allocation of limited public funds' without possible discrimination on such grounds attracts the manifestly without reasonable foundation standard of review.[53]

Rules can be formulated with exceptions, and when so formulated their context-sensitivity increases. Incorporating exceptions into a rule means introducing more complexity into the X of the formula. In laying down principles for determining the standard of review for administrative decisions, the Canadian Supreme Court in *Vavilov* laid down a rule—that is, the reasonableness standard of review shall apply to the review of administrative decisions—but carved out a few exceptions: where the legislature provides an appeal mechanism to a court or explicitly prescribes by statute what standard the courts should apply; 'constitutional questions'; 'general questions of law of central importance to the legal system as a whole'; and 'questions related to the jurisdictional boundaries between two or more administrative bodies'.[54] The court was of the view that this approach would provide greater certainty than multifactorial analysis while allowing for sufficient context-sensitivity: a 'general rule of reasonableness review, when coupled with these limited exceptions, offers a comprehensive approach to determining the applicable standard of review'.[55]

The use of rules should be distinguished from the use of presumptions. Both presumptions and rules can lead to what have been called 'spatial' approaches[56]—the carving out of wholesale areas of adjudication that warrant high or low degrees of deference—but their locations on the formalism spectrum differ, holding other things constant. The relationship between the X and the Y in the formula differs between decision-making based on rules and that based on presumptions. Whilst X decisively renders Y in a rule, X is a mere rule of thumb for rendering Y in a presumption.[57] Unlike rule-based decision-making, presumptions do not bar judges from balancing the normative considerations that underpin the rule, but merely raise 'the confidence level required to justify taking an action other than that indicated by the rule of thumb'.[58] Depending on how high the confidence level is raised, judges may still engage with the underlying balancing to various degrees. However, it will never be to as high a degree as when the presumption is absent. To ascertain whether a presumption is rebutted, the court may simply take a 'perfunctory glimpse' rather than a 'careful look' at the reasons underpinning the presumption.[59] Frederick Schauer writes that rules of thumb are 'transparent to their

[53] *Kong Yunming v The Director of Social Welfare* [2013] HKCFA 107, (2013) 16 HKCFAR 950 [40]–[41].

[54] *Vavilov* (n 38) [17], [34]–[35].

[55] ibid [17].

[56] Hunt (n 45) 346.

[57] Schauer (n 10) 77–78.

[58] ibid 108; Aileen Kavanagh, *Constitutional Review under the UK Human Rights Act* (CUP 2009) 217.

[59] Schauer (n 10) 91.

substantive justifications' while allowing 'their very existence' as rules of thumb to determine 'whether rules should be set aside when the results they indicate diverge from the results indicated by direct application of their substantive justifications'.[60] Decision-making using rules of thumb, he further suggests, meets the demands of both workability and context-sensitivity: it 'takes account of the virtues of rules without ... elevating those rules into an absurd position of formal importance purely for formality's sake'.[61] Dean Knight similarly argues that presumptions 'provide a degree of predictability which make the forensic process more predictable', while retaining 'judicial discretion and explicitly allow[ing] the particular circumstances to be given effect to if that is necessary'.[62]

Presumptions have been used by judges for determining when, how, and how much to defer. For example, in the pre-*Vavilov* era, the Canadian Supreme Court held in the administrative law context that the following issues 'generally' attract a reasonableness standard: 'questions of fact, discretion and policy as well as questions where the legal issues cannot be easily separated from the factual issues' and 'where a tribunal is interpreting its own statute or statutes closely connected to its function'.[63]

The three techniques—factorial analysis, presumptions, and rules—can be used in combination.[64] For example, in *R (on the application of SC, CB and 8 children) v Secretary of State for Work and Pensions and others*[65] the UK Supreme Court stipulated multifactorial analysis alongside presumptions of a high or low degree of deference when certain matters are involved.[66] Combinations are also prevalent in the literature. King combines his multifactorial analysis with a default position of judicial minimalism. If the result of factorial analysis 'appears cacophonous', the court should presumptively resort to a set of techniques on judicial incrementalism that 'provide a rough heuristic for approximating the result that would respect' such analysis.[67] Julian Rivers argues that the burden of proof should presumptively be on the public authority to demonstrate necessity and balance but that that presumption can be rebutted when factorial analysis dictates a different result. At the same time, he stipulates that the burden should be reversed in the following categories of cases: 'cases in which rights conflict'; '[c]ases turning on arbitrary, but unavoidable, distinctions of degree'; cases that involve 'minor limitations of rights in pursuit of important but diffuse public goods'; and cases that involve 'procedurally-rigorous judgments of proportionality by well-qualified public bodies'.[68]

60 ibid 97.
61 ibid.
62 Knight (n 31) 256–57.
63 *Dunsmuir* (n 4) [51]–[54]. See also *Vavilov* (n 38) [7] and [228] revisiting the jurisprudence.
64 cf Knight (n 31) 256–57.
65 [2021] UKSC 26, [2022] AC 223 [157]–[161].
66 ibid [158]–[161].
67 King, *Judging Social Rights* (n 28) 147.
68 Julian Rivers, 'The Presumption of Proportionality' (2014) 77(3) MLR 409, 428–31.

To conclude, rules, presumptions, and factorial analysis are in order of increasing flexibility and correspondingly decreasing certainty and workability, holding other things constant, and can be used in combination to alleviate the downside of applying each technique in a standalone manner. The greater the extent to which formalism is appropriate, the more the courts should rely on techniques on the rule-based end of the spectrum.

IV. Division of Work Amongst Deference Devices

The second set of techniques relates to the mapping of the normative considerations underlying deference onto specific devices. I suggest two ways of such mapping. The first enhances workability by reducing the possibility of the normative considerations underlying each device pulling in opposite directions, thereby assuaging the difficulty of determining how specific devices should be used. The second enhances workability by providing a structure that facilitates judicial reasoning. I now explain each suggestion in turn.

One challenge to the workability of deference is that the normative considerations that underlie deference may pull in different directions. In those circumstances, judges have to assign weights to the different normative considerations and balance them in order to determine whether, and if so how, to relax certain deference devices. The challenge of weighing and balancing factors that pull in different directions has been widely recognized. The UK Supreme Court in *SC* recognized that '[i]n any given case', a 'range of factors which tend to heighten, or lower, the intensity of review ... may be present, possibly pulling in different directions, and the court has to take them all into account in order to make an overall assessment ... [S]ome factors have greater weight than others.'[69] Torstein Eckhoff remarks that 'a weighing of reasons which pull in different directions can give rise to considerable doubt and scruples'.[70] One technique that alleviates this difficulty is to institute some division of work amongst the devices, that is, to map the normative considerations underlying deference onto specific devices so as to minimize the number of considerations that determine the use of each device, and hence the possibility of conflict between those considerations in relation to each device. Such a division of work alleviates the difficulty of determining how specific devices should be used.[71]

This approach was employed by Mark Elliott for both analytical and practicability reasons. On his account, the burden and standard of proof and standard

[69] *R (on the application of SC, CB and 8 children)* (n 8) [99].

[70] Eckhoff (n 31) 208.

[71] Lim and Chan (n 3) 108–09. Although admittedly it may not significantly alleviate the difficulty of ascertaining what the overall outcome of the case will be, given that multiple devices may be at play.

of review (what he calls 'intrinsic deference') are determined solely by the importance of the right concerned, whilst the giving of weight (what he calls 'adjudicative deference') is determined by the relative institutional and constitutional competence of the court and the original decision-maker in deciding the issue.[72] Elliott argues that this division of work supplies 'a form of analytical (as well as descriptive) granularity that is helpful, in that it enables the concerns that animate calls for deference to be invested with degrees of relevance and weight that reflect the full range of issues—normative, constitutional and institutional—that are in play', a granularity that cannot be captured by approaches based on 'a single doctrinal standard'.[73] This argument is premised on the difficulty of weighing and balancing conflicting normative considerations, although Elliott did not explicitly express such a premise. In the absence of such difficulty, there would be no reason for approaches based on a single doctrinal standard to be unable to capture the 'full richness' of the underlying normative considerations.[74] The single standard would simply need to reflect the outcome of the weighing and balancing of all relevant considerations. Precisely because of the difficulty of weighing and balancing, however, such approaches are not feasible. Mapping different considerations onto different deference devices alleviates this difficulty and contributes to 'temper[ing] an open-textured approach that is appropriately sensitive to [the] underlying concerns with one that recognises the practical need to avoid reducing the field to a state of unhelpful shapelessness'.[75] For the reasons explained in Chapter 4, the precise division advocated by Elliott (ie intrinsic deference determined solely by the importance of the right, and adjudicative deference by relative institutional and constitutional competence) falls foul of the internal logic behind the deference devices.[76] Nonetheless, his insight that a division of work amongst the devices can alleviate practicability concerns remains valid.

A division of work amongst deference devices was also deployed by the Canadian Supreme Court in *Vavilov*, partly to address practicability concerns. In order to 'bring greater coherence and predictability'[77] into the deference framework, aspects of which had hitherto been 'unclear and unduly complex',[78] the court held that from then on the standard of review would be determined solely by considerations of the legislative allocation of power and rule-of-law considerations.[79] Relative expertise should no longer be taken into account in determining

[72] Mark Elliott, 'From Bifurcation to Calibration: Twin-Track Deference and the Culture of Justification' in Hanna Wilberg and Mark Elliott (eds), *The Scope and Intensity of Substantive Review: Traversing Taggart's Rainbow* (Hart 2015) 65–82.

[73] ibid 84.

[74] ibid.

[75] ibid 75.

[76] Text to nn 68–73 in Chapter 4.

[77] *Vavilov* (n 38) [10].

[78] ibid [21].

[79] ibid [10].

the standard of review because it is difficult to assess, although it would be relevant in determining whether a standard of review has been discharged (in the parlance of this book, how much the giving of weight device should be used).[80] Again, for the reasons explained in Chapter 4,[81] the exclusion of expertise considerations from determination of the standard of review is arbitrary from the internal logic point of view, but the insight that we can map normative considerations onto deference devices is one that is worth exploring.

Based on the arguments developed in Chapter 4, I have two suggestions for how such mapping can be achieved without compromising the internal logic of deference. First, as explained in that chapter, certain considerations can be expressed through the burden and/or standard of proof, but not through the standard of review, namely, the prior probability theory, the relative difficulties of proof, and minimizing the social costs of an erroneous ruling.[82] In contrast, the relative ability and legitimacy of the original decision-maker and the court to determine the rights issue can be expressed through both the burden and standard of proof and the standard of review. In addition, considerations concerning such ability and legitimacy can also be expressed through the giving of weight device. Accordingly, it would make sense to have the burden and standard of proof focus on accommodating considerations that uniquely underpin them, leaving the standard of review and the giving of weight device to be determined by considerations of relative ability and legitimacy. This suggestion would not completely obviate the need to weigh and balance conflicting considerations, but would reduce such need in relation to the application of specific devices without sacrificing their internal logic.

In addition to this way of dividing work amongst the devices, another means of work division is possible, although its aim is not to reduce the risk of conflict between the normative considerations that underlie the same device, but rather to provide a structure for judicial reasoning, thereby enhancing workability. According to the analysis in Chapter 4,[83] there can be a division of work between the standard of review and the giving of weight device along temporal lines. The standard of review enters the scene earlier than the giving of weight device. It has to be set before the court can closely examine the merits of the case. Further, it inevitably has to be set according to doctrinal classifications that are visible to the court before it closely examines the merits. These doctrinal classifications are based on indicators of the balance of, say, expertise and legitimacy reasons for deference. As Chapter 2 explains, indicators (which are by nature factors rather than grounds for deference) at best only approximate the degree of deference that is actually due in the circumstances.[84] In contrast, the giving of weight

[80] ibid [27]–[31].
[81] See section III.2 of Chapter 4.
[82] See section III.4 of Chapter 4.
[83] See section IV of Chapter 4.
[84] See section III of Chapter 2 and section II.

device enters the scene once the court has a better idea of whether the normative justifications for deference indeed exist in the case in question, and it can accommodate deference concerns that arise or become clear to the court only at this relatively late stage. The device can therefore be used to fine-tune the level of deference accorded,[85] thereby bringing it closer to the level that is actually due in the circumstances. Based on this temporal consideration, there can be a division of work between the standard of review and giving of weight device. The standard of review is to be determined according to the doctrinal classifications that are indicators of the balance of considerations of relative ability and legitimacy, whereas the giving of weight device can be deployed to adjust the amount of deference granted.

An illustrative example of the last-mentioned division of work is in order. Suppose that the court needs to assess whether a seven-year residency requirement for obtaining social welfare is a proportionate limitation on the right to equality.[86] Assume that the fact that the measure under challenge is a socio-economic matter involving the allocation of scarce resources is an indicator that the court is less likely than the decision-maker to be correct about, and has less legitimacy to decide, the rights issue at stake, a reason for diluting the standard of review from correctness to manifestly without reasonable foundation. The court may dilute the standard of review in such fashion based on that reason, but the degree of deference manifested may not precisely reflect the actual degree warranted by the balance of competence and legitimacy considerations in the circumstances. When the court engages closely with the merits of the case—asking, for example, whether the residency requirement in question is manifestly without reasonable foundation—it can assess whether the original decision-maker indeed, say, adopted a democratic procedure in introducing the requirement and indeed, say, has more expertise than the court to determine the matter. If the answers to the questions are negative, the court can rigorously demand cogent arguments from the primary decision-maker to demonstrate that the measure is not manifestly without reasonable foundation. Alternatively, if the answers are positive, the court can give more weight to the primary decision-maker's arguments.

V. Clear and Reliable Indicators

As section II explains, how formalist a prescription (of 'if X [the trigger], then Y [the consequence for a certain device(s) for deference]') is depends on whether the prescription takes the form of a rule, presumption, or factorial analysis and on

[85] Paul Craig, 'Varying Intensity of Judicial Review: A Conceptual Analysis' [2022] PL 442, 446–47.
[86] Adapted from the facts of *Kong Yunming* (n 53).

how clear the X and Y in the prescription are. Section II further explains that the X may rely on categories and distinctions that serve as indicators of the existence of the justification for Y. The third set of techniques is designed to enhance the clarity of such indicators, as well as their reliability to indicate the existence of a justification for Y. Where more formalism is desirable, the court should rely on clearer and more reliable indicators. This section's key suggestions can be summarized as follows. First, because clarity and reliability are highly context dependent, the court should ensure that prescriptions for deference remain open to review and should not blindly import prescriptions from other jurisdictions. Second, where more practicability is desired, the court should avoid relying on indicators that are vague and require highly evaluative judgments, but should instead rely on indicators that cover fewer grounds for deference and are closer to those grounds, and it should also avoid conflicts between prescriptions. Finally, spatial approaches are not necessarily unjustified.

In the following, I first discuss clarity before moving on to a discussion of reliability.

1. Clarity

For a prescription to be able to guide, judges and litigants must be able to identify certain features as instances of a category stated in the trigger of that prescription. They must have a common understanding of the membership of the category at least in relation to the typical cases that come before the court.[87] For example, in the jurisdictions under study, there is usually no disagreement over whether a decision being challenged is an eligibility condition for social welfare benefits. Perfect common understanding is not possible, but there has to be a close enough common understanding at least in relation to the usual cases for the prescriptions to guide. Prescriptions that rely on categories for which such common understanding is lacking are therefore to be avoided. In this chapter, I use 'clear indicators' and 'clear categories' (and the like) merely as shorthand for indicators and categories for which such common understanding is present.

Whether such common understanding exists is highly contextual. The meaning of a phrase may be clear to audiences in one jurisdiction but not in another, in one human rights context but not in another, and at one point in time but not at another. The less sharp the boundaries of categories are, and the more their application relies on evaluative concepts,[88] the less likely common understanding is to be attained. Let me illustrate by way of two commonly used indicators.

[87] cf Schauer (n 10) 138; HLA Hart, *The Concept of Law* (3rd edn, OUP 2012) 123–26.

[88] See eg Timothy AO Endicott, *Vagueness in Law* (OUP 2000) ch 2, 126–31; Jeremy Waldron, 'Vagueness in Law and Language: Some Philosophical Issues' (1994) 82 Cal L Rev 509, 512–14, 516–29.

The first is the distinction between 'law' or 'rights' on the one hand and 'policy' or 'politics' on the other. Case law is replete with remarks to the effect that questions of policy or politics, as opposed to questions of law or rights, attract a high degree of deference. The policy or politics label is given as a reason for strong deference. For example, in *R (Williamson and others) v Secretary of State for Education and Employment and others*, Lord Nicholls remarked that 'Parliament was entitled to take this course [ie ban corporal punishment in schools] because this issue is one of broad social policy. As such it is pre-eminently well suited for decision by Parliament. The legislature is to be accorded a considerable degree of latitude....'[89] Similarly, in *Iarnród Éireann v Ireland*, the Irish Supreme Court remarked that it could not accept the validity of a challenge to a statute that apportioned liability between wrongdoers because 'for the Oireachtas so to provide is within its competence in what is truly an area of policy'.[90]

To understand what is meant by the distinction between law/rights and policy/politics, we need to first set aside an obvious non-starter,[91] that is, that the realms of law/rights and policy/politics are entirely separate. Lord Hoffmann's remark in *A v Secretary of State for the Home Department* ('*Belmarsh*') that '[W]e are not dealing here with matters of social or economic policy ... We are dealing with actions ... which affect the rights and freedoms of the individual'[92] could be read as suggesting such a separation. This view of law/rights and policy/politics—seeing the two as distinct and non-overlapping—is problematic in the rights adjudication context because in that context the courts are asked precisely to assess the constitutionality of policy choices made by executive and legislative authorities. The legal question that the courts need to assess in rights adjudication involves an evaluation of the government's policy choices; hence, the nature of the question before the court necessarily involves both realms. If any legal question that touches on policy choices would attract a high degree of deference, then the distinction would be virtually meaningless: a high degree of deference would be needed in all cases. Therefore, to make sense of the law/rights versus policy/politics distinction as a prescription for a high or low degree of deference in the rights adjudication context, it is necessary to understand the distinction in another way.

The distinction can alternatively be understood as suggesting a *spectrum* on which the properties of politics/policy and law/rights exist, with one end occupied by purely political matters and the other by purely legal matters. This understanding seems compatible with that of some judges. For example, in *Belmarsh*, Lord Bingham phrases the distinction in the following way: '[t]he more purely political ... a question is, the more appropriate it will be for political resolution and the

[89] [2005] UKHL 15, [2005] 2 AC 246 [51] (Lord Nicholls).

[90] [1996] 3 IR 321, 376. See also Brian Foley, *Deference and the Presumption of Constitutionality* (Institute of Public Administration 2008) 140.

[91] cf Foley (n 90) 87–88.

[92] [2004] UKHL 56, [2005] 2 WLR 87 [108] (Lord Hoffmann).

less likely it is to be an appropriate matter for judicial decision. The smaller, therefore, will be the potential role of the court....'[93] Similarly, in *Paul Rodney Hansen v The Queen*, the New Zealand Supreme Court remarked that 'there is a spectrum which extends from matters which involve major political, social, or economic decisions at the one end to matters which have a substantial legal content at the other. The closer to the legal end of the spectrum, the greater the intensity of the court's review is likely to be.'[94]

Unlike the view that sees law and politics as distinct and non-overlapping, this understanding of the distinction makes sense in the rights adjudication context. However, as has been widely acknowledged, the distinction has been 'applied in an inconsistent ... manner'.[95] Contrast, for example, *R (on the application of Carson) v Secretary of State for Work and Pensions*, in which the UK House of Lords treated the eligibility criteria in a pension scheme as a policy and political matter attracting a high degree of deference,[96] with *R (Elias) v Secretary of State for Defence*, in which the English and Welsh Court of Appeal treated the eligibility criteria in an ex gratia compensation scheme as not amounting to a political matter worthy of such deference.[97] That the distinction would be applied in an inconsistent manner is unsurprising given that it requires the courts to answer such questions as whether a matter is so significantly political as to warrant a high degree of deference, questions that hinge on concepts with highly imprecise boundaries. This second reading of the law versus politics distinction is therefore an example of non-clarity in situations in which the application of a category requires the application of concepts whose boundaries are highly imprecise.

Consider also the commonly used category of 'complex' or 'difficult' judgments made by the executive or legislature, which the courts have said indicates that a high degree of deference is due. For example, in *Divito v Canada (Public Safety and Emergency Preparedness)*, the Canadian Supreme Court stated that a large degree of deference should be accorded 'given the complex social and political problems being tackled'.[98] Likewise, in *Patrick Hyland v Minister for Social Welfare*, the Irish High Court remarked that given that 'the legislation is of its nature difficult and complex', a high degree of deference must be granted.[99]

The concepts of 'complexity' and 'difficulty' require the court to assess whether a rights issue is too difficult for it to handle, a value judgment that hinges on concepts with imprecise boundaries. There is bound to be considerable disagreement over a given matter's level of complexity and difficulty and over what level thereof suffices

93 *Belmarsh* (n 92) [29].
94 [2007] NZSC 7, [2007] 3 NZLR 1 [116] (Tipping J).
95 See eg King, *Judging Social Rights* (n 28) 124–25.
96 [2005] UKHL 37, [2005] 4 All ER 545 [17], [45], [78], [80].
97 [2006] EWCA Civ 1293, [2006] 1 WLR 3213 [289]–[294] (Arden LJ).
98 2013 SCC 47, [2013] 3 SCR 157 [85] (LeBel and Fish JJ).
99 [1989] IR 624, 631; Foley (n 90) 153.

to render a matter sufficiently complex and difficult to warrant a high degree of deference. These and other categories and distinctions for which common understanding of their application is likely to be absent should therefore be avoided if certainty and workability are to be enhanced.

I acknowledge that it may not be feasible to ask courts to completely exclude the aforementioned law/rights versus politics/policy distinction or the concept of 'complex judgments' from their reasoning, given the prevalence of such a distinction and concept. Nevertheless, even if courts retain them in their reasoning, they should endeavour not to give the misimpression that the distinction and concept can, as they stand, offer meaningful guidance on deference. Whilst it may be acceptable for a court to use these notions as conclusory labels, they should not be presented as 'obviat[ing] the need for a method of analysis'.[100] For example, rather than simply remarking that 'because the matter involved is a policy matter, a high degree of deference is warranted', courts should explain *why*, independent of the law and policy labels, they consider the matter to warrant a high degree of deference.

2. Reliability

To enhance the ability of formalist prescriptions to do individual justice, the reliability of the indicators needs to be increased. The reliability of an indicator refers to how closely it reflects the actual level of deference that the balance of reasons for deference yield in that instance. The higher the probability that the set of facts referred to in the indicator reflects the justification for the consequence of deference stated in the prescription, the lower the deference error rate and the more reliable the indicator. Error occurs when the indicator suggests a certain level of deference, but the balance of reasons in that instance does not actually warrant a level of deference approximate to that level. In other words, the indicator is overinclusive.[101]

Take the aforesaid prescription on distribution of social welfare benefits as an example. The prescription states that when the decision being challenged is an allocative policy on social welfare benefits, the court should dilute the standard of review to manifestly without reasonable foundation. If the balance of reasons for deference that underlie the standard of review (eg the relative ability and constitutional legitimacy of the court and primary decision-maker to determine the rights issue at hand) justifies a high degree of deference in that standard in, say, 95 per cent of cases concerning social welfare allocation policies, then the aforesaid indicator—that is, policies allocating social welfare benefits—is highly reliable.

[100] King, *Judging Social Rights* (n 28) 124.

[101] See eg Paul Daly, 'The Unfortunate Triumph of Form over Substance in Canadian Administrative Law' (2012) 50 Osgoode Hall LJ 317, 342.

Conversely, if such balance points to a high degree of deference in, say, only 10 per cent of such cases, then the deference-related error rate of relying on the prescription is high, and the indicator is unreliable.

Under-inclusivity occurs when there are instances other than those suggested by the indicator that warrant the level and means of deference stated in the prescription. For example, one might say that the prescription on social welfare policy is under-inclusive because it does not exhaust all situations warranting a dilution of the standard of review to manifestly without reasonable foundation. However, under-inclusivity is not an *error* of the prescription on social welfare policy itself, and, contrary to some commentators' views,[102] is not a problem for the overall scheme of deference if the courts have other ways (eg other prescriptions) to accommodate other situations calling for a similar level and means of deference.

A few further observations about the reliability of indicators are in order. First, formalist prescriptions can be devised at various levels of generality. For example, one could stipulate a rule on deference for all human rights cases in relation to all devices, a rule on deference for all human rights cases in relation to the standard of review alone, and a rule on social welfare policies and in relation to the standard of review alone. The higher the level of generality, the larger the number of grounds for deference that the indicator needs to cover. There are at least three dimensions along which the generality of a prescription can vary. The first is the number of grounds for deference. For example, one could prescribe national security matters as an indicator of superior constitutional legitimacy on the part of the government, but not of its superior ability to arrive at correct outcomes. The second dimension is the number of devices, which indirectly affects the number of grounds an indicator covers. For example, one could prescribe national security matters as an indicator of strong deference for the burden of proof, standard of proof, standard of review, and giving of weight rather than for just one of these devices. In that case, the indicator would have to indicate the balance of the grounds for deference that underlie all of the aforementioned devices rather than just one of them. The third dimension is the number of issues covered by the indicator, which, like the number of devices, indirectly affects the number of grounds for deference covered by the indicator. The larger the number of issues—or, in the parlance of Canadian practice, the less the question of deference is 'segmented'[103]—the greater the number of grounds for deference the indicator has to cover. One could prescribe that national security matters lead to a high degree of deference in relation to proportionality analysis but not in relation to rights definition analysis. In that case, the indicator would need to reflect the balance of deference reasons underlying the proportionality test, but not that underlying rights definition analysis.

[102] See eg ibid 348.

[103] David Mullan, 'Unresolved Issues on Standard of Review in Canadian Judicial Review of Administrative Action—The Top Fifteen' (2013) 42 Advoc Q 1, 64–68.

Second, the larger the number of grounds for deference that an indicator needs to cover, the more difficult it is likely to be to design a reliable indicator. When multiple grounds for deference are involved, how much deference is due requires a summation of the deference called for by those grounds. The exercise is harder still when the grounds pull deference in opposite directions, in which case the precise calibration of whether, and if so, how much, deference is due becomes even more challenging. The upshot of the two aforementioned observations is that the higher the level of generality at which an indicator is formulated, the more difficult it is likely to be to devise reliable indicators. The challenge is compounded in situations in which there is a strong likelihood of the grounds pulling in different directions. As Daly remarks, '[d]elegated decision-makers can be more or less democratically legitimate, relative to one another, relative to the different types of decision that they render, and relative to reviewing courts'.[104] Coming up with a reliable indicator of the level of deference due a particular decision-maker in all circumstances is more challenging than formulating one for a specific circumstance.

Third, although the task of formulating an indicator is more challenging when the underlying grounds are likely to pull in different directions than when they are likely to point in the same direction, it is not impossible. The fact that the grounds pull in different directions does not in itself invalidate an indicator in that particular instance. An indicator is valid when it represents the *conclusion* on the *balance* of the underlying grounds for deference, which is a function not just of the *impact* of deference or non-deference on such grounds but also of the relative *weight* of those grounds. An indicator may accurately reflect a high degree of deference even when one ground—say, the legitimacy ground—pulls against deference if another ground—say, the correct outcomes ground—pulls towards deference and is a lot weightier than the legitimacy ground in the circumstances.

Fourth, whether an indicator is reliable is an empirical question and is highly context dependent. National security matters may be a reliable indicator of a high level of deference in one jurisdiction but not in another in which the security institutions are less competent. A controversial issue on sexual mores and changing social attitudes may be a reliable indicator of remedial deference in a jurisdiction in which the legislature is sensitive to individual rights and changes in societal attitudes, but not in a jurisdiction in which the legislature lacks such sensitivity. The reliability of indicators can also change over time.[105] As explained above, a generalization may be falsified or strengthened over time. The replacement of competent personnel with incompetent personnel at national security institutions would render national security matters unreliable as an indicator of a high degree of deference on the outcome ground for deference. The implication is twofold: evaluations of indicator reliability must be contextual and empirically based, and, to

[104] Paul Daly, *A Theory of Deference in Administrative Law: Basis, Application and Scope* (CUP 2012) 106.

[105] Schauer (n 10) 35.

ensure that indicators are valid, they should not be blindly imported from other jurisdictions and should remain open to review.[106]

Fifth, it should be clear from the foregoing observations that 'spatial approaches' to deference, that is, the carving out of wholesale subject areas as warranting high or low levels of deference, are not *necessarily* unjustified. A key criticism of such approaches centres around the fact that the indicators used in spatial approaches may be wrong in particular cases and only approximate the level of deference due in others.[107] As acknowledged in section II, this is a necessary price to pay for the workability and predictability that such indicators can bring. Whether use of a particular indicator is justified depends on the factors highlighted in section II. Observations on the general unreliability of indicators, such as the following remark by Tom Hickman, therefore have to be tested against empirical evidence:

> [i]t is unsafe to reason from more specific generalisations or categories of cases, such as that the case ... raises an issue of public morals, or concerns a ministerial decision ... to the conclusion that weight should be afforded, because such generalisations will *very often* not be true.[108]

In a context in which the risk of judicial error on questions of deference is high, and reliable indicators on deference can be identified, a spatial approach in the form of bright-line rules or presumptions on deference may well be justified, all things considered. Hence, at an abstract level, spatial approaches should not be ruled out;[109] such approaches would be unjustified only if the balance of factors highlighted in section II suggested that the costs to context-sensitivity they brought about outweigh their benefits to practicability.

Sixth, an indicator's distance from the underlying grounds for deference varies. Some indicators are directly that of a balance of such grounds, whilst others are indicators of indicators of such grounds. There can be tiers of indicators, a point that has been touched upon in section III and in Chapter 2.[110] For example, predictive judgments on human behaviour may be an indicator that the executive has greater ability to arrive at correct decisions in a matter, but national security matters may be an indicator of, inter alia, the existence of such predictive judgments. Indicators that are closer to the balance of the ultimate grounds for deference are likely to

[106] cf King, *Judging Social Rights* (n 28) 148, 301–03.

[107] See eg Hunt (n 45) 348–49.

[108] Tom Hickman, *Public Law after the Human Rights Act* (Hart 2010) 137–38, emphasis added.

[109] This does not mean that their use should not be eschewed in particular contexts where the balance of factors weighs against them. I therefore take no view on whether the prevalent views in the literature against spatial approaches in the United Kingdom are justified other than to highlight that any views for or against such approaches have to be tested against empirical evidence. For said views in the literature, see eg Hunt (n 45); Young (n 43); Kavanagh, *The Collaborative Constitution* (n 34) 281–95; Kavanagh, *Constitutional Review* (n 58) part II; Aileen Kavanagh, 'Defending Deference in Public Law and Constitutional Theory' (2010) 126 LQR 222; Jeff King, *Judging Social Rights* (n 28).

[110] See section V of Chapter 2.

be more reliable than indicators that are higher up the ladder, assuming that the latter are not indicators of other features relevant to that balance. This is because in that case the latter are subject to a further probability discount. For example, if 90 per cent of predictive judgments reflect the superior ability of the government to arrive at correct decisions, and 70 per cent of national security decisions contain predictive judgments, then the probability of national security matters reflecting the superior ability of the government to arrive at correct decisions is 90 per cent × 70 per cent = 63 per cent, assuming that national security matters are not an indicator of any other features relevant to the presence or absence of such superior ability. However, this proviso may not be true. National security matters may be taken as an indicator of superior ability to arrive at correct decisions for reasons other than that it may contain predictive judgments.

Finally, formalist prescriptions are better able to guide when there are fewer conflicts between the prescriptions. Conflicts occur when, for example, the prescriptions overlap but pull deference in different directions. For example, if one prescription states that socio-economic matters involving the allocation of scarce resources attract the manifestly without reasonable foundation standard of review and another states that cases involving suspect grounds of discrimination attract a correctness review on the 'no more than necessary' formula, and if socio-economic decisions can involve discrimination on suspect grounds, then a conflict can arise between the two rules. The conflict can be resolved by, say, erecting a hierarchy between the two prescriptions. That is what happened in Hong Kong, where the courts decided that the latter prescription takes priority such that when socio-economic decisions involve discrimination on suspect grounds, they attract the more rigorous standard of review.[111]

Let us now apply the aforementioned observations to examine the commonly used indicator of the 'balancing of competing interests'. Case law is full of remarks to the effect that government decisions that require 'a balance to be struck' between 'competing interests' should attract a high degree of deference because the political authorities have more legitimacy than the courts to strike that balance. For example, in *Chaoulli v Quebec (Attorney-General)*, the Canadian Supreme Court held that 'courts must show deference' in 'situations in which the government is required to mediate between competing interests....'[112] Similarly, in *Tuohy v Courtney*, the Irish Supreme Court held that because 'the Oireachtas ... is essentially engaged in a balancing of constitutional rights and duties', the courts should not intervene unless the impugned law is 'so contrary to reason and fairness as to constitute an unjust attack on some individual's constitutional rights'.[113] Applying the earlier observations in this section, this indicator of the 'mediation of competing interests' stands out

111 *Kong Yunming* (n 53) [40]–[41].
112 2005 SCC 35, [2005] 1 SCR 791 [94] (Deschamps J).
113 [1994] 3 IR 1, 47 (Finlay CJ); Foley (n 90) 129.

for being overly inclusive by a wide margin across all constitutional rights contexts. Given that most, if not all, decisions being challenged in rights adjudication require a balancing of a right and an interest or the interests of competing groups, the deployment of the aforementioned indicator in a rule context would require a high level of deference across many human rights contexts. However, whilst the balance of deference reasons may point to a high level of deference in some of those contexts, there are a large number in which it would not. For example, the legitimacy ground for deference may be weak when the individual right at stake is highly important, calling for stronger judicial supervision. Hence, the indicator of the mediation of competing interests clearly over-shoots by a wide margin in human rights cases, and should not be used as a trigger in a rule for the benefit of indicator reliability.

To conclude, where more formalism is desired, courts should rely on clearer and more reliable indicators of deference. Because both clarity and reliability are context dependent, courts should not blindly adopt indicators from other jurisdictions and should ensure that the indicators they employ remain open to review. To enhance clarity, courts should avoid relying on overly vague or highly evaluative indicators. To enhance reliability, they should rely on indicators that cover fewer grounds for deference and are closer to those grounds. Courts should also not automatically assume that spatial approaches are problematic and avoid setting conflicting prescriptions.

VI. Gradating and Bundling of Devices

Section V proposes ways of striking a balance between practicability and flexibility in formulating the X in an 'If X (the trigger), then Y (the consequence in relation to a certain device(s) for deference)' prescription. The present section considers a set of techniques for striking that balance in formulating the Y in the prescription. Such consequence is stated in the form of certain means of relaxing or strengthening the application of a deference device(s). The cruder these means are, the more easily implementable they are, but also the less likely they are to precisely reflect the level of deference due and the way in which it should be exhibited. This section suggests three ways of enhancing the practicability of Y: setting finite scales that rely on fewer standards (of, say, review) and rely less on evaluative judgments, setting finite scales for the giving of weight device, and developing levels of scrutiny that combine various devices.

1. Setting of finite scales

One technique for rendering the means of adjusting the devices more practicable is to delineate 'a number of pre-defined standards', which is more workable than relying on 'a continuum of limitless possibilities'.[114] Knight calls these 'finite scales' and 'infinite scales', respectively, and argues that the former is 'more likely to exact control of judicial discretion and ensure operational coherence'.[115] A finite scale, he further argues, ensures 'panoptic flexibility', noting that 'any loss of flexibility associated with limited precision is marginal'.[116] The ease with which a finite scale can be implemented is a function of the number of standards and the extent to which common understanding of the meaning of those standards can be developed. Regarding the former, the greater the number of standards, the less workable and predictable they are, given that 'cognitive capacities are typically inadequate to sustain a fine-grained schema of deference standards'.[117] Experience from the jurisdictions under study also seems to suggest that three is the maximum number of standards of review that a court is able to handle insofar as the capacities of the courts in those jurisdictions are concerned. Settled doctrine in the jurisdictions has coalesced around two to three standards of review and proof, and scholars' suggestions rarely go beyond three.[118] However, the extent to which the scale can guide also depends on the extent to which the addressees of those standards have a common understanding of the standards' meaning, an issue to which we now turn.

Common understanding of what certain standards (of, say, review) require is likelier to be achieved when those standards require little evaluative judgment on the part of the court. In none of the jurisdictions under study have there been any difficulties implementing the burden of proof because it is binary, and the act of adjusting it is straightforward: the court places the burden on either the applicant or the public body defendant. There is also less need for evaluative judgment when the standard is tied to the outcome of an issue or to a procedural requirement. This latter approach is incorporated by Rivers into his scheme of standards of review, which are listed in decreasing order of deference: the court can 'simply accept the assertion'; accept the assertion under oath; 'require the authority to reveal the factual basis for its judgements'; or 'require a certain degree of rigour in the fact-finding process'.[119] However, more qualitative judgments would be needed for standards that rely on assessments of the cogency of reasons, sufficiency of evidence, or egregiousness of error.[120] When evaluative judgments are needed, common understanding is more likely to be attained for extremes, such as 'clearly

[114] Knight (n 31) 187.
[115] ibid 187–89.
[116] ibid 189.
[117] Jacob E Gersen and Adrian Vermeule, 'Chevron as a Voting Rule' (2007) 116(4) Yale LJ 676, 687.
[118] cf Dixon, *Responsive Judicial Review* (n 48) 130–31 and Rosalind Dixon, 'Calibrated Proportionality' (2020) 48(1) FL Rev 92, 113–22, which propose four standards of scrutiny.
[119] Rivers, 'Proportionality and Variable Intensity' (n 23) 203.
[120] Daly, *A Theory of Deference* (n 104) 166–78. Daly argues that although the relevancy of reasons is also 'not quantifiable', it is 'more tangible than a burden of justification based on magnitude [of error]', and proposes that in addition to correctness and unreasonableness a third standard be introduced—decision to be 'upheld unless unsupported by relevant reasoning and evidence'. On distinction between cogency and sufficiency, see Daly, *A Theory of Deference* (n) 137–62.

erroneous' and 'correctness' standards. Jacob Gersen and Adrian Vermuele rightly observed that '[l]egal language can capture the idea of the best legal answer and can indicate the idea of deference when decisions under review are not clearly erroneous ... [but] [m]ore fine-grained standards of deference ... are difficult to express'.[121]

The Canadian experience with standards of review in administrative law is instructive in this regard. The adding of a third standard[122]—unreasonableness *simpliciter*—to the two-standard model comprising correctness and patent unreasonableness has proved difficult for judges and litigants alike. Courts have struggled to distinguish unreasonableness *simpliciter* from patent unreasonableness, with divergent approaches having been developed.[123] In the end, for both analytical and practical reasons, the Canadian Supreme Court in *Dunsmuir* decided to collapse the two variants of reasonableness review into one, namely, unreasonableness: 'the three-standard model is too difficult to apply to justify its retention'.[124]

2. Finite scales for the device of giving of weight?

One question that has thus far received scant attention is whether it is possible to develop a finite scale for the giving of weight device. The general assumption seems to be that it is not possible, that the scale for this device necessarily ranges 'from a gram to a tonne',[125] that any denomination is possible,[126] and hence that application of the device is inherently malleable. This subsection probes this assumption.

Let us begin by asking whether, and if so when, the giving of weight device should be rendered more predictable and workable. The question requires a recap of what role the device can perform. As explained in Chapter 4[127] and section IV, it can perform two key roles. First, it can function as a residual device. Whilst the burden of proof, standard of review, and standard of proof have to be determined before the merits of the case are closely examined, the giving of weight device comes into play only when the court examines those merits closely. Accordingly, the giving of weight device is able to accommodate normative considerations of deference that are not apparent to the court when it determines the burden of proof, standard of proof, and standard of review.

121 Gersen and Vermeule (n 117) 686–87.

122 *Canada (Director of Investigation and Research) v Southam Inc* [1997] 1 SCR 748.

123 *Dunsmuir* (n 4) [37]–[41]; See eg Deborah K Lovett QC, 'That Enigmatic Curial Deference and the Continuing and Most Curious Search for Legislative Intent—What to Do, What to Do?' 17 CJALP 207, 217–27.

124 *Dunsmuir* (n 4) [44]–[45].

125 Hickman (n 108) 138.

126 Knight (n 31) 233.

127 See section IV of Chapter 4.

Second, the device can serve to fine-tune the level of deference granted by the earlier devices to bring it closer to the level actually warranted in the circumstances. If the devices that entered the scene earlier all operated by way of a small number of finite standards based on doctrinal categories, the level of deference that can be accorded will necessarily be crude. The giving of weight device can bring the level accorded closer to that actually warranted because the actual level due will be much more apparent to the court by the time the device enters the scene (ie when the court examines the merits closely). However, it can perform this role only if it operates in a manner that is more fine-grained than the earlier devices.

In contexts in which the need for workability and predictability outweighs the need to preserve the giving of weight device's ability to perform these two roles, the device may as well be discarded. However, if it is to be retained and the importance of the second role's performance is not too high, then the question of developing finite scales for the device becomes pertinent. One way of developing workable standards for the giving of weight device is to adopt Rivers' aforementioned scheme, which ties finite standards to outcome and procedural requirements.

3. Bundling of devices

In addition to gradating individual devices, another way of rendering the application of the devices more workable and predictable is to develop levels of scrutiny with different combinations of ways in which the various devices are to be applied. The trigger in the rule would lead to an adjustment of numerous (or all) devices rather than a single device. The application of various devices would come as a 'package'. This approach was advocated by Janneke Gerards. She developed tiers of scrutiny that affect the burden of proof, standard of review and giving of weight: 'marginal review' would, inter alia, place the burden of proof on the applicant, who would have to demonstrate that the measure 'will not and cannot have the desired effects' with 'clear and uncontested evidence'; and 'strict scrutiny', which, inter alia, requires an *ex nunc* rather than *ex tunc* review, would place the burden of proof on the primary decision-maker, which would have to 'demonstrate the adequacy of the measure as a means to obtain a certain goal by adducing conclusive evidence and by pointing out that the effectiveness of the instrument has been duly investigated in preparing the decision or regulation'.[128] Gerards' standards contain evaluative judgments that may not be suitable if a high level of workability and predictability is required, but the idea of bundling devices together as a package would save the courts and litigants from having to determine the level of deference and method of manifestation for each and every device.

[128] Janneke Gerards, 'Pluralism, Deference and the Margin of Appreciation Doctrine' (2011) 17(1) ELJ 80, 88.

VII. Conclusion

This chapter has considered how the method of determining when, how, and how much to defer can be made more practicable for judges and litigants without undue compromise of the normative impulse for deference. It has established that there is an inevitable trade-off between making methods of deference more practicable and making them more flexible to account for variations in the deference due across contexts. It has also explained that to enhance the practicability of methods of deference, courts have to rely more on formalist decision-making. The following guidelines can be distilled:

1) How much formalism concerning deference is appropriate for a legal system depends on whether more or less of it would advance the system's goals. The following factors are typically relevant.[129] The more competent and well-informed judges are in making deference assessments and the more resources the court has, the less need there is for formalist rules. The more accurate generalizations on deference are, the more formalist decision-making can be relied upon. The more serious a rights violation is, the more flexibility there should be to achieve individual justice, and hence the less formalism there should be.
2) Rules, presumptions, and factorial analysis are in decreasing order of formalism. To enhance practicability, the court should rely more on techniques towards the formalist end of the spectrum.[130]
3) To enhance practicability, the court can map certain normative considerations onto specific devices by:
   a) determining the burden and standard of proof solely by way of considerations regarding prior probability, the relative difficulties of proof, and minimizing the social costs of an erroneous ruling;[131]
   b) determining the standard of review solely by doctrinal classifications that reflect the court and primary decision-maker's relative ability and legitimacy to determine the rights issue and using the giving of weight device to fine-tune the amount of deference due in the circumstances.[132]
4) To enhance practicability, the court should rely on clearer and more reliable indicators of deference.
   a) Because clarity and reliability are context dependent, the court should ensure that prescriptions for deference remain open to review and should not blindly import prescriptions from other jurisdictions.[133]

[129] Section II.
[130] Section III.
[131] Text to n 82.
[132] Text to nn 83–85.
[133] Sections V.1 and V.2.

b) Where more practicability is desired, the court should avoid relying on indicators of deference that are vague or require highly evaluative judgments (such as the law/rights versus policy/politics distinction and the concept of 'complex and difficult judgments')[134] or that overshoot by a wide margin (eg where 'a balance is to be struck between competing interests');[135] should rely on indicators that cover fewer grounds for deference and are closer to those grounds; and should avoid formulating conflicting prescriptions. Spatial approaches are unjustified, all things considered, only if the balance of factors highlighted in section II (some of which are recapped in point 1 in this section) suggest so, that is, that the costs to individual justice they brought about outweigh their benefits to practicability.[136]

5) To enhance the clarity of the consequences of deference for the various devices, the court can:
   a) develop finite scales that rely on fewer standards (of, say, review) and rely less on evaluative judgments;[137]
   b) develop such finite scales for the giving of weight device by linking them to outcome and procedural requirements;[138] and/or
   c) develop levels of scrutiny that combine various devices.[139]

Having set out various techniques for balancing practicability and context-sensitivity, we are ready to conclude the book. The final chapter, Chapter 7, suggests four ways of combining the techniques and shows how they can be applied using the case of Hong Kong, summarizes and draws together the arguments of the book, and suggests directions for future research.

134 Section V.1.
135 Section V.2.
136 Section V.2.
137 Section VI.1.
138 Section VI.2.
139 Section VI.3.

7
Conclusion

I. Introduction

This book has sought to answer two underexplored questions on judicial deference in human rights adjudication. The first is how courts should give effect to the reasons for deference. The second is how to render the method of determining when, how, and how much to defer more workable for judges and more predictable for litigants without undue compromise of the method's ability to appropriately reflect the reasons for deference in a particular case. The answers to these questions enable us to formulate methods of deference that both fulfil the reasons for deference (ie fulfil what I call the 'internal logic' of deference) and are practicable (ie address what I call 'external constraints' on deference). In this concluding chapter, I first trace the main arguments of the book, and then illustrate the way in which the various techniques proposed in Chapter 6 can be applied using the case of Hong Kong. Next, I draw a connection between the demands of internal logic and those of external constraints. Finally, I outline the significance of the book, its applicability, and directions for future research.

II. Summary of the Book

The book begins by laying the groundwork for answering the two focal questions by defining deference and discussing the reasons the courts have for deference and the devices available to them for exercising it. In Chapter 1, I define deference as occurring when a court grants leeway to the legislature or executive—leeway that it would not have granted if it had merely considered the balance of reasons bearing on the rights issue at hand—for reasons arising from the comparative institutional position of the court and the two political branches of government. Chapter 2 then explains that in polities that satisfy certain background conditions, the courts have three sets of grounds for exercising deference: grounds that relate to arriving at the correct outcome on the rights issue at hand, grounds that relate to respect for constitutional legitimacy, and a residual category of grounds that relate to other considerations that the courts should take into account in adjudication.

I then introduce, in Chapter 3, six devices available to the courts for exercising deference: the burden of proof, standard of proof, standard of review, giving of weight to views, choice of interpretation (ie adopting an interpretation of a

Deference in Human Rights Adjudication. Cora Chan, Oxford University Press.
DOI: 10.1093/9780198921677.003.0007

constitutional provision that affords the executive or legislature more decision-making room), and choice of remedy. Because the first four devices operate by relaxing the court's review of a prior decision or view, whereas the final two do not, I refer to the first four devices as 'review devices' to distinguish them from the final two.

With this groundwork laid—deference defined and the reasons and devices for deference identified—Chapters 4–5 then address the first of the book's two questions. These chapters probe into how the courts should use the six devices to fulfil the reasons they have for deferring in a given case. Chapter 4 focuses on the qualitative aspect of this internal logic analysis. It compares the type of reasons for deference that the various devices and their application to various issues can express and makes the following key points. First, when the court needs to give effect to the original decision-maker's superior ability to arrive at correct answers on, or to its stronger legitimacy to determine, the rights issue at hand, it can in principle do so by adjusting the burden of proof, standard of proof, or standard of review. However, it should choose one device over another when such values can be served by, or are better served by, that device. For example, when the comparison of expertise is between the applicant and the public body defendant alone (eg in cases of conflicting expert evidence) and the court's relative competence vis-à-vis the defendant is irrelevant, then the court should defer through the standard of proof, which is a device that regulates a three-way relationship (that amongst the court, the defendant, and the applicant), rather than through the standard of review (which exclusively regulates the court–defendant relationship).

Second, if the court needs to give effect to the considerations underlying prior probability theory, address the relative difficulties of proof faced by the litigation parties, or minimize the social costs of an erroneous ruling, then it should adjust the burden and standard of proof rather than the standard of review. Third, the giving of weight device can generally be used to give effect to the normative considerations that underlie the burden and standard of proof and standard of review.

Fourth, if the court needs to defer for reasons that were not apparent to it when it determined the burden and standard of proof and standard of review, then it can rely on the giving of weight device, which enters the scene later than the former devices. Fifth, when the facts giving rise to reasons for deference call for the use of a review device rather than the choice of interpretation and remedy devices (or vice versa) or for deference to be accorded on one substantive issue rather than another, then that device or deference on that issue should be deployed.

Chapter 5 focuses on the quantitative aspect of the internal logic analysis, analysing how the six devices should be used to express the appropriate degree of deference. I make four key arguments in the chapter. First, both the range and granularity of deference that the burden of proof can express are smaller/less than those of the other devices. Second, the degree of deference exerted by the standard of proof, standard of review, and giving of weight can be compared by assessing how much additional presumptive weight the court affords the primary decision-maker's proposition. Third, in the polities covered by this study, when deference at the definition and limitation stages is exercised in ways that lead to favourable outcomes for the primary decision-maker at those stages, the amount of deference manifested at the three stages—definition, limitation, and remedy—is in decreasing order. Fourth, I offer a definition of double counting: it occurs when the court gives undue additional weight to a ground (as defined in Chapter 2) served by deference. Understood as such, deference using more than one device is neither a sufficient nor necessary condition for double counting, and the concerns over double counting expressed in the literature may be overstated. Courts should, however, be alert to the risk of double counting in three non-exhaustive situations, namely, when the court defers over and above recognizing the appeal versus review distinction in the absence of evidence of a rigorous decision-making process; when more than one device is used in highly deferential ways within the same limb of the proportionality test for the same spatial reason; and when deference is given on proportionality issues at the rights definition stage.

Following the analysis of internal logic in Chapters 4 and 5, Chapter 6 then examines the second of the book's two questions, that is, how methods of deference can address the external constraints of practicability without undue compromise of the internal logic of the devices. The chapter notes that there is an inevitable trade-off between making methods of deference more flexible to accommodate the internal logic across various deference contexts and making them more workable and predictable in response to external constraints. How the balance between context-sensitivity and practicability is to be struck depends on the goals of the given legal system and typically hinges on a number of factors, including whether reliable indicators of how the devices should be used are available, the competence of the judges in question to make a decision on deference and the judicial resources available.

Chapter 6 then proposes four sets of techniques for striking a balance between the practicability and context-sensitivity of the methods of deference.

The first is the use of rules, presumptions, and factorial analysis, which are in decreasing order of practicability. To enhance practicability, courts should rely more on techniques towards the rule-based end of the spectrum than on those towards the factorial analysis end.

The second set of techniques is a division of work amongst the devices. To enhance practicability, courts can map certain normative considerations onto specific devices to reduce the risk of the normative considerations underlying one device pulling in opposite directions. For example, they can determine the burden and standard of proof solely by way of considerations on prior probability, the relative difficulties of proof and minimizing the social costs of an erroneous ruling, considerations that can be manifested exclusively by these devices, and the standard of review solely by considering the relative ability and constitutional legitimacy of the court and primary decision-maker to decide an issue. Furthermore, courts can institute a division of work amongst the devices based on their temporal sequence, which could serve to enhance structured judicial reasoning. For example, the standard of review can be determined by doctrinal classifications that reflect relative expertise and constitutional legitimacy, whereas the giving of weight device, which enters the scene later than the standard of review, can be used to fine-tune the amount of deference granted in the circumstances.

The third set of techniques is aimed at enhancing the clarity and reliability of the indicators of deference. An example of an indicator used in UK case law is a decision under challenge being an eligibility condition for social welfare benefits, which is taken to indicate a high degree of deference in the standard of review. Whether an indicator is clear and reliable is context dependent. An indicator that is clear and reliable in one timeframe or polity may not be so in another. Accordingly, courts should keep indicators open to review and should not indiscriminately import them from other jurisdictions. Further, to enhance practicability, courts should avoid relying on indicators that are overly vague or require highly evaluative judgments (such as the law/rights versus policy/politics distinction and the concept of 'complex and difficult' judgments) or that overshoot by a wide margin (eg a high degree of deference whenever 'a balance is to be struck between competing interests'). They should also avoid formulating conflicting prescriptions on deference. Spatial approaches are not necessarily unjustified. They would be so only if the balance of factors for determining how much rule-based decision-making there should be suggests that they are unjustified, that is, if the costs to context-sensitivity brought about by the spatial approach outweigh its benefits to practicability.

The fourth and final set of techniques involves enhancing the clarity of the consequences of deference for the devices. This set includes developing cruder scales for the devices that rely less on evaluative judgments, developing such scales for the giving of weight device, and developing tiers of review that combine various devices.

III. Illustrations: Four Models

I now demonstrate how the techniques proposed in Chapter 6 can be put into practice by combining them into four models: the algorithmic model, stable model, elastic model, and amorphic model. A couple of preliminary points about the analysis are in order. First, the four models represent four points on a spectrum of formalism, presented in decreasing order, with model 1 (algorithmic) being the most formalist and model 4 (amorphic) the least.

Second, they are but four *examples* of how the techniques can be combined; other combinations are possible. Courts can develop models of deference along the lines suggested by the four models in accordance with the factors that determine the degree of rule-based decision-making desirable for a given polity or context. Moreover, the application of the various models need not be distinguished by subject matter, as I propose they be in this section.

Third, the models differ in terms of the degree to which they rely on rules, presumptions, and factorial analysis (the first set of techniques), the degree of reliability their indicators are expected to have (the third set of techniques), and the degree to which devices are bundled up and gradated (the fourth set of techniques). However, all four models equally utilize the second set of techniques on the division of work and eschew the use of unclear indicators highlighted in the discussion of the third set of techniques above, techniques that will help to ensure a minimum degree of workability in all of the models. The four models are summarized in Table 7.1.

Fourth, I use Hong Kong to illustrate how the models could be applied. The choice is justified because, as section II of Chapter 6 reveals, the degree of formalist

Table 7.1 Summary of the four models

	1. The algorithmic model	**2. The stable model**	**3. The elastic model**	**4. The amorphic model**
Reliance on rules	High: a rule for all devices in all three stages of adjudication	Moderately high: at the limitation stage, a rule for the burden and standard of proof and standard of review; factorial analysis for the giving of weight	Moderately low: at the limitation stage, a rule for the burden and standard of proof; a presumption for the standard of review; factorial analysis for the giving of weight	Low: factorial analysis for all devices in all three stages of adjudication
Reliability of indicators expected	High	High	High for rules, moderate for presumptions	Low
Use and gradation of the giving of weight device	Device not used	Device used and gradated	Device used and not gradated	Device used and not gradated
Bundling of devices	High: all devices at all three stages of adjudication bundled up	Moderate: devices of burden and standard of proof and standard of review at limitation stage bundled up	Moderate: devices of burden and standard of proof and standard of review at limitation stage bundled up	Low: all devices determined on a case-by-case basis

decision-making that is warranted depends on a host of factors, including whether reliable indicators of how the devices are used are available, the competence of the judges in question to make a decision on deference, the amount of judicial resources available, and the ease with which judicial errors can be rectified and the likelihood thereof, all of which are highly context dependent and whose judgments require familiarity with the institutional and constitutional environment. Of the jurisdictions covered by this book, Hong Kong is the one with which I am most familiar. My observations about how these factors are likely to fare are therefore likelier to be correct than observations in relation to the other jurisdictions.

Fifth, the sole purpose of this section is to illustrate how the four models can be applied to the real world with reference to several fairly uncontroversial empirical assumptions. My purpose is not to *prove* any institutional *facts* in relation to any polity. My empirical observations in relation to Hong Kong are tentative (albeit not controversial), and my justifications for applying a particular model in a particular context are defeasible (although plausible given that the underlying empirical assumptions are not controversial). More conclusive observations can be drawn only upon a systematic investigation of the comparative competences and constitutional legitimacy of the courts, executive, and legislature in the jurisdiction concerned, as well as of the reliability of the prescriptions for deference in that jurisdiction. In the final section of this chapter, section V, I highlight examples of empirical data that are needed to draw conclusive observations using the ideas in this book, as well as several directions for future research.

Finally, the observations drawn for Hong Kong cannot be taken as observations for other jurisdictions. The institutional and constitutional landscape of each polity varies. The answer to the question of which model is applicable, and when, must be answered afresh in relation to each jurisdiction.

With these points in mind, let us now examine each model in turn.

1. Model 1: the algorithmic model

In the first model, a single rule is relied upon for all devices across the rights definition, limitation, and remedial stages, and the giving of weight device is not used. Once the trigger for the rule is present, the consequences for all of the deference devices in all three stages of adjudication are clear. There would be no need for the court to determine the use of each individual device. This model offers the most predictability amongst the four models. However, it is unlikely to be commonly used for specific subject matters. The indicator needed in the model's rule is an indicator at a high level of generality: an indicator of the balance of considerations that underlie all devices for deference across all three stages of adjudication. Such an indicator is unlikely to be very reliable, although, as my illustration below shows, it is possible to come up with a reliable indicator even at this level of generality. The algorithmic model may be suitable in, for example, jurisdictions or subject areas in which the courts are generally unreliable in making judgments about whether to defer or judicial resources are tight such that case-by-case analysis of deference cannot be conducted. In any case, the algorithmic model may be adopted as a 'default model'; that is, the other models can be designated for specific subject areas, and the algorithmic model may be applicable in areas not covered by those models.

One possible application of the model in Hong Kong is in cases that challenge measures limiting the rights of sexual minority groups. The limitation of such rights is a reliable indicator of the balance of considerations underlying all devices. Let us look at the burden and standard of proof at the limitation stage first. There are usually no difficulties of proof on the part of the primary decision-maker. Also, there are usually no reasons to believe that the social cost of an erroneous ruling for the applicant would be any greater than that of an erroneous ruling against it.[1] It would thus be safe to assume that as a general matter the burden of proof in such cases should be on the primary decision-maker and that the standard of proof should be the usual civil standard of a balance of probabilities.

Let us now turn to the standard of review, which is determined by the relative expertise and constitutional legitimacy of the primary decision-maker and the courts. As Chapter 2 explains,[2] the executive and legislative branches of the Hong Kong government are highly insensitive to the rights of sexual minority groups. Such insensitivity is demonstrated in official policy,[3] in members' public remarks,[4] and in case law that reveals the absence of rationality in measures against sexual minority groups.[5] The courts generally fare better in making judgments of proportionality regarding sexual minority rights and have a strong constitutional role to protect such rights given the insensitivity of the other two branches. Hence, the most rigorous form of the proportionality test—the no more than necessary formula coupled with a correctness review—should generally be applicable. Fine-tuning using the giving of weight device is not proposed given that the relative competence reasons would generally be in favour of the court in this area.

[1] See eg discussion in *Ng Hon Lam Edgar v The Hong Kong Housing Authority* [2021] HKCFI 1812, [2021] 3 HKLRD 427 [61]–[79]; *Infinger, Nick v The Hong Kong Housing Authority* [2020] HKCFI 329, [2020] 3 HKC 41 [51].

[2] Text to n 73 in Chapter 2.

[3] For example, there is no legislation prohibiting discrimination on the ground of sexual orientation.

[4] See eg 'Policy against LGBT discrimination involve national security: Junius Ho' The Standard (Hong Kong, 10 Feb 2022) <https://www.thestandard.com.hk/breaking-news/section/4/187007/Policy-against-LGBT-discrimination-involve-national-security:-Junius-Ho> accessed 20 April 2022.

[5] Eg in *Leung TC William Roy v Secretary for Justice* [2006] HKCA 360, [2006] 4 HKLRD 211 [51]; *Secretary for Justice v Yau Yuk Lung Zigo* [2007] HKCFA 50, [2007] 3 HKLRD 903 [27], the government failed to present a legitimate aim for differential criminal law treatment in relation to buggery. In *Director of Immigration v QT* [2018] HKCFA 28, (2018) 21 HKCFAR 324 [90]–[99] and *Leung Chun Kwong* [2019] HKCFA 19, (2019) 22 HKCFAR 127 [67]–[77], a rational connection in the differential treatment of same-sex couples was found to be lacking. In *Ng Hon Lam Edgar* (n 1), the differential treatment thereof was found to fail the second to fourth limbs of the proportionality test.

Let us now consider the rights definition stage and the choice of remedies. The political branches have long been insensitive to sexual minority rights and will likely remain so given the way in which they are returned,[6] which ensures that they are biased in favour of morally conservative, pro-government groups. Therefore, insofar as its purposive interpretative approach allows, the court need not be overly concerned with granting the future executive and legislature the leeway to define sexual minority rights. There may be reasons to grant a remedy that gives the government greater scope to respond, such as a remedy that allows it to reform related areas of law in one go. However, the Hong Kong government's track record of exercising the discretion granted by such deferential remedies is poor. As Chapter 2 shows, the executive and legislature have failed even to fulfil the court's remedial order to reform the law to allow transsexual persons to marry in their post-operative gender.[7] This poor track record offers reasons for the courts to grant non-deferential remedies in future.

In sum, that the case in question challenges a measure that limits sexual minority rights is a reliable indicator of non-deference on all of the devices. In addition, asking the courts to rely on a rule on deference may be more desirable than asking them to determine the devices afresh on a case-by-case basis, because there is a risk that some judges may be influenced by the strong hostility of the political branches and some sections of the public towards the rights of sexual minorities and thus arrive at overly deferential standards. The proposed algorithmic model therefore seems more desirable, and is in fact partly reflected in current practice. It is established doctrine that where suspect grounds of discrimination (eg on the basis of sexual orientation or gender identity) are involved, the courts should apply the no more than necessary standard of review.[8] The Hong Kong courts have also granted a non-deferential definition of right in some cases concerning sexual minority rights[9] and dealt with the risk of the government failing to heed a court order to reform the law by stipulating a remedial interpretation that kicks in upon such failure.[10] The giving of weight device formally remains in place but is rarely used. What I have done here is to systematically set out a rule not only for the standard of review but also for all of the other devices, as well as to exclude the giving of weight device.

[6] See Improving Electoral System (Consolidated Amendments) Ordinance 2021, Ord No 14 of 2021 A437.

[7] See the discussion of *W v Registrar of Marriages* [2013] HKCFA 39, [2013] 3 HKC 375 in text to n 73 of Chapter 2.

[8] *Fok Chun Wa and another v The Hospital Authority and another* [2012] HKCFA 34, (2012) 15 HKCFAR 409 [77].

[9] Although the generous approach is not consistently adopted. Contrast *W* (n 7) with *MK v The Government of HKSAR* [2019] HKCFI 2518, [2019] 5 HKLRD 259.

[10] *W* (n 7) [147]–[150]. More recently, the CFA ruled in *Sham Tsz Kit v Secretary for Justice* [2023] HKCFA 28 and [2023] HKCFA 31 that the Hong Kong government must devise a scheme for legally recognizing same sex partnerships. The court gave the government two years to formulate such a scheme but retained supervisory jurisdiction.

2. Model 2: the stable model

In the second model, a single rule is relied upon for the devices of burden of proof, standard of proof, and standard of review at the limitation stage. Once the trigger within the rule is present, the consequences for all three devices are clear, and there would be no need for the court to determine the use of each device. The fine-tuning of deference can be performed using the giving of weight device, which is determined on a case-by-case basis via multifactorial balancing. To achieve a greater degree of predictability, however, the device needs to be gradated along the lines explained in section VI(2) of Chapter 6.

The stable model is suitable for situations in which a highly reliable indicator can be found for the balance of considerations underlying the burden of proof, standard of proof, and standard of review at the limitation stage and in which the courts would be likelier to arrive at correct judgments on deference by relying on the rules of these devices than by engaging in multi-factorial balancing every time.

One category of cases in Hong Kong appears to meet these conditions, namely, cases in which electoral laws limiting the right to vote or stand for election are being challenged. The courts tend to accord a large degree of deference to laws that involve 'political judgments' on the basis that they have less expertise and legitimacy than the government to make such judgments,[11] although the concept of 'political judgments' has never been defined. In *Kwok Cheuk Kin v Secretary for Constitutional and Mainland Affairs*, in assessing whether a ban on legislators who had resigned from standing in a by-election, the Court of Final Appeal (CFA) stipulated a presumption of deference for 'political judgments'.[12] In the end, the court diluted the 'no more than necessary' standard of review to that of 'manifestly without reasonable foundation', and afforded the legislature considerable weight in deciding whether the ban met that diluted standard.[13]

Let us now take a closer look at what form of deference electoral laws warrant. According to the arguments in section V(1) of Chapter 6, *Kwok Cheuk Kin* is non-commendable in at least one respect, that is, its reliance on the overly vague concept of 'political judgments' as an indicator that a high degree of deference is due. Hence, the proposal made here is to rely on a more concrete concept, such as electoral laws that impinge on the right to vote or stand for election. Experience suggests that the Hong Kong government faces no serious difficulties of proof in this area and that there are no special reasons for believing that the social cost of an erroneous ruling for the applicant would be any greater than that of an erroneous ruling against it. Accordingly, electoral laws appear to be a reliable indicator that

[11] See eg *Wong Chi Fung v Secretary for Justice* [2016] HKCFI 1047; [2016] 3 HKLRD 835.
[12] [2017] HKCFA 44, (2017) 20 HKCFAR 353 [42].
[13] ibid [55]–[59].

the government bears the burden of justifying, on a civil standard of proof, electoral laws that impinge on the right to vote or stand for election.

As for the standard of review, existing practice seems to overestimate the relative constitutional legitimacy of the legislature. The court in *Kwok Cheuk Kin* failed to give sufficient weight to the fact that one of the most fundamental rights—the right to vote and stand for election—was involved or to that fact that such involvement strengthened the court's legitimacy to scrutinize the matter. The relative constitutional legitimacy of the court in this area is arguably even stronger following the 2021 electoral reform introduced by the Chinese government,[14] which has greatly weakened political opposition in the legislature. Decisions taken by a legislature returned in such a manner lack the imprimatur of a major political camp. Furthermore, in most cases the courts do not lack the expertise to assess the proportionality of an electoral measure. A rule of a rigorous 'no more than necessary' test applied with a correctness standard of review would therefore make sense.

Nonetheless, there are a number of variables in this type of case. Electoral laws may on rare occasions involve judgments that the courts have little experience in making. For example, in *Kwok Cheuk Kin*, the CFA indicated its lack of insight on the predictive question of whether the system of resignation would be abused, and the legislature's integrity undermined, if the ban were not in place.[15] Legislators, who have experience of working with one another, would be able to predict the behaviour of their counterparts more accurately than the courts. Another variable is prudential considerations. Electoral laws have the potential to become politically sensitive as they pertain to one of the Chinese government's core concerns: control of democratic developments in Hong Kong. Both the Chinese and Hong Kong governments would likely prefer the courts to accord a large degree of weight to electoral arrangements passed by the pro-government legislature. Recalcitrant judicial decisions risk attracting a backlash that might affect the courts' long-term ability to do justice. However, the degree of such risk varies with the nature of the case in question. Some judicial challenges go to the core of the electoral system more than others. For example, the judicial expansion of electoral rights in village elections,[16] or of prisoners' rights,[17] would have much less of an impact than the abolition of corporate voting in Legco elections.[18] Variation in the strength of prudential imperatives and in the relative institutional competences can be accommodated by the giving of weight device, which is gradated in the stable model.

[14] See n 6.

[15] *Kwok Cheuk Kin* (n 12) [41], [50], [55]–[57].

[16] *Secretary for Justice and others v Chan Wah and others* [2000] HKCFA 43, [2000] 3 HKLRD 641.

[17] *Chan Kin Sum v Secretary for Justice* [2008] HKCFI 1081, [2009] 2 HKLRD 166.

[18] *Chan Yu Nam v Secretary for Justice* [2010] HKCA 364, [2012] 3 HKC 38. Simon NM Young, 'Judicial Review of Elections in Hong Kong: Resolving a Contradiction' in Po Jen Yap (ed), *Judicial Review of Elections in Asia* (Routledge 2016).

There is at least one reason to guide judges with a rule on the bundled-up devices of the burden and standard of proof and standard of review rather than to expect them to determine these devices from scratch in every case. In recent years, the Hong Kong courts have tended to be highly deferential across the board in challenges against electoral laws.[19] Hence, asking them to determine deference on a case-by-case basis would likely lead to over-deference.

3. Model 3: the elastic model

Model 3 is distinguished from model 2 in that rules are used in conjunction with presumptions and the giving of weight device is non-gradated, thereby allowing for greater flexibility. The burden and standard of proof are determined by way of a rule, whereas the standard of review is determined by way of a presumption, and a non-gradated giving of weight device is determined on a case-by-case basis using factorial analysis. Compared with model 2, the elastic model is suited to situations in which the indicators for the use of the devices are less (but still fairly) reliable.

One possible area of application for the model in Hong Kong would be cases that challenge policies on the distribution of social welfare benefits that do not involve suspect grounds of discrimination. In many such cases the primary decision-maker faces difficulties proving that the line should be drawn exactly where it is.[20] Hence, it would make sense for cases of this type to attract a lower than civil standard of proof, say, a reasonable basis for belief, at least in relation to the third limb of the proportionality test.

As for the standard of review, the courts currently accord a large degree of deference via the manifestly without reasonable foundation standard, claiming that they lack both the expertise and a constitutional mandate to determine socio-economic matters.[21] Insofar as expertise is concerned, such a claim seems to be refuted by the courts' own record, which shows that the courts indeed have the ability to evaluate the available evidence to assess whether a social welfare measure is necessary.[22] Insofar as relative legitimacy is concerned, given the democratic deficit of the executive branch (and hence that of the makers of the socio-economic policies concerned), the democratic warrant of such policies cannot be automatically assumed, but would be present if the policies were the result of a genuine consultative process, which is sometimes the case. Because any difficulties of proof on the policy-makers' part would already have been taken into account through a lower standard

[19] *Wong Chi Fung* (n 11); *Leung Lai Kwok Yvonne v The Chief Secretary for Administration and others* [2015] HKCFI 929.

[20] See eg *Fok Chun Wa* (n 8) [71]–[74].

[21] ibid [71].

[22] See eg *Yao Man Fai George v Director of Social Welfare* [2010] HKCFI 537 [47]–[105].

of proof, a presumption of a rigorous 'no more than necessary' standard of review would be appropriate. If there are very strong expertise and legitimacy reasons for deference, the presumption may be rebutted and a less demanding standard of review adopted. In the bulk of cases, however, it is expected that any deficiency in the court's expertise and legitimacy to assess whether a policy is no more than necessary can be taken into account through a non-gradated giving of weight device on a case-by-case basis. Unlike sexual minority rights, this is not an area in which the executive and legislature are insensitive and non-responsive, and thus if there are any concerns regarding the wide-ranging ramifications of a policy change they could be accommodated by granting a deferential remedy.

The elastic model represents a partial change from current practice, whereby the courts rely on a rule stipulating that socio-economic matters that do not involve suspect grounds of discrimination attract the manifestly without reasonable foundation standard of review. What I am proposing here is that the standard of proof be lowered as a rule and the rigorous form of the standard of review be adopted as a presumption. In line with current practice, flexibility is maintained through a case-by-case determination of a non-gradated giving of weight device. The model can counteract the courts' overly sweeping deferential approach on the standard of review in this type of case. A presumption of a non-deferential standard would force the courts to reason through why deference—and hence a departure from the presumption—is warranted, providing a doctrinal structure that would facilitate arrival at the right judgment on deference.

4. Model 4: the amorphic model

This final model lies on the least formalist end of the spectrum. It eschews the use of rules and presumptions and asks the courts to determine on a case-by-case basis the use of all deference devices across the three stages of adjudication. The amorphic model maximizes flexibility at the cost of coherence and predictability. Given the need for workability, it is unlikely to be suitable for many specific contexts in the real world, but it may be adopted in situations in which the considerations underlying the devices are so context dependent that no generalization is possible. The model may also be adopted as a default model that is applicable when no other model applies if, inter alia, the courts are generally competent in making judgments on deference, judicial errors are easily rectified, and judicial resources are abundant.

One possible area of application in Hong Kong is in cases in which national security measures taken by the executive are being challenged. This suggestion may seem surprising given that national security is one of the few subject matters widely considered to attract a high degree of deference across the board. I do not know whether it should indeed attract such deference as a general matter, but in the specific context of Hong Kong, there are reasons to believe that a case-by-case approach would be more suitable.

In Hong Kong, it is difficult to come up with any generalizations on the balance of reasons that determine deference in the national security context. Neither the courts nor the government have had much experience handling national security matters. The recently enacted National Security Law[23] (NSL) established a national security committee in Hong Kong and designated sections within the police, prosecution and courts to handle national security cases.[24] Little is known about the credibility and competence of these institutions to strike a balance between rights and security.[25] It is unclear at this stage to what extent the government will rely on undisclosed evidence in national security cases and to what extent it will face difficulties of proof in such cases. It is also not entirely clear where the burden of proof should lie, noting that the NSL has reversed that burden in relation to bail cases.[26] Nevertheless, the courts do not seem handicapped in terms of constitutional legitimacy. Given weak political opposition in the legislature, amongst other institutional characteristics of the jurisdiction, the courts seem to be the sole institutional channel for ensuring that executive measures do not overreach on rights in the national security arena. In short, in light of Hong Kong's limited experience with national security cases, except perhaps with respect to the relative constitutional legitimacy of the courts and executive (which comes down in favour of the courts), it is difficult to generalize about the balance of the imperatives underlying the burden and standard of proof and standard of review at this juncture.

Moreover, the prudential reasons for deference in national security cases can vary greatly depending, inter alia, on how politically sensitive the applicants/defendants are and what aspects of the security system are being challenged. A case involving high-profile, politically sensitive figures has higher stakes than a case involving unknown individuals, and a challenge against the substantive aspects of a decision may have higher stakes than a challenge against its procedural aspects. A non-deferential review of a high-stakes case may attract a political backlash, but that of a low-stakes case may be off the political authorities' radar. Whilst national security cases as a whole can be considered a relatively politically sensitive area in Hong Kong, the pull of prudential reasons for deference in such cases can in fact

[23] The Law of the People's Republic of China on Safeguarding National Security in the Hong Kong Special Administrative Region, LN 136 of 2020, B2345 (in Chinese) ('NSL'); an unofficial translation is available at https://www.gld.gov.hk/egazette/pdf/20202448e/egn2020244872.pdf (last accessed 16 April 2024).

[24] NSL, ss 16, 18, 44.

[25] One of the few judicial assessments of the credibility of the government in the security context is *Chu Woan-Chyi and others v Director of Immigration* [2009] HKCA 316, [2009] 6 HKC 77 [108]–[119], [157] in which the court heavily criticized the executive's way of handling records that form the basis of its intelligence assessments and expressed dissatisfaction with the government's 'coyness' and 'inconsistency' during the litigation.

[26] NSL, s 42.

vary widely. A non-gradated giving of weight device would be able to accommodate such variation.

In addition to the difficulty of coming up with reliable indicators, there are two further reasons to adopt a more flexible approach. First, important rights are typically at stake in the national security context. There is thus, in general, a stronger constitutional imperative on the part of the courts to scrutinize individual cases carefully. Second, national security is an area in which judicial resources do not seem to be tight. There are not very many national security cases (at least for now), and there is no evidence that the designated judges are unable to handle the workload. The courts therefore appear able to afford sufficient time to a close, case-by-case deference examination. Nevertheless, there is a risk that the courts will be overly deferential when asked to decide questions of deference without the assistance of rules and presumptions given the institutional controls that the NSL imposes on national security judges.[27] However, on balance, more flexibility seems to be warranted in this context, at least at this early stage of the NSL era.

IV. Relationship Between Internal Logic and External Constraints

Having summarized the main arguments of the book and illustrated how the techniques in Chapter 6 can be put into practice, I now explicitly draw a connection amongst the three core chapters of the book, that is, Chapters 4, 5, and 6. As already noted in Chapter 6, there is an inevitable trade-off between making methods of deference more flexible to meet the demands of internal logic and rendering them more capable of addressing practicability constraints. Following the analysis of both internal logic (in Chapters 4 and 5) and external constraints (in Chapter 6 and section II of this chapter), we are now in a position to see why such a trade-off is inevitable and why certain suggestions made in the discussions on internal logic may have to give way if we are to follow the suggestions on addressing external constraints.

One example of why the former suggestions may have to give way to the latter relates to the use of bright-line rules on deference, use that inevitably sacrifices context-sensitivity. If, for example, in accordance with the algorithmic model outlined above, rules on deference are adopted across the board in all three stages of adjudication, then the court will not be able to deviate from the means and amount of deference prescribed by those rules, even if the context requires otherwise. Assume, as my example of Hong Kong does, that bright-line rules that prescribe a low level of deference—including the non-deferential 'minimal impairment' proportionality standard of review—are adopted in all cases concerning

[27] ibid s 44.

sexual minority rights. Then, even if the court lacks the relative expertise to assess whether a measure is minimally impairing in a particular such case, it will have to stick with the non-deferential minimal impairment formula notwithstanding its relative incompetence. Doing so would run contrary to the suggestion in Chapter 4 that courts should defer on an issue if (and only if) deference is due on that issue, say, because the court in question lacks the expertise to adjudicate the issue.

Another example concerns the suggestion about introducing a division of work amongst the devices. On the one hand, Chapter 6 suggests that one way of making methods of deference more practicable is to allow the burden and standard of proof to be determined exclusively by considerations on prior probability, the relative difficulties of proof, and minimizing the social costs of an erroneous ruling, leaving the standard of review to address considerations of the relative expertise and legitimacy of the court and primary decision-maker. Yet, on the other hand, Chapter 4 suggests that in some situations it may be more suitable to use the standard of proof in lieu of the standard of review to address considerations of relative expertise and legitimacy. For example, if the comparison of expertise and legitimacy involves a three-way comparison (ie court, defendant, applicant), then the standard of proof (being a three-way device) would be more suitable for expressing such competence reasons for deference than the standard of review (which exclusively regulates the court–defendant relationship). In such a situation, the suggestion in Chapter 4 cannot be followed if the court adopts the division of work suggested in Chapter 6.

Hence, not all of the suggestions in the internal logic analysis can be taken on board if the methods of deference are to be made more practicable. Nevertheless, the proposals in Chapter 6 are designed to minimize the compromises to those suggestions.

V. Applicability, Significance, and Future Research Directions

The ideas in this book are applicable to judicial deference in qualified rights adjudication in jurisdictions that apply a three-stage framework for adjudicating such rights. Under this framework, courts first assess whether there has been a prima facie limitation of a right (the rights definition stage) and, if so, then examine whether the limitation is justified under a proportionality test (the rights limitation stage). If the limitation fails the proportionality test, the court proceeds to a decision on what remedies, if any, to grant (the remedial stage). The book draws on the case law of Canada, Hong Kong, Ireland, Israel, New Zealand, and the United Kingdom, which are common law jurisdictions that embrace the three-stage framework and a structured proportionality test. This choice of jurisdictions was made for the practical reason that these jurisdictions provide the elaborate reasoning on methods of deference required for this study.

However, in principle, my ideas are also applicable to civil law jurisdictions and to common law jurisdictions that do not apply the proportionality test in a structured way, as long as they adopt the three-stage framework for adjudicating qualified rights. Moreover, although the book focuses on the adjudication of constitutional rights, its ideas may also illuminate deference in other adjudicative contexts (eg in administrative law or criminal law) because at least some of the devices for deference, as well as their nature and techniques for rendering them more practicable, appear to be relevant to these other contexts as well. One potential direction for future research would therefore be to assess whether, and if so how, the ideas herein could be adapted to other contexts and jurisdictions.

The book has both theoretical and practical import. Its conceptual analysis illuminates understanding of the nature of the reasons and devices for deference, the relationship between such reasons and devices, and the complex considerations involved in formulating methods of deference that are both workable and faithful to the normative impulse underlying deference. This analysis makes an original and significant contribution to the literature and will be of interest to academics and practitioners alike. I have also sought to offer guidance to judges who may wish to put the theoretical arguments into practice. Readers can refer to the final sections of Chapters 4–6 for the key takeaway points for judges. Although the guidance is meant for judges, it is equally useful for policymakers who wish to formulate policies on judicial deference.

This leads me to the question of which institution—the courts, the legislature, or the executive—should be tasked with determining the methods of deference that the courts should apply. That question is not answered in this book. Although I analyse how appropriate prescriptions on deference can be formulated for the courts, the question of which institution should formulate those prescriptions is a distinct one. As an analogy, some court procedures are formulated by the courts, and some by legislators. In the jurisdictions studied herein, questions of deference are determined primarily by the courts, but that should not be taken as a foregone conclusion. It is possible to envisage methods of deference being laid down in advance by the legislature or executive instead. Which institution should be tasked with formulating methods of deference depends, inter alia, on the relative competence of the three institutions in coming up with appropriate methods, which hinges on their ability to gather the empirical data needed to formulate a method of deference that meets the requirements of internal logic and external constraints outlined in this book. As the discussion in Chapter 6 reveals, such data include information on the relative competence of the courts, executive, and legislature to assess substantive rights issues (information that is needed to enable the formulation of reliable rules on deference and to evaluate such reliability); their relative competence to assess when, how, and how much to defer; and the judicial resources available (information that is needed to determine the extent to which the courts should rely on bright-line rules on deference).

Two related directions for future research would therefore be fruitful. The first would be to discern what empirical data are needed to formulate methods of deference that meet the demands of both internal logic and external constraints and systematically collect those data in relation to particular polities. The findings of such research would assist whichever institution is tasked with formulating methods of deference—be it the courts, the legislature, or the executive. The second would be to discern the criteria for determining which institution should be responsible for formulating methods of deference and then apply those criteria to particular polities to determine which institution is best positioned to formulate those methods. The two proposed research directions are related because a study proceeding along the lines of the first—including determining what data are needed to formulate appropriate methods of deference—is needed to some extent for a study proceeding along the lines of the second, which would require a determination of which institution has the ability to gather such data. The amount of information available for the first study would also inform the second: if plenty of data are available to determine what methods of deference are appropriate, then it may not matter much which institution is responsible for such determination.

To conclude, this book constitutes a step towards rendering judicial deference more principled, workable, and predictable. To maximize the potential of the arguments herein, efforts could be made to explore their applicability beyond the qualified rights context, to analyse which institution should be tasked with formulating methods of deference, and to collect the empirical data needed to fully apply the book's ideas.

Bibliography

Alexy R, *A Theory of Constitutional Rights* (OUP 2010)
Allan TRS, 'Human Rights and Judicial Review: A Critique of "Due Deference"' (2006) 65 CLJ 671
Allan TRS, 'Deference, Defiance and Doctrine: Defining the Limits of Judicial Review' (2010) 60 U Toronto LJ 41
Allan TRS, 'Judicial Deference and Judicial Review: Legal Doctrine and Legal Theory' (2011) 127(Jan) LQR 96
Allan TRS, *The Sovereignty of Law: Freedom, Constitution, and Common Law* (OUP 2013)
Barak A, *Proportionality: Constitutional Rights and Their Limitations* (CUP 2012)
Barak A, 'A Research Agenda for the Future' in Vicki C Jackson and Mark Tushnet (eds), *Proportionality: New Frontiers, New Challenges* (CUP 2017)
Barber NW, *The Principles of Constitutionalism* (OUP 2018)
Bell J, 'Rethinking the Story of Cart v Upper Tribunal and Its Implications for Administrative Law' (2019) 39(1) OJLS 74
Bickel AM, *The Least Dangerous Branch: The Supreme Court at the Bar of Politics* (2nd edn, Yale University Press 1986)
Biehler H and Donnelly C, 'Proportionality in the Irish Courts: the Need for Guidance' (2014) 3 EHRLR 272
Bilchitz D, 'Necessity and Proportionality: Towards A Balanced Approach' in Liora Lazarus, Christopher McCrudden, and Nigel Bowles (eds), *Reasoning Rights: Comparative Judicial Engagement* (Hart Publishing 2014)
Bobbitt P, *Constitutional Fate: Theory of the Constitution* (OUP 1982)
Brady ABP, 'Proportionality, Deference and Fundamental Rights in Irish Administrative Law; The Aftermath of Meadows' (2010) 32 Dublin U LJ 136
Brady ABP, *Proportionality and Deference under the UK Human Rights Act: An Institutionally Sensitive Approach* (CUP 2012)
Bridge N, 'Presumptions and Burdens' (1949) 12(3) MLR 273
Butler AS, 'Limiting Rights' (2002) 33 Victoria U Wellington L Rev 113
Canon BC, 'A Framework for the Analysis of Judicial Activism' in Stephen C Halpern and Charles M Lamb (eds), *Supreme Court Activism and Restraint* (Lexington Books 1982)
Carolan E, *The New Separation of Powers: A Theory for the Modern State* (OUP 2009)
Carter A, *Proportionality and Facts in Constitutional Adjudication* (Hart 2021)
Chan C, 'Proportionality and Invariable Baseline Intensity of Review' (2013) 33(1) LS 1
Chan C, 'Deference, Expertise and Intelligence-gathering Powers' (2013) 33(4) LS 598
Chan C, 'The Burden of Proof Under the Human Rights Act' [2014] JR 46
Chan C, 'A Preliminary Framework for Measuring Deference in Rights Reasoning' (2016) 14(1) ICON 851
Chan C, 'Can Hong Kong Remain a Liberal Enclave within China? Analysis of the Hong Kong National Security Law' [2021] PL 271
Choudhry S, 'So What is the Real Legacy of Oakes? Two Decades of Proportionality Analysis under the Canadian Charter's Section 1' (2006) 34 Sup Ct L Rev 501
Choudhry S and Roach K, 'Putting the Past Behind Us? Prospective Judicial and Legislative Constitutional Remedies' (2003) 21 Sup Ct L Rev 205
Choudhry S and Hunter CE, 'Measuring Judicial Activism on the Supreme Court of Canada: A Comment on *Newfoundland (Treasury Board) v. NAPE*' [2003] 48(3) McGill L J 525

Christiano T, 'Democracy', *The Stanford Encyclopedia of Philosophy* (Fall 2018 Edition), Edward N Zalta (ed), <https://plato.stanford.edu/archives/fall2018/entries/democracy/>

Cohen-Eliya M and Porat I, *Proportionality and Constitutional Culture* (CUP 2013)

Cohen-Eliya M and Stopler G, 'Probability Thresholds as Deontological Constraints in Global Constitutionalism' (2010) 49 Colum J Transnl L 75

Cohn M, 'Judicial Activism in the House of Lords: A Composite Constitutionalist Approach' (2007) PL 95

Cohn M and Kremnitzer M, 'Judicial Activism: A Multidimensional Model' (July 2005) 18(2) CJLJ 333

Craig P, *UK, EU and Global Administrative Law: Foundations and Challenges* (CUP 2015)

Craig P, *Administrative Law* (8th edn, Sweet & Maxwell 2016)

Craig P, 'Varying Intensity of Judicial Review: A Conceptual Analysis' [2022] PL 442

Daly P, 'Standards of Review in Irish Administrative Law After Meadows v Minister for Justice, Equality and Law Reform' (2010) 32 Dublin U LJ 379

Daly P, *A Theory of Deference in Administrative Law: Basis, Application and Scope* (CUP 2012)

Daly P, 'The Unfortunate Triumph of Form over Substance in Canadian Administrative Law' (2012) 50 Osgoode Hall LJ 317

Daly P, 'Struggling Towards Coherence in Canadian Administrative Law? Recent Cases on Standard of Review and Reasonableness' (2016) 62 McGill LJ 527

Daly P, 'The Vavilov Framework and the Future of Canadian Administrative Law' (2020) Ottawa Faculty of Law Working Paper No 2020-09, <https://ssrn.com/abstract=3519681> accessed 20 April 2022

David L, 'Resource Allocation and Judicial Deference on Charter Review: The Price of Rights Protection According to the McLachlin Court' (2015) 73(1) U Toronto Faculty L Rev 35

Davidov G, 'Judicial Deference and the Constitutional Protection of Rights' (1998) Thesis submitted in conformity with the requirements for the degree of LLM at University of Toronto <https://tspace.library.utoronto.ca/handle/1807/16154> accessed 20 April 2022

Davidov G, 'The Paradox of Judicial Deference' (2000-2001) 12 NJCL 133

Davidov G and Reichman A, 'Prolonged Armed Conflict and Diminished Deference to the Military: Lessons from Israel' [2010] 35(4) L & Soc Inquiry 919

Delaney EF, 'Analyzing Avoidance: Judicial Strategy in Comparative Perspective' (2016) 66 Duke LJ 1

Dindjer H, 'What Makes an Administrative Decision Unreasonable?' (2021) 84(2) MLR 265

Dixon R, 'The Supreme Court of Canada, Charter Dialogue, and Deference' (2009) 47 Osgoode Hall LJ 235

Dixon R, 'Constitutional "Dialogue" and Deference' in Geoffrey Sigalet, Grégoire Webber, and Rosalind Dixon (eds), *Constitutional Dialogue: Rights, Democracy, Institutions* (CUP 2019)

Dixon R, 'The Forms, Functions, and Varieties of Weak(ened) Judicial Review' (2019) 17(3) ICON 904

Dixon R, 'Calibrated Proportionality' (2020) 48(1) FL Rev 92

Dixon R, *Responsive Judicial Review: Democracy and Dysfunction in the Modern Age* (OUP 2023)

Dixon R and Issacharoff S, 'Living to Fight another Day: Judicial Deferral in Defense of Democracy' [2016] Wis L Rev 683

Dotan Y, 'Deference and Disagreement in Administrative Law' (2020) 71(4) Adm L Rev 761

Doyle O and Hickey T, *Constitutional Law: Text, Cases and Materials* (2nd edn, Clarus Press 2019)

Dworkin R, *Taking Rights Seriously* (first published 1977, Duckworth 2005)

Dwyer D, *The Judicial Assessment of Expert Evidence* (CUP 2008)

Dyzenhaus D, 'The Politics of Deference: Judicial Review and Democracy' in Michael Taggart (ed), *The Province of Administrative Law* (Hart 1997)

Dyzenhaus D, 'Constituting the Rule of Law: Fundamental Values in Administrative Law' (2002) 27 Queen's LJ 445

Dyzenhaus D, 'Dignity in Administrative Law: Judicial Deference in a Culture of Justification' (2012) 17(1) Rev Const Stud 87

Eckhoff T, 'Guiding Standards in Legal Reasoning' (1976) 29(1) CLP 205
Edwards RA, 'Judicial Deference under the Human Rights Act' (2002) 65(6) MLR 859
Ekins R, *The Nature of Legislative Intent* (OUP 2012)
Elliott M, 'Proportionality and Deference: the Importance of a Structured Approach', in Christopher Forsyth, Mark Elliott, Swati Jhaveri, Anne Scully-Hill, and Michael Ramsden (eds), *Effective Judicial Review: A Cornerstone of Good Governance* (OUP 2010)
Elliott M, 'From Bifurcation to Calibration: Twin-Track Deference and the Culture of Justification' in Hanna Wilberg and Mark Elliott (eds), *The Scope and Intensity of Substantive Review: Traversing Taggart's Rainbow* (Hart 2015)
Ely JH, *Democracy and Distrust: A Theory of Judicial Review* (HUP 1980)
Endicott TAO, *Vagueness in Law* (OUP 2000)
Endicott TAO, *Administrative Law* (3rd edn, OUP 2015)
Fallon RH, 'Foreword: Implementing the Constitution' (1997) 111 Harv L Rev 54
Flood CM, 'The Evidentiary Burden for Overturning Government's Choice of Regulatory Instrument: The Case of Direct-to-Consumer Advertising of Prescription Drugs' (2010) 60 U Toronto LJ 397
Fisher E and Shapiro SA, *Administrative Competence: Reimagining Administrative Law* (CUP 2020)
Foley B, *Deference and the Presumption of Constitutionality* (Institute of Public Administration 2008)
Foley B, 'The Proportionality Test: Present Problems' (2008) 1 JSIJ 67
Foley B, 'The BUPA Ireland Case and Constitutional Litigation' (2010) 45 IJ 230
Foster CE, *Science and the Precautionary Principle in International Courts and Tribunals: Expert Evidence, Burden of Proof and Finality* (CUP 2011)
Fuller LL, *The Morality of Law* (Yale University Press 1964)
Fuller LL, 'The Forms and Limits of Adjudication' (Dec 1978) 92(2) Harv L Rev 353
Gardbaum S, 'Limiting Constitutional Rights' (2007) 54 UCLA L Rev 789
Gardbaum S, *The New Commonwealth Model of Constitutionalism: Theory and Practice* (CUP 2013)
Gardiner G, 'The Reasonable and the Relevant: Legal Standards of Proof' (2019) 47(3) Philosophy & Public Affairs 288
Geiringer C, 'Sources of Resistance to Proportionality Review of Administrative Power under the New Zealand Bill of Rights Act' (2013) 11 NZ J Public and Intl L 123
Gerards J, 'Pluralism, Deference and the Margin of Appreciation Doctrine' (2011) 17(1) ELJ 80
Gersen JE and Vermeule A, 'Chevron as a voting rule' (2007) 116(4) Yale LJ 676
Goold B, Lazarus L, and Swiney G, 'Public Protection, Proportionality, and the Search for Balance' [2007] 10/07 Ministry of Justice Research
Greer S, 'Constitutionalizing Adjudication under the European Convention on Human Rights' (2003) 23(3) OJLS 405
Greer S, '"Balancing" and the European Court of Human Rights: A Contribution to the Habermas-Alexy Debate' (2004) 63(2) CLJ 412
Hamer D, 'The Presumption of Innocence and Reverse Burdens: A Balancing Act' (2007) 66(1) CLJ 142
Hamer D, 'Presumptions, Standards and Burdens: Managing the Cost of Error' (2014) 13 Law, Probability and Risk 221
Hardcastle L, 'Proportionality Analysis by the Canadian Supreme Court' in Mordechai Kremnitzer, Talya Steiner, and Andrej Lang (eds), *Proportionality in Action: Comparative and Empirical Perspectives on the Judicial Practice* (CUP 2020)
Hart HLA, *The Concept of Law* (3rd edn, OUP 2012)
Hickman T, 'The Substance and Structure of Proportionality' (2008) PL 694
Hickman T, *Public Law after the Human Rights Act* (Hart 2010)
Ho HL, *A Philosophy of Evidence Law* (OUP 2008)
Hogg PW, 'Interpreting the Charter of Rights: Generosity and Justification' (1990) 28(4) Osgoode Hall LJ 817

Hooper H, 'Trust As A Core Principle of the Constitution' (2022) 81(2) CLJ 228
Hughes J and MacDonnell V, 'Social Science Evidence in Constitutional Rights Cases in Germany and Canada: Some Comparative Observations' (2013) 32 NJCL 23
Hunt M, 'Sovereignty's Blight: Why Public Law Needs "Due Deference"' in Nicholas Bamforth and Peter Leyland (eds), *Public Law in a Multi-Layered Constitution* (Hart 2003)
Jackson VC, 'Thayer, Holmes, Brandeis: Conceptions of Judicial Review, Factfinding, and Proportionality' (2017) 130 Harv L Rev 2348
Joseph PA, *Constitutional and Administrative Law* (Thomson Reuters, 2014)
Jowell J, 'Judicial Deference and Human Rights: A Question of Competence' in Paul Craig and Richard Rawlings (eds), *Law and Administration in Europe: Essays in Honour of Carol Harlow* (OUP 2003)
Jowell J, 'Judicial Deference: Servility, Civility or Institutional Capacity?' [2003] PL 592
Kavanagh A, *Constitutional Review under the UK Human Rights Act* (CUP 2009)
Kavanagh A, 'Defending Deference in Public Law and Constitutional Theory' (2010) 126 LQR 222
Kavanagh A, 'Judicial Restraint in the Pursuit of Justice' (2010) 60 U Toronto LJ 23
Kavanagh A, 'Reasoning About Proportionality Under the Human Rights Act 1998: Outcomes, Substance and Process' (2014) 130 LQR 235
Kavanagh A, 'The Constitutional Separation of Powers' in David Dyzenhaus and Malcolm Thorburn (eds), *Philosophical Foundations of Constitutional Law* (OUP 2016)
Kavanagh A, *The Collaborative Constitution* (CUP 2023)
Kenny D, 'Proportionality, the Burden of Proof, and Some Signs of Reconsideration' (2014) 52 IJ 141
Kenny D, 'Remedial Innovation, Constitutional Culture, and the Supreme Court at a Crossroads' (2017) 40 Dublin U LJ 85
Kenny D, 'Proportionality and the Inevitably of the Local: A Comparative Localist Analysis of Canada and Ireland' (2018) 66 AJCL 537
King J, 'Institutional Approaches to Judicial Restraint' (2008) 28(3) OJLS 409
King J, *Judging Social Rights* (CUP 2012)
Knight DR, *Vigilance and Restraint in the Common Law of Judicial Review* (CUP 2018)
Komesar NK, *Imperfect Alternatives: Choosing Institutions in Law, Economics and Public Policy* (University of Chicago Press 1994)
Kumm M, 'Institutionalising Socratic Contestation: The Rationalist Human Rights Paradigm, Legitimate Authority and the Point of Judicial Review', (2007) 1(2) EJLS 153
Kumm M, 'The Idea of Socratic Contestation and the Right to Justification: The Point of Rights-Based Proportionality Review' (2010) 4(2) LEHR 141
Kyritsis D, 'What is Good about Legal Conventionalism' (2008) 14 LEG 135
Kyritsis D, *Where Our Protection Lies: Separation of Powers and Constitutional Review* (OUP 2017)
Lawson G and Seidman GI, *Deference: the Legal Concept and the Legal Practice* (OUP 2020)
Leckey R, *Bills of Rights in the Common Law* (CUP 2015)
Legg A, *The Margin of Appreciation in International Human Rights Law: Deference and Proportionality* (OUP 2012)
Lewans M, *Administrative Law and Judicial Deference* (Hart Publishing 2018)
Lim E and Chan C, 'Problems with Wednesbury Unreasonableness in Contract Law: Lessons from Public Law' (2019) 135 LQR 88
Lindquist SA and Cross FB, *Measuring Judicial Activism* (OUP 2009)
Lovett DK, 'That Enigmatic Curial Deference and the Continuing and Most Curious Search for Legislative Intent—What to Do, What to Do?' (2004) 17 CJALP 207
Marshall WP, 'Conservatives and the Seven Sins of Judicial Activism' (2002) 73 U Colom L Rev 1217
Mashaw JL, *Reasoned Administration and Democratic Legitimacy: Reasoned Administration and Democratic Legitimacy* (CUP 2018)
McCauliff CMA, 'Burdens of Proof: Degrees of Belief, Quanta of Evidence, Or Constitutional Guarantees' (1982) 35 V and L Rev 1293

McLean J, 'Legislative Invalidation, Human Rights Protection and s 4 of the New Zealand Bill of Rights Act' (2001) 2001 NZ L Rev 421
McLean K, *Constitutional Deference, Courts and Socio-Economic Rights in South Africa* (Pretoria University Law Press 2009)
Miller BW, 'Justification and Rights Limitations' in Grant Huscroft (ed), *Expounding the Constitution: Essays in Constitutional Theory* (CUP 2008)
Möller K, *The Global Model of Constitutional Rights* (OUP 2012)
Mullan D, 'Unresolved Issues on Standard of Review in Canadian Judicial Review of Administrative Action—The Top Fifteen' (2013) 42 Advoc Q 1
Munday R, *Cross and Tapper on Evidence* (13th edn, OUP 2018)
Nance DA, *The Burdens of Proof: Discriminatory Power, Weight of Evidence, and Tenacity of Belief* (CUP 2016)
Panaccio CM, 'In Defence of Two-Step Balancing and Proportionality in Rights Adjudication' (2011) 24 CJLJ 109
Perry S, 'Second-order Reasons, Uncertainty and Legal Theory' (1988–89) 62 S Cal L Rev 913
Petersen N, 'The Construction of Judicial Deference and the Use of Scientific Evidence in Constitutional Jurisprudence' (on file with author)
Petrie N, 'Indications of inconsistency' (2019) 78(3) CLJ 612
Phillipson G, 'Deference, Discretion, and Democracy in the Human Rights Act Era' (2007) 60 CLP 40
Poole T, 'The Reformation of English Administrative Law' (2009) 68(1) CLJ 142
Rawls J, *Political Liberalism* (Expanded edition, Columbia University Press 2005)
Raz J, *Practical Reasons and Norms* (Hutchinson 1975)
Raz J, *The Morality of Freedom* (OUP 1986)
Raz J, 'Disagreement in politics' (1998) 43 Am J Juris 25
Raz J, *Practical Reasons and Norms* (OUP 1999)
Redmayne M, 'Expert Evidence and Scientific Disagreement' (1996–97) 30 UC Davis L Rev 1027
Redmayne M, 'Standards of Proof in Civil Litigation' (1999) 62(2) MLR 167
Redmayne M, 'Objective Probability and the Assessment of Evidence' (2003) 2 Law, Probability and Risk 275
Ribeiro G, 'Can there be a Burden of the Best Explanation?' (2018) 22(2) Intl J of Evidence & Proof 91
Rivers J, 'Proportionality and Variable Intensity of Review' [2006] CLJ 174
Rivers J, 'The Presumption of Proportionality' (2014) 77(3) MLR 409
Roach K, *The Supreme Court on Trial: Judicial Activism or Democratic Dialogue* (Revised edn, Irwin Law Inc 2016)
Roach K, 'Remedies for Laws that Violate Human Rights' in John Bell, Mark Elliott, Jason NE Varuhas, and Philip Murray (eds), *Public Law Adjudication in Common Law Systems: Process and Substance* (Hart 2016)
Roach K, *Constitutional Remedies in Canada* (2nd edn, Thomson Reuters 2019)
Sager LG, *Justice in Plainclothes: A Theory of American Constitutional Practice* (Yale University Press 2004)
Sathanapally A, *Beyond Disagreement: Open Remedies in Human Rights Adjudication* (OUP 2012)
Saunders KW, 'The Mythic Difficulty of Proving a Negative' (1985) 15 Seton Hall L Rev 276
Schauer F, *Playing by the Rules: A Philosophical Examination of Rule-Based Decision-Making in Law and in Life* (OUP 1991)
Schlag P, 'Rules and Standards' (1985) 33 UCLA L Rev 378
Soper P, *The Ethics of Deference: Learning from Law's Morals* (CUP 2002)
Stein A, *Foundations of Evidence Law* (OUP 2005)
Steiner T, 'Proportionality Analysis by the Israeli Supreme Court' in Mordechai Kremnitzer, Talya Steiner, and Andrej Lang (eds), *Proportionality in Action: Comparative and Empirical Perspectives on the Judicial Practice* (CUP 2020)
Stephenson S, *From Dialogue to Disagreement in Comparative Rights Constitutionalism* (The Federation Press 2016)

Stone A, 'The Limits of Constitutional Text and Structure: Standards of Review and the Freedom of Political Communication' (1999) 23 Melb U L Rev 668

Stone A, 'Proportionality and Its Alternatives' (2020) 48(1) FL Rev 123

Stone Sweet A, 'The Necessity of Balancing: Hong Kong's Flawed Approach to Proportionality, and Why it Matters' (2020) 50 HKLJ 541

Stone Sweet A and Mathews J, 'Proportionality Balancing and Global Constitutionalism' (2008–09) 47 Colum J Transnl L 72

Stone Sweet A and Mathews J, *Proportionality Balancing & Constitutional Governance: A Comparative & Global Approach* (OUP 2019)

Sunstein CR, 'Foreword: Leaving Things Undecided' (1996) 110(4) Harv L Rev 6

Sunstein CR and Vermeule A, 'Interpretation and Institutions' (2003) 101 Mich L Rev 885

Taggart M, 'Proportionality, Deference, Wednesbury' (2008) 2008 NZ L Rev 423

Teo M, 'Proportionality as Epistemic Independence' [2022] PL 245

Thayer JB, 'The Origin and Scope of the American Doctrine of Constitutional Law' (1893) 7(3) Harv L Rev 129

Tushnet M, *Taking the Constitution Away from the Courts* (Princeton University Press 1999)

Tushnet M, 'New Forms of Judicial Review and the Persistence of Rights—And Democracy-based Worries' (2003) 38 Wake Forest L Rev 813

Tushnet M, 'Alternative Forms of Judicial Review' (2003) 101 Mich L Rev 2781

Urbina FJ, *A Critique of Proportionality and Balancing* (CUP 2017)

Van der Schyff G, *Limitation of Rights: A Study of the European Convention and the South African Bill of Rights* (Willem-Jan van der Wolf 2005)

Varuhas JNE, 'Taxonomy and Public Law' in Mark Elliott, Jason NE Varuhas, and Shona Wilson Stark (eds) *The Unity of Public Law?: Doctrinal, Theoretical and Comparative Perspectives* (Hart 2018)

Vermeule A, *Judging Under Uncertainty: An Institutional Theory of Legal Interpretation* (Harvard UP 2006)

Waldron J, 'Vagueness in Law and Language: Some Philosophical Issues' (1994) 82 Cal L Rev 509

Waldron J, *Law and Disagreement* (OUP 1999)

Waldron J, 'The Core of the Case Against Judicial Review' (2006) 115(6) Yale LJ 1346

Webber G, *The Negotiable Constitution: On the Limitation of Rights* (CUP 2009)

Webber G, 'On the Loss of Rights' in Grant Huscroft, Bradley W Miller, and Grégoire Webber (eds), *Proportionality and the Rule of Law: Rights, Justification, Reasoning* (CUP 2014)

Weinrib EJ, *Corrective Justice* (OUP 2012)

Wilberg H, 'The Bill of Rights in Administrative Law Cases: Taking Stock and Suggesting Some Reassessment' (2013) 25 NZU L Rev 866

Williams R, 'Structuring Substantive Review' [2017] PL 99

Wiseman D, 'Managing the Burden of Doubt: Social Science Evidence, the Institutional Competence of Courts and the Prospects for Anti-Poverty Charter Claims' (2014) 33 National Journal of Constitutional Law 1

Yam J, 'Judging Under Authoritarianism' MLR, forthcoming. Early access: https://onlinelibrary.wiley.com/doi/10.1111/1468-2230.12861

Yap PJ, 'Remedial Discretion and Dilemmas in Asia' (2019) 69(Supp 1) U Toronto LJ 84

Yap PJ and Lin CC, *Constitutional Convergence in East Asia* (CUP 2021)

Young AL, 'In Defence of Due Deference' (2009) 72(4) MLR 554

Young AL, 'Will You, Won't You, Will You Join the Deference Dance?' (2014) 34(2) OJLS 375

Young AL, *Democratic Dialogue and the Constitution* (OUP 2017)

Young EA, 'Judicial Activism and Conservative Politics' [2002] 73 U Colom L Rev 1139

Young SNM, 'Judicial Review of Elections in Hong Kong: Resolving a Contradiction' in Po Jen Yap (ed), *Judicial Review of Elections in Asia* (Routledge 2016)

Yowell P, *Constitutional Rights and Constitutional Design: Moral and Empirical Reasoning in Judicial Review* (Hart 2018)

'Policy against LGBT discrimination involve national security: Junius Ho' The Standard (Hong Kong, 10 Feb 2022) <https://www.thestandard.com.hk/breaking-news/section/4/187007/Policy-against-LGBT-discrimination-involve-national-security:-Junius-Ho> accessed 20 April 2022.

Index

Tables are indicated by an italic *t* following the page/paragraph number